Key Sources in Comparative and World Literature

Key Sources

in Comparative

and World Literature

An Annotated Guide to Reference Materials

George A. Thompson, Jr.

with the assistance of
Margaret M. Thompson

FREDERICK UNGAR PUBLISHING CO.
New York

To Bessie and David

Library of Congress Cataloging in Publication Data

Thompson, George 1941–
   Key Sources in Comparative and World Literature

   Includes indexes.
   1. Literature—History and criticism—Bibliography.
2. Bibliography—Bibliography—Literature. 3. Reference
books—Literature. I. Thompson, Margaret M. II. Title.
Z6511.T47 1982 [PN523]   016.809   82-40253
ISBN 0-8044-3281-3

PN
523
T47
1982

TABLE of CONTENTS

• INTRODUCTION •

This bibliography will be found useful by people who are doing
research in comparative literature or in the literatures written in the
languages of Western Europe, including English. It should be most useful
to graduate students who are undertaking major research projects but are
not yet familiar with the full variety of reference materials and sources
of bibliographic and other information available to them. Professors of
literature and other experienced researchers will find little here in
their fields of expertise with which they are not already familiar, but
they may, perhaps, be introduced to some valuable new general sources,
such as Arts and Humanities Citation Index [1/13], or to sources on periods, literatures, authors or other topics which are outside their usual
interests. In addition, they will find an office copy of this guide useful as a teaching tool, when directing the research of their students.

The reference sources listed in this guide cover comparative, general and European or world literature [section 1]; literature in Greek
and Latin, including the medieval and modern periods [section 2]; the
Romance literatures, with separate sections on French, Italian and Hispanic literatures [sections 3 through 6]; German literature [section 7];
and literature in English [section 8]. In addition, there is a section
on the other literatures of Europe, with Russian being treated in most
detail [section 9], and one on the literatures of the Orient [section
10]. The final section of the book covers the related disciplines,
chiefly in the arts and humanities, listing only the most basic sources,
selected and commented on with reference to their value for literary
research. The types of reference sources listed include bibliographies
and reviews of research; handbooks and encyclopedias, including biographical collections; dictionaries of critical terms; guides and indexes to
themes and plots; histories and other surveys; and, for the more than
160 writers covered, concordances and other indexes.

There are certain topics not covered by this guide. Expositions on

the methods of literary study or the theory of literary criticism are not
listed. Bibliographies of literary works are also omitted, with the
exception of bibliographies of translations into English of works in foreign languages. Other topics are covered selectively. Within the traditional sphere of comparative literary studies, the topic of international
literary relations and influences is touched on only in reference to the
influence of the classical literatures on later literatures. The section
on literature in English, although it is the largest section in the book,
is nonetheless highly selective; I hope soon to cover the English literatures in a separate volume. The subsection on Spanish-American literature does not attempt to list the bibliographies, handbooks and histories
of the individual literatures of the Spanish-American countries. Topics
are also covered only as far as suitable material is available; therefore
the sections on the various literatures are not of a uniform size, some
periods are more fully covered than others, and certain specific themes
and major writers could not be included at all. Finally, reference works
which are general in scope--national bibliographies, lists of books in
print, language dictionaries, universal encyclopedias and biographical
collections, and so forth--are altogether omitted; they may be looked for
in the general reference guides listed at 11/115 through 11/119.

The space gained by these systematic omissions and limitations has
been given chiefly to several special features. One is the annotations.
Most entries are annotated at least briefly, and many have annotations
which are specific and detailed, and often give an express comparison
with other similar sources, or at least some data from which a comparison
may be inferred. Another feature is the references to book reviews found
at the end of many of the entries. These are not to be taken as complete
lists, but are rather only the reviews which I have actually read in the
course of my research. Finally, an important feature is the attention
paid to individual writers and anonymous works, topics which have been
omitted from most recent guides to specific national literatures.

The overall organization of the book places the items cited in sections and subsections, according to their subject, and arranges the subsections in a logical sequence. Naturally, some topics and groups of

books fell into order readily, while others did not. The Hispanic and English sections were troublesome; the nature of the materials cited impelled me to place Yiddish literature in the section with Hebrew literature, rather than with German; and so forth. However, the organization of the book is clarified by the systematic tables of contents which precede each section of the book and outline its arrangement. These outlines are noted in the general table of contents on p. v. In addition, there is a detailed subject index on pp. 369-83. The items in each subsection are also presented in a logical sequence, with those works which seem most likely to be useful placed first, and those which are more specialized or otherwise limited offered last. There is an index of editors, compilers and other scholars on pp. 343-57 and a selective index of titles on pp. 357-68.

Approximately one-third of the entries in this guide are bibliographies. It may seem that so many bibliographies on overlapping topics must be redundant, and indeed, for a limited project needing the support of only a few studies, any bibliography will do. (For these occasions, Humanities Index [1/12] offers a simple yet precise subject index and the convenience of limiting its coverage to those journals most likely to be found in academic libraries.) But if one needs to find as many studies as possible, or only a few studies, but exactly the right ones, or ones on a very limited topic, then it is important to be familiar with a variety of bibliographies, because each may offer some feature not offered by the others: annotations, subject indexes, a scheme of organization, or a breadth of range in terms of either the types of sources included or the number of years of research scanned. The index which is best for one purpose may not be best for another, and for some project the combined coverage of several bibliographies may be necessary.

The subject arrangement of this book, reinforced by the subject index, helps to make the variety of resources listed in this guide accessible. However, no degree of elaboration of either the arrangement or the index can guarantee that every useful source on any topic will always be found immediately. Someone working on Marcel Proust may think to look in the section of general bibliographies, where the MLA International

<u>Bibliography</u> [1/9] will be found, among other things, or he may look in the section of general bibliographies on French literature, or he may look for Proust in the subject index, from which he will be directed to Graham's bibliography [4/95]. Anyone who does only one of these things will miss what is offered by the other two possibilities; anyone who does all three, but no more, will still miss the annotated lists of articles on modern world literature in each issue of <u>Twentieth Century Literature</u> [1/174], the very valuable <u>French XX</u> bibliography on modern French literature [4/67], and Kearney's <u>Continental Novel</u> [1/92], which, among other conveniences, offers some indexing of passages from general studies of modern literature, the novel, and so forth. Anyone doing research on a theme will be directed from the subject index to a number of useful works, including bibliographies, handbooks and materials on some specific major themes, but not to the general bibliographies which are described in the annotation as being arranged or indexed so as to direct attention to studies of themes, nor to the general handbooks which include articles on themes. The full usefulness of the sources cited in this guide will be realized the more as one becomes familiar with its contents, and familiar with the sources to which it refers.

Most of the terms used in the annotations are defined in standard dictionaries. I have tried to be consistent in reserving the word "author" for literary figures who are the object of study, while using "scholar" for writers of critical and other studies. I have used the word "concordance" for an index of the words used by an author which places each word in the context of the line or sentence in which it occurs, thus making it easier to recognize figurative uses or quotations or translations from other writers; I have used the term "word index" for indexes which do not reproduce contexts. By "classified arrangement" I mean a list in which the items are placed in a systematic order, and in which considerations like alphabetical order play a secondary role, if any. A "cumulative bibliography" is one in which a number of independent lists are combined into a single sequence; a "collected bibliography" reprints such lists in one volume or set, but does not reorganize them. Finally, "dissertations as found in DAI" [<u>Dissertation Abstracts</u>

<u>International</u> and its predecessors] means that the coverage of doctoral dissertations is limited largely to those from universities in the U. S., and is not even complete for those, since a few universities and departments (such as the literature departments of Harvard) do not submit their dissertations to DAI even now, and its "international" aspect is recent and quite haphazard.

Several people in particular have been helpful to me in this project. Mary Henry has called my attention to a number of sources on the Hispanic literatures, several of which I have chosen to include. Arnold Markowitz made some very useful suggestions based on his experience as a bibliographer and editor. Prof. Doris Guilloton was kind enough to read a section of the manuscript and made some valuable comments on it. Prof. Robert J. Clements has been encouraging throughout my work.

Among librarians who have helped me to solve particular problems I might mention Jean Longland of the Hispanic Society of America, Fred Muratori of Cornell, Robert Bailey and Barbara McCorkle of Yale, Shane Vitemb of Goethe House, Robert Connolly of Columbia's Casa Italiana, Vicki Hendricks of Syracuse University, and Stanley Nash, Patrick McGuire and Rikki Twersky of New York University. Most of the reference librarians in the reference room and the periodicals center of the New York Public Library and the reference room of Butler Library, Columbia University, have given me help at one time or another.

Jana Stevens, Kathy Hartzler and their staff in the acquisitions department of the Bobst Library, and Mike Hannon, Evelyn Abramowitz, Helen Yakalis and the splendid clerks and students in the serials department there, have made it possible that much of the material which I have consulted for this project has been conveniently available to me.

• ABBREVIATIONS of PERIODICAL TITLES •

[An "x" following the page number in the citations of book reviews indicates the relevant pages from a longer review.]

AGald	Anales galdosianos
AHR	American Historical Review
AL	American Literature
Alighieri: Rassegna bibliografica dantesca	
ALR	American Literary Realism
AmLS	American Literary Scholarship
Apollo: a Journal of the Arts	
ArchR	Architectural Review
Art Bull	The Art Bulletin
AUMLA	Journal of the Australian Universities Language and Literature Association
BCom	Bulletin of the Comediantes
BH	Bulletin Hispanique
BHR	Bibliothèque d'Humanisme et Renaissance
BHS	Bulletin of Hispanic Studies
BJA	British Journal of Aesthetics
BlakeN	Blake: An Illustrated Quarterly
BSOAS	Bulletin of the School of Oriental and African Studies [of the University of London]
CASS	Canadian-American Slavic Studies
CHum	Computers and the Humanities
CL	Comparative Literature
ClassJ	Classical Journal
ClassP	Classical Philology
ClassR	Classical Review
ClassW	Classical World
ClioI	Clio: An Interdisciplinary Journal
CLS	Comparative Literature Studies
ConL	Contemporary Literature
CSP	Canadian Slavonic Papers
DHS	Dix-huitième siècle
Drama: The Quarterly Theatre Review	
ECS	Eighteenth-Century Studies [Davis, Calif.]
EcumR	Ecumenical Review
EG	Études germaniques
EHR	English Historical Review
Encounter [London, Engl.]	
English [London, Engl.]	
ES	English Studies: A Journal
ETJ	Educational Theatre Journal
FilmC	Film Comment
Films in Review	
FLQ	Film Library Quarterly
FMLS	Forum for Modern Language Studies
Folklore	

FR	French Review
FS	French Studies
G&R	Greece and Rome
GL&L	German Life and Letters
GQ	German Quarterly ["m" after page ref. indicates the separately-paged membership issue]
GRM	Germanisch-Romanische Monatsschrift
GSLI	Giornale storico della letteratura italiana
Hispania	
HistRel	History of Religion
HJR	Henry James Review
HLAS	Handbook of Latin American Studies
HR	Hispanic Review
IQ	Italian Quarterly
IS	Italian Studies
Isis: International Review Devoted to the History of Science and Its Cultural Influences	
Italica	
IUR	Irish University Review
JAAC	Journal of Aesthetics and Art Criticism
JAAR	Journal of the American Academy of Religion
JAF	Journal of American Folklore
JAsiat	Journal asiatique
JASt	Journal of Asian Studies
JBiblLit	Journal of Biblical Literature
JEGP	Journal of English and Germanic Philology
JHI	Journal of the History of Ideas
JHP	Journal of Hispanic Philology
JHS	Journal of Hellenic Studies
JJQ	James Joyce Quarterly
JML	Journal of Modern Literature
JRomSt	Journal of Roman Studies
JSSR	Journal for the Scientific Study of Religion
JTS	Journal of Theological Studies
LALR	Latin American Literary Review
LE&W	Literature East and West
[The] Library: A Quarterly Journal of Bibliography	
LR	Les Lettres romanes
LRN	Literary Research Newsletter
MAE	Medium AEvum
M&L	Music and Letters
MD	Modern Drama
MiltonQ	Milton Quarterly
MLJ	Modern Language Journal
MLN	Modern Language Notes
MLR	Modern Language Review
Monatshefte: Für deutschen Unterricht	
Moreana: Bulletin Thomas More	
MusicR	Music Review
MusicalQ	Musical Quarterly

MusicalT   Musical Times
N&Q   Notes and Queries
Notes: Journal of the Music Library Association
NYRB   New York Review of Books
Opera
PhilosB   Philosophical Books
Philosophy
PoeS   Poe Studies
PTL: A Journal for Descriptive Poetics and Theory
QJFS   Quarterly Journal of Film Studies
RAL   Research in African Literatures
REG   Revue des études grecques
RelSt   Religious Studies
Ren&R   Renaissance and Reformation
RenQ   Renaissance Quarterly
RES   Review of English Studies
Review [Blacksburg, Va.]
RHLF   Revue d'histoire littéraire de la France
RLC   Revue de littérature comparée
RLJ   Russian Language Journal
Romania
RPh   Romance Philology
RR   Romanic Review
Scan   Scandinavica
SCN   Seventeenth-Century News
Scriblerian   Scriblerian and the Kit-Cats
Scriptorium: Revue internationale des études relatives aux manuscripts
SEEJ   Slavic and East European Journal
SEER   Slavonic and East European Review
ShakS   Shakespeare Studies [Knoxville, Tenn.]
ShawR   Shaw Review
SlavR   Slavic Review
SN   Studia Neophilologica
SPCT   Studi e problemi di critica testuale
Speculum: A Journal of Medieval Studies
SpNews   Spenser Newsletter
SQ   Shakespeare Quarterly
SS   Scandinavian Studies
Studio   Studio International
Symposium
TLS   Times Literary Supplement
UTQ   University of Toronto Quarterly
VQR   Virginia Quarterly Review [Reviews in a separately-
                    paged section, here designated with a '.]
WLWE   World Literature Written in English
YCGL   Yearbook of Comparative and General Literature
YES   Yearbook of English Studies
YWES   Year's Work in English Studies
YWMLS   Year's Work in Modern Language Studies

I

COMPARATIVE, GENERAL and INTERNATIONAL LITERATURES

OUTLINE

● ●   COMPARATIVE LITERATURE   ● ●

● BIBLIOGRAPHIES ●

1/1 "Revue de revues." In Canadian Review of Comparative Literature,
     1 (1974)--.
In issue no. 3 (the Summer issue). 7 (1980): 253-365, for 1979. 378
     entries in 3 broad categories (Histoire et relations littéraires;
     Théorie littéraire et methodes d'études; La littérature et les
     autres arts.) Subject index, from 5 (1978), of names and other
     topics, using English or French terms. Relations littéraires: 2+
     cols., clearly subdivided. Deconstruction and construction: 3
     refs. Lists arts. from appr. 100 journals, incl. some in E.
     European langs. Abstracts in English or French. Early install-
     ments similar but smaller, covering fewer journals.

1/2 "Bibliography of Comparative Literature in Britain." In Compar-
     ative Criticism, 1 (1980)--.
List of books and arts. by British scholars, from 1975.

1/3 Baldensperger, Fernand, and Werner P. Friederich. Bibliography of
     Comparative Literature. Chapel Hill: 1950. (U. of North Carolina
     Studies in Comparative Literature, 1) 705 pp.
Unannotated list of books and arts. in the langs. of W. Europe, chiefly,
     and chiefly on the literatures of W. Europe. 18 pp. section on
     Oriental literatures, mostly their influence on European writers.
     13 pp. section on Slavic literatures.
Classified arrangement. 4 main sections, divided, subdivided and di-
     vided again. I: Generalities, Intermediaries, Thematology, Liter-
     ary Genres; II: The Orient, Antiquity, Judaism, Early Christianity,
     Mohammedanism; III: Aspects of Western Culture: Modern Christian-
     ity, Literary Currents, International Literary Relations, Collec-
     tive Influences; IV: The Modern World. Section I is in 7 parts,
     each in from 3 to 11 subdivisions. Part 6, Literary Themes, is in

11 subdivisions, incl. Individual Authors, Individual Motifs, and
Collective Motifs, all further divided by topic, listed alphabetically. Section IV is in 13 parts; Part 7, French Contributions,
68 pp., in 25 sections, incl. French influences upon England,
Italy, etc., and the influence of 13 individual writers on European literatures.

No indexes. The influence of Montaigne on later writers is IV/7/14 (3
cols.), but arts. on the influence of earlier writers on Montaigne,
his use of various themes, his knowledge of the classics, etc.,
would be scattered elsewhere in the book.

1/4 "Annual Bibliography." In Yearbook of Comparative and General
     Literature, 1 (1952)-19 (1970).

Meant to supplement Baldensperger and Friederich (1/3)

1/5 "Bibliographie." In Revue de littérature comparée, 1 (1921)-34
     (1960).

Irregular, up to 4/yr. Also issued separately, 1949-1959. This jour-
     nal now carries a brief section listing the contents of other
     recent journals.

1/6 Betz, Louis P. La littérature comparée: Essai bibliographique.
     Strasbourg: Trübner, 1904. 410 pp.

2nd ed., rev. Fernand Baldensperger.

1/7 Jellinek, Arthur L. Bibliographie der vergleichenden Literatur-
     geschichte. Berlin: Duneker, 1903.

Vol I: publs. of 1902-03. 76 pp. No more publ.

● DISSERTATIONS ●

1/8 "Completed Doctoral Dissertations in Comparative Literature." In
     American Comparative Literature Assn. Newsletter.

9:1 (Fall, 1976):23-33, for 1974-75. No more publ.

● ●   GENERAL and INTERNATIONAL LITERATURE   ● ●

●   BIBLIOGRAPHIES   ●

1/9   <u>MLA</u> <u>International</u> <u>Bibliography</u> <u>of</u> <u>Books</u> <u>and</u> <u>Articles</u> <u>on</u> <u>the</u> <u>Modern</u>
<u>Languages</u> <u>and</u> <u>Literatures</u>.   1921--.

Annual. At present, and since 1969, this has been divided into 3 sections, or "volumes," each with a separate table of contents, list
of journal abbreviations, and index of scholars. The sections are:
I: General, English, American, Medieval and Modern Latin, and
Celtic literatures, and folklore; II: European, Asian, African, and
Latin American literatures; and III: general linguistics and languages.

Classified arrangement. Limited use of cross-refs. No subject index.
Lists books, arts. from journals and from certain books, and diss.
as listed in <u>DAI</u>. Very few, very brief annotations. Covers general literary studies and the various literatures of the medieval
and modern world; does not cover classical Greek or Latin, but does
cover those literatures in medieval and modern times. The sections
on each literature are usually divided into a general subsection
and period subsections. The period subsections are themselves divided into a section of general studies and sections on the individual authors. This arrangement makes it easy to survey the
studies of particular writers, but since only the sections on
Chaucer and Shakespeare are subdivided by the titles of their
works, it is not easy to locate studies of a specific piece. The
arrangement is burdensome for anyone interested in a literary theme
or form, or a topic in critical theory. In the 1978 bibl., the
subsection "Themes and Types" (one of 6 subsections under General
Literature and Related Topics) was in 21 parts, incl. Arthurian,
Epic and Allegory, but not incl. Faust, Tragedy or Symbol. Studies
of Faust would have to be looked for under the heading "Other
Themes." There are also Arthurian listings in the Medieval subsections of the English and French sections, but there are no

cross-refs. between these sections, nor any note indicating that
there will be entries concerning the Arthurian theme in the sections on various authors, like Chrétien, Malory or Tennyson. (The
cross-refs. are always to specific studies, cited only by entry
number. Most are at the end of an author section and most refer
to an entry in another author section.) The MLA plans major
changes in the indexing of the bibl. beginning with the vol. for
1981 (expected in late 1982) which will be intended to improve its
usefulness in this respect.

From 1921 through 1955 this bibl. was called "American Bibliography"
and listed studies by American scholars only. Therefore other
bibls. must be used to find studies by British, European or other
foreign scholars from those years. Through 1966 this bibl. was
largely devoted to W. European literatures and langs., although
from 1950 there had been a relatively small section on E. European
studies and from 1956 there had been a small section on Oriental
and African studies. Recent vols. have listed studies in not only
the langs. of W. and E. Europe, but also Hebrew, Arabic, Japanese,
etc.

There is no other bibl. which covers all the literatures of the world
as thoroughly as does the present-day MLA International. However,
there are a number of other bibls. listing research on a specific
literature, period, movement, theme or author, which may, even for
recent years, list studies not in the MLA, or arrange their contents more conveniently, or offer a feature (such as descriptive
or evaluative notes or a subject index) not found in the MLA.
Many of these bibls. are listed elsewhere in this book. Even
though the MLA's coverage of recent publications will usually be
adequate, it is still important to be familiar with the alterna-
tives.

This bibl. has recently become available for searching by computer,
beginning with the contents of the 1976 vol. The MLA plans to
extend this accessibility back to the early 1970s. But this service is of extremely limited usefulness. It is based on matching

a name or word or a combination of names or words against the
names and words occurring in the headings of each section and
subsection of the bibl. and in the titles of the books and arts.
listed and in the infrequent notes. Foreign lang. titles are
seldom translated or annotated. A search for "Arthur" and "Arthurian" would retrieve all the titles in the 3 Arthurian sections, however their titles were worded, and any other title con-
taining either word, regardless of whether or not they really
concerned the Arthurian theme. It would not retrieve German
titles about König Artus nor any title from the Malory or other
author sections which concerned the Arthurian theme but which did
not contain these two words. Forethought and ingenuity in phras-
ing the query can reduce this imprecision to some extent. Nonetheless, although this service may be useful to locate some studies of an elusive topic, one difficult to find in the printed
bibls. because of their arrangement, it would be impossible to be
assured that one had found all the items that one might have found
by a sufficiently careful search of the likely sections of the
printed bibls.

1/10 MLA Abstracts of Articles in Scholarly Journals. 1972-77.
Covers 1970-75. Discontinued. Abstracts of certain arts. cited in the
    MLA Bibl., chiefly in English. Arrangement is parallel to that of
    the Bibl. Vols. for 1972-75 had a subject index with headings
    like Society, Themes, Influence Study, all specifically subdivided.

1/11 Bulletin signalétique 523: Histoire et sciences de la littérature.
    24 (1970)--.
4/yr., and cumulative index of authors and other subjects, and of schol-
    ars. Each issue is arrange by subject and has its own index. The
    main divisions are: 1): Généralités; 2): Sciences de la littéra-
    ture (in 4 sections, incl. Poétique, divided and subdivided, and
    Littérature comparée, in 6 divisions;) and 3): Histoire de la litté-
    rature (arranged geographically, then by period). Lists arts.

from more than 500 journals in the langs. of W. and E. Europe.
Most entries have a brief abstract. The subject index is very
specific, but cites entry numbers only. 32 (1978): Narrateur: 1
col., every entry qualified with the name of an author (R. Ellison,
Rabelais) or other topic (Fou, et--with ref. to Erasmus and Luther). This continues indexes which were more general in scope,
beginning in 1947.

1/12 Humanities Index. 1974/75--.
4/yr., and annual cumulation. Covers about 300 of the most widely-read
   journals in the humanities, nearly half of which are exclusively
   or in part concerned with literature. Alphabetical arrangement,
   by subject and scholar, with many cross-refs. Substantial appen-
   dix listing book revs. Very useful for listing arts., chiefly in
   English, from major journals, within 4 to 6 months of publ. Also
   very useful for its use of exact subject headings, e. g., **Storms** in
   Literature or Petrarch--Influence, which identify studies which may
   be lost or difficult to find in other bibls. Previously called
   Social Sciences and Humanities Index (1965-74) and before that International Index to Periodicals, which began in 1907.

1/13 Arts and Humanities Citation Index. 1977--.
3/yr. The 3rd issue is a cumulative 4 vol. set. Covers appr. 1100
   journals in the arts and humanities. Sections: 1): an author listing of recent arts.; 2): an index to the names and other words in
   the titles of the recent arts.; and 3): the citation index, an
   author index to all materials cited in the notes and bibls. of the
   arts. in section 1. The citation index is meant to permit one to
   trace recent arts. which apply, refute or extend a fact, interpre-
   tation or theory advanced in an earlier art., book or diss., but
   since it lists all cited materials it also offers references to
   studies of particular poems, novels and other literary works (incl.
   the Bible and the Koran), as well as operas, films, ballets, musi-

cal compositions (classical, jazz, folk, etc.), and paintings, buildings, and other works of art. Lists book revs. Since 1980 has incl. selective indexing of appr. 5000 journals in the social sciences and sciences.

1/14 Current Contents: Arts and Humanities. 1 (1979)--.
Weekly. Lists the complete contents (incl. book revs., fiction and poems) of the most recent issues of many journals, incl. a number in literature. Also lists arts. in certain recent books. Indexes in each issue, incl. scholars, and the names and other words appearing in the titles of the arts. A note under each journal title indicates the langs. used in that issue. Titles of all arts. are given in English, with no indication as to which are in a foreign lang.--a problem when the journal is bilingual. It is intended to provide a means of browsing through journals efficiently and within a few months of their publication.

1/15 Essay and General Literature Index. 1934--.
Now 2/yr. and annual cumulation. Indexes by author, title and subject arts. publ. in selected books, incl. many in literature and the other humanities, since 1900.

1/16 Index to Social Sciences and Humanities Proceedings. 1979--.
4/yr. and annual cumulation. A list of publ. conference proceedings (incl. ones appearing in journals), with the papers presented and their authors. Indexes incl. a "Category Index," listing the conferences by discipline; a list of names and other words from the titles of the papers; and authors and editors.

● REVIEW of RESEARCH ●

1/17 The Year's Work in Modern Language Studies. 1 (1929/30)--.
Review essays, citing books and arts. in English and in other langs. as appropriate. At present covers medieval and neo-Latin, and Romance,

Celtic, Germanic and Slavonic literatures and langs. Coverage
in the past has varied, but has always excl. literature in English
and the Oriental and African langs. No section on general or comparative literature, although studies of a comparative nature may
be noted throughout the book. Most literatures are discussed in a
series of essays by different specialists, each covering a century
or other period. 41 (1979), publ. 1981, 1260 pp. French literature: 200 pp., in 9 sections, incl. 20 pp. on the 16th c. and 3
pp. on Rabelais, which cite studies in French and English only.
Since 30 (1968) there has been a detailed but incomplete subject
index, noting themes, genres, etc. 39 (1977): Petrarchism: 10
entries; Politics: appr. 1 col., all specifically qualified ("in
Balzac," etc.); the double (theme): 4 entries.

YWMLS is most useful as a means of surveying trends and fashions in
scholarship, and for summaries of or comments on journal arts.
There is considerable variation in content among the chapters,
some noting studies of cultural and social history and others
not, all covering publs. in 2 langs., but some in 3 and a few in
4. Some chapters annotate most entries, often with several sentences, while others merely cite many studies and annotate others
with but a word or a phrase. The comments are often evaluative.
On a descriptive level the comment will often indicate the exact
subject of the study, the major works referred to, its point of
view, or its relation to a previous study. As a simple list of
literary studies, this is probably seldom as complete as the lists
in the MLA, yet one may find studies cited in YWMLS which are not
in the MLA.

BHS 53 (1976):85; Romania 98 (1977):522; RPh 34 (1980-81):138-39

● HANDBOOKS, ENCYCLOPEDIAS, etc. ●

1/18 **Cassell's Encyclopaedia of World Literature**. N. Y.: Morrow,
1973.

Rev. and enlarged. J. Buchanan-Brown, ed. 1st ed. 1953, S. H. Stein-

berg, ed. 3 vols. I: signed arts. on national literatures,
genres, movements, critical terms, etc. Japanese Literature: 2
1/2 cols., plus 2 1/2 cols. bibl.; Expressionism: 1 1/2 cols., 1/2
col. bibl.; Satire: 3 cols., with particular reference to classical, English, French and Italian writers, but no bibl. II and
III: biographies. Dante: 3 cols., 2/3 col. bibl.; G. Grass: 1/2
col., 1/3 col. bibl.; Li Po: 1/2 col., bibl. of English and German
transls., French and English studies.

YWMLS 73:217--"good up-to-date bibls.," with ref. to Spanish entries;
73:292; 74:361--"the arts. remain valuable for their good sense
and concise information, but it is a pity that the revision of
some was not more thorough," with ref. to Portuguese entries.

1/19 Princeton Encyclopedia of Poetry and Poetics. Princeton, N. J.:
Princeton U. Pr., 1974. 992 pp.

Ed. by Alex Preminger, with Frank J. Warnke and O. B. Hardison, Jr.
Enlarged ed. (The 1965 ed., unrevised, with an 84 pp. suppl. of
additional arts.) "About 1000 individual entries ranging from
twenty to more than 20,000 words, dealing with the history,
theory, technique and criticism of poetry." (Pref.) Signed arts.
on national literatures, forms, movements, schools, critical and
technical terms, etc., but not on individual poets or critics.
Many cross-refs. Metaphor: 10 cols., plus 1/2 col. bibl.; Satire:
4 cols., 1/3 col. bibl., with ref. to Classical and English literature; Japanese poetry: 16+ cols., 1 col. bibl.

YWMLS 75:147; MLJ 50 (1966):226-27; SEEJ ns 10 (1966):231-33

1/20 Shipley, Joseph T., ed. Encyclopedia of Literature. N. Y.:
Philosophical Library, 1946.

2 vols. 1188 pp. Signed arts. on national literatures.

1/21 Van Tieghem, Philippe and Pierre Josserand, eds. Dictionnaire des
littératures. Paris: PUF, 1968.

3 vols. 4349 pp. Mainly biographies (Chaucer: 2/3 p., Boileau: 1 2/3

pp.) Also movements, themes, national literatures, etc.
FS 24 (1970):87-88

1/22 Dictionnaire universel des lettres. Paris: SEDE, 1961. 952 pp.
Pierre Clarac, ed. "4000 arts.; 1500 on authors, 2200 on works."
    (Pref.) Also arts. on technical terms, etc. Entries on works
    listed under the French transl. of the title. Brief arts.

1/23 Kleines literarisches Lexikon. Bern & München: Francke, 1969-72.
4th ed., rev. by Horst Rüdiger and Erwin Koppen. 1st ed. 1946-48, by
    Otto Oberholzer and Heinrich Mahlberg. 3 vols. in 4. I: authors,
    through the 19th c.; II, pt. 1 and 2: 20th c. authors; III: sub-
    jects. Covers German and world, chiefly western, literature.
LR 29 (1976):96-97; Monatshefte 67 (1975):314

1/24 Wilpert, Gero von. Lexikon der Weltliteratur. Stuttgart: Kröner,
    1975-80.
2nd ed. 1st ed. 1963-68. 2 vols. I: Biographisch-bibliographisches
    Handwörterbuch nach Autoren und anonymen Werken. 1793 pp.
    II: Hauptwerke der Weltliteratur in Charakteristiken und Kurzinter-
    pretationen. 1343 pp. See also his Sachwörterbuch (1/48). Brief
    entries, few more than 1 col. Vol. I: unsigned arts., with bibls.;
    II: signed arts., under German title. Index of national litera-
    tures, giving roster of authors. Index of authors. Note that
    anonymous works are covered by arts. in both vols.

1/25 Die Weltliteratur: biographisches, literarhistorisches und
    bibliographisches Lexikon in Übersichten und Stichwörtern. Wien:
    Hollinek, 1951-54.
3 vols. 2119 pp. Suppl., 2 vols., 467 pp., [A-O; no more publ?]
    1968--. Erich Frauwallner, H. Giebisch and E. Heinzel, eds. Brief
    arts. on writers, anonymous works and national literatures. Index
    of names.

1/26 Enciclopedia Garzanti della letteratura. n. p.: Garzanti, 1972.
      963 pp.
Mainly biographies and critical terms.

1/27 Kratkaia literaturnaia entsiklopediia. Moskva: Sovetskaia Ent-
      siklopediia, 1962-78.
Alexsei A. Surkov, ed. 9 vols. Index to set in vol. 9. Signed arts.,
      most with bibls. Biographies, national literatures, etc. "It
      takes in the whole of world lit., stressing . . . the U. S. S. R.,
      and the lits. of the Soviet nationalities receive the full treat-
      ment. The non-Soviet oriental lits. are also notably well catered
      for." YWMLS 62:548-49. Note also: Literaturnaia entsiklopediia,
      1929-39, vols. 1-9 and 11 only.
SlavR 39 (1980):104-10--a history and evaluation of the project

1/28 Sáinz de Robles, Federico Carlos. Ensayo de un diccionario de la
      literatura. Madrid: Aguilar, 1964-67.
3rd ed. 1st ed. 1949. 3 vols. I: Términos, conceptos, "ismos" lite-
      rarios. Incl. arts. on national literatures, movements, etc.
      1218 pp. II: biographies of Spanish and Spanish-American writers.
      4th ed., 1973, 1338 pp. III: biographies of foreign writers,
      mainly western. 1268 pp.

1/29 Svenskt Litteraturlexikon. Lund: Gleerup, 1970. 643 pp.
2nd ed. 1st ed. 1964. Terms relevant to European literature and biog-
      raphies of Swedish writers only.
YWMLS 64:606--"130 recognized specialists"

● BIOGRAPHIES ●
[Many of the handbooks listed above contain biographical entries, as do
      many of the handbooks to specific literatures, periods and forms.]

1/30 Penguin Companion to European Literature. N. Y.: McGraw-Hill,
      1969. 908 pp.

Mostly brief biographical entries, with bibls.

1/31 Kunitz, Stanley J. and Vineta Colby. European Authors, 1000-1900:
    A Biographical Dictionary of European Literature. N. Y.: Wilson,
    1967. 1016 pp.
"Nearly 1000 writers of 31 different literatures" (Pref.), excl. English
    and American. Most arts. about 2 cols., some longer.

1/32 Index to the Wilson Authors Series. N. Y.: Wilson, 1976. 72 pp.
Lists the entries in 1/30, 1/179, and 1/180, and 3 other works.

1/33 Dictionnaire biographique des auteurs de tous les temps et de tous
    les pays. Paris: SEDE, 1957-58.
2 vols. Illustrated. Bibl. of books only with most entries. Balzac:
    11 cols., incl. 12 illus. and 5 cols. of remarks by Goethe, G.
    Sand, Bernanos, and others.

● CRITICAL TERMS ●
[Many of the handbooks listed above incl. entries for critical and tech-
    nical terms.]

1/34 Ruttkowski, Wolfgang V. and R. E. Blake. Glossary of Literary
    Terms in English, German and French, with Greek and Latin Deriva-
    tions of Terms, for the Student of General and Comparative Litera-
    ture. Bern & München, Francke, 1969. 68 pp.
No definitions. Tables of equivalent terms, in classified order. 780
    numbered entries. Indexes of terms in German, English and French.

1/35 Elkhadem, Saad. The York Dictionary of English-French-German-
    Spanish Literary Terms and Their Origin. Fredericton, N. B.: York
    Pr., 1976. 154 pp.
Arranged by English term, giving brief definitions of terms from rhet-
    oric, prosody, etc., related English terms, and equivalents in
    the other langs. Indexes in French, German and Spanish.

1/36 Escarpit, Robert, ed. Dictionnaire international des termes
      littéraires.   Berne: Francke, 1979--.
Few but lengthy signed arts. in English or French, giving etymology,
      definition, equivalent terms (in German, Russian, Arabic, Japanese,
      etc.) and history. Allégorie: 3+ pp.; Autobiographie: 7 pp.; Ba-
      roque: 9 1/2 pp. Incl. terms from Arabic, Japanese, etc. A proto-
      type fascicle covering the letter "L" was publ. in 1973. 2 fasci-
      cles, 192 pp., through middle of letter "B" publ. to date.
YWMLS 79:662-63--v fav as regard "the substance of the arts.", less so
      as regard the bibls.

1/37 Abrams, Meyer H. A Glossary of Literary Terms. N. Y.: Holt,
      Rinehart Winston, 1981. 220 pp.
4th ed. 1st ed. 1941, by Dan S. Norton and Peters Rushton. Rather long
      arts. (few less than 1/2 p., many several pp. or more), most con-
      taining discussions of a number of related terms. Point of View:
      3 pp., with a bibl. of 4 books and 1 art. Index of terms, incl.
      those imbedded in longer arts.
ECS 5 (1971-72):196--v unfav, ref. to 3rd ed.

1/38 Beckson, Karl E. and Arthur Ganz. Literary Terms: A Dictionary.
      N. Y.: Farrar, Straus and Giroux, 1975. 280 pp.
2nd ed. 1st ed., as A Reader's Guide to Literary Terms, 1961.
VQR 52 (1976):26'-28'--dismissive

1/39 Cuddon, J. A. A Dictionary of Literary Terms. London: Deutsch,
      1977. 745 pp.
Pref claims coverage of terms from 20 langs. Rev. ed., 1979, 761 pp.
YWES 77:1; TLS, Aug. 12, 1977, p. 979--v unfav

1/40 Ducrot, Oswald and Tzvetan Todorov. Encyclopedic Dictionary of
      the Sciences of Language. Baltimore & London: Johns Hopkins U.
      Pr., 1979. 380 pp.
Transl. by Catherine Porter of the 2nd, 1973, French ed., with revs. by

the authors. More than 50 signed arts., with bibls., on linguistics and literary theory. Literary Genres (by Todorov): 3 pp., and
1/2 p. bibl. Significant terms within the arts. are in bold-face
type. Index of terms.
MLN 95 (1980):1054-55; YWMLS 74:204--the French ed.

1/41 Fowler, Roger, ed. A Dictionary of Modern Critical Terms. London
      and Boston: Routledge, Kegan Paul, 1973. 208 pp.
Fewer than 150 signed arts. on forms, movements and other basic terms.
      Satire: 1 p., with ref. to English literature.
YWES 73:403-05

1/42 Holman, C. Hugh. A Handbook to Literature. Indianapolis: Bobbs-
      Merrill, 1980. 537 pp.
4th ed. 1st ed., by W. F. Thrall and A.Hibbard, 1936. "More than 1560
      entries" (Pref.), most less than 1 p., without bibls. Terms from
      English usage, applicable to English and American literature. some
      entries from film; some themes (Grail, but not Faust); some move-
      ments and circles. Structuralism: 1/2 p., but no terms from
      structuralist vocabulary.
AmLS 79:533--"indispensible"; AL 53 (1981):162

1/43 Lanham, Richard A. A Handlist of Rhetorical Terms: A Guide for
      Students of English Literature. Berkeley & Los Angeles: U. of
      California Pr., 1968. 148 pp.
List of terms mainly from Greek and Latin, with brief definitions and
      exemplary quotations from English literature.

1/44 Shipley, Joseph T., ed. Dictionary of World Literary Terms:
      Forms, Technique, Criticism. Boston: The Writer, 1970. 466 pp.
Previous ed. as Dictionary of World Literature, 1953. Brief arts.,
      unsigned, sometimes up to several pp. "Critical Surveys," pp. 367-
      453: 10 essays on the history of criticism in Greece, Rome, medi-
      eval Europe, Russia and modern Europe.

1/45 Angenot, Marc. Glossaire practique de la critique contemporaine.
      Ville La Salle: Hurtubise/HMH, 1979. 223 pp.
2nd ed. 1st ed., Glossaire de la critique littéraire contemporaine,
      1972. List of critics cited incl. Barthes, Derrida, Goldmann and
      Todorov.

1/46 Greimas, A. J. and J. Courtés. Sémiotique: Dictionnaire raisonné
      de la théorie du langage. Paris: Hachette, 1979. 424 pp.
Arts. from 1 paragraph to 5 or more cols. Gives English equivalents.
      Narratif (schéma . . .): nearly 7 cols., with cross-refs. to 8
      other terms. Mythologie: 2/3 col.

1/47 Morier, Henri. Dictionnaire de poétique et de rhétorique. Paris:
      PUF, 1975. 1210 pp.
2nd ed. 1st ed. 1961. Rhetorical terms, metrics, forms, etc. Hiatus:
      11 pp.; Sonnet: 30 pp. Illus. with graphs, musical staffs, etc.
RHL 77 (1977):676-79

1/48 Wilpert, Gero von. Sachwörterbuch der Literatur. Stuttgart:
      Kröner, 1969. 865 pp.
5th ed. 1st ed. 1955. Terms, incl. forms, movements, etc. Sometimes
      lengthy arts., with bibls. and cross-refs. to his Lexikon der Welt-
      literatur (1/23). 6th ed., 928 pp., 1979.

1/49 Marchese, Angelo. Dizionario di retorica e di stilistica. Mila-
      no: Mondadori, 1978. 309 pp.
Entries from a few lines to a page, rarely longer. Segno: 3+ pp.

1/50 Głowiński, Michał, et al. Słownik terminów literackich. Wrocław,
      etc.: Zakład Narodowy im Osslińkich, 1976. 577 pp.
Brief signed entries, few longer than a page, on major movements of
      European literature, and technical and rhetorical terms. Gives
      equivalent terms in English, French, German and Russian, with in-
      dexes to those langs. "Covers not only lit. but also several

neighboring fields (linguistics, aesthetics, etc.) YWMLS 76:848

1/51 Campos, Geir. Pequeno dicionário de arte poética. São Paulo:
    Cultrix, 1978. 181 pp.
3rd ed. 1st ed. 1960. Brief entries.
YWMLS 79:427

1/52 Moisés, Massaud. Dicionário de termos literários. São Paulo:
    Cultrix, 1974. 520 pp.
Entries up to several pages. Rhetorical terms, forms, movements, etc.

1/53 Marino, Adrian. Dictionar de idei literare. Bucuresti: Eminescu,
    1973--.
Vol. 1: A-G, 1087 pp. 27 entries, covering genres, literary periods and
    modes, movements, etc. Bibls. (in the form of notes) are "massive,
    though not all-inclusive." (Based largely on rev. by T. A. Perry
    in YCGL 23 [1974]:106-08).

1/54 Timofeev, Leonid Ivanovich. Slovar' literaturovedcheskikh ter-
    minov. Moscow: Prosveshchenie, 1974. 509 pp.
Signed arts., 1 col. to several pages, many with brief bibls.

1/55 Diccionario de términos e "ismos" literarios. Madrid: Porrua
    Turanzas, 1977. 192 pp.
Very brief entries on forms, meters and other technical terms. "Dic-
    cionario de 'ismos' literarios," by José Ortega, pp. 147-84: essays
    on 10 movements.
BHS 55 (1978):350-51--mixed; RPh 34 (1980):345-47--unfav

1/56 Hozven, Roberto. "Glosario de literatura." In Atenea 432 (1975):
    130-211.
Glossary proper is pp. 154-206. Appr. 250 entries, up to 1/2 p., rarely
    longer, citing Aristotle, Barthes, Freud, Jakobson, etc.

● HISTORIES ●

1/57 A Comparative History of Literature in the Western Languages.
1 vol. to date. Ulrich Werner Weisstein, ed. Expressionism as an
International Literary Phenomenon. Paris: Didier, 1963. See 1/
196. Other vols. still in preparation.

1/58 Literature and Western Civilization. London: Aldus, 1972-76.
6 vols. David Daiches and Anthony Thorlby, eds. I: The Classical
World. 1972. 557 pp. II: The Mediaeval World. 1973. 725 pp.
III: The Old World: Discovery and Rebirth. 1974. 624 pp. IV: The
Modern World: Hopes. 1975. 716 pp. V: The Modern World: Real-
ities. 1972. 626 pp. VI: The Modern World: Reactions. 1976.
621 pp. Signed arts. on the literatures of the western nations and
general topics in western literature, as well as culture and history. Index in each vol.

1/59 Friederich, Werner P., with David H. Malone. Outline of Comparative Literature from Dante Alighieri to Eugene O'Neill. Chapel
Hill: U. of North Carolina Pr., 1954. (U. of North Carolina
Studies in Comparative Literature, 11) 451 pp.
Covers "the flow of forms and ideas" and "the dissemination of cultural
values" among the countries of W. Europe, chiefly, esp. the influence (incl. translations) of major authors and the use of specific
themes and styles. Index of names and other subjects.

1/60 Van Tieghem, Paul. Histoire littéraire de l'Europe et de l'Amé-
rique de la Renaissance à nos jours. Paris: Colin, 1946. 426 pp.
2nd ed. 1st ed. 1941. By period and genre. Covers the literatures of
W. and E. Europe, incl neo-Latin. Index of names.

1/61 Cohen, John M. A History of Western Literature. Chicago: Aldine,
1963. 381 pp.
Rev. ed. 1st ed. 1956. From the 12th to the mid 20th c. Incl. Russia

and Latin America, but excl. literature in English. Chronology.

1/62 Histoire des littératures. Paris: Gallimard, 1977-78. (Encyclo-
    pédie de la Pléiade)
New ed. 3 vols. 1st ed. 1955-58. Raymond Queneau, ed. I: Littéra-
    tures anciennes, orientales et orales. 2024 pp. II: Littératures
    occidentales. 2128 pp. III: Littératures françaises, connexes et
    marginales. 2112 pp. Signed arts. on the various literatures.
    Bibls. with each chapter, chiefly books. Lengthy chronological
    tables in each vol. Index of names, with brief identifying notes,
    and of titles, mostly in French versions, in each vol.

1/63 Neues Handbuch der Literaturwissenschaft. Frankfurt am Main:
    Athenaion, 1972--.
Klaus von See, general ed. The volumes to date:
1:     Röllig, W., et al. Altorientalische Literaturen. 1978. 330 pp.
    Literatures of the Near East.
3:     Fuhrmann, Manfred, et al. Römische Literatur. 1974. 332 pp.
    Through the 2nd c. AD.
8:     Erzgräber, Willi, et al. Europäisches Spätmittelalter. 1978.
    792 pp. Covers 1250-1500.
9-10: Buck, August, et al. Renaissance und Barock. 1972. 2 vols.
    Covers the 16th and 17th c.
11-13: Hinck, Walter, et al. Europäische Aufklärung. 1974--. 3 vols.
    projected. The 18th c.
17:    Lauer, Reinhard, et al. Europäischer Realismus. 1980. 517 pp.
    Covers 1830-1880.
18-19: Kreuzer, Helmut, et al. Jahrhundertende-Jahrhundertwende. 1976.
    2 vols. Covers 1870-1918.
21-22: Hermand, Jost, et al. Literatur nach 1945. 1979. 2 vols.
 Every vol. differs in scope, arrangement, indexing, etc. The vols. may
    be arranged by nation or by form or theme, and sometimes both. All
    vols. or sets have an index of names, and a few have an index

of other subjects. All are illus. None have bibls., but there are
notes after each chapter.
RES ns 31 (1980):332-34; MLR 75 (1980):937-39; Speculum 56 (1981):128-
31--critical of balance; YWMLS 79:664-65 [All ref. to vol. 8]

1/64 Einsiedel, Wolfgang von, ed. Die Literaturen der Welt in ihrer
mündlichen und schriftlichen Überlieferung. Zurich: Kindler, 1964.
1402 pp.
Arts. with bibls. on the literatures of the world, arranged geographi-
cally. English: 40 pp.; Greek (ancient and modern): 38 pp.; Mon-
golian: 9 pp. Identical with vol 7 of Kindlers Literatur-Lexikon
(1/132).

• CHRONOLOGIES •

1/65 International Federation of Modern Languages and Literatures. Répertoire chronologique des littératures modernes. Paris: Droz,
1935. 413 pp.
Paul van Tieghem, ed. Covers 1455-1900. Incl. Celtic and neo-Latin, and
the literatures of E. Europe, the U. S. and Latin America.

1/66 Weil, Gonthier and Jean Chassard. Les Grandes dates des littéra-
tures étrangères. Paris: PUF, 1969. 128 pp.
Not seen.
FS 25 (1971):366

1/67 Spemann, Adolf. Vergleichende Zeittafel der Weltliteratur vom
Mittelalter bis zur Neuzeit. Stuttgart: Spemann, 1951. 160 pp.
From the 12th c. to 1939. 1150-1850, pp. 9-40; 1850-1939, pp. 40-115.
Covers E. Europe, some Latin American countries, (but not Chile or
Brazil), Japan and India (but not China or the Arabic countries).
Index.

1/68 Paxton, John and Sheila Fairfield. Calendar of Creative Man.

N. Y.: Facts on File, 1979. 497 pp.
Charts in 8 cols., 500 AD to 1970. **Covers literature**, dance and drama,
   music, the arts (in 3 cols.), history, and **inventions and discover-**
   ies. Incl. E. Europe; incl. Asia, not extensively. Events are
   described in 1 or 2 sentences of doubtful value.

1/69 Brett-James, Antony. The Triple Stream: Four Centuries of Eng-
   lish, French and German Literature, 1531-1930. Cambridge, Engl.:
   Bowes & Bowes, 1953. 178 pp.
Indexes of English, French and German authors and titles.

● CRITICISM, STYLISTICS and SCHOOLS of CRITICISM ●
[Dictionaries of critical terminology are 1/34-1/56.]
● BIBLIOGRAPHIES ●

1/70 Hall, Vernon. Literary Criticism: Plato through Johnson. N. Y.:
   Appleton-Century-Croft, 1970. 119 pp.
Selective list of books and arts. in English, French, German, Italian
   and Spanish, in 4 sections, by period, each largely devoted to
   early and modern eds. of individual critics and studies of their
   work. Index of scholars.

1/71 Eckhard, Michel. Poetics in Periodicals. Poétique à travers les
   périodiques. Tel Aviv: Porter **Israeli Inst. for Poetics and Semi-**
   otics, 1977. (Papers on Poetics and Semiotics, 6) 69 pp.
Covers 1974. No more publ. Pp. 10-44: alphabetical list of critics.
   Pp. 45-69: classified subject index in 16 sections, all subdivided.
   Section 1: Meaning and Literature, in 10 divisions, incl. 1:6, Am-
   biguity. Potentially a very useful bibl.; it is a pity it has not
   been continued.

1/72 "Annual Bibliography." In Style, 1 (1967)--.
14 (1980):138-59. Lists arts. and diss. as found in DAI, in English
   only. Brief abstracts. Classified arrangement, under 8 headings,

incl. Rhythm and Sound, and Imagery, Diction and Figures of Speech.
Incl. general and theoretical studies and studies of specific authors and works, incl. French, German, etc. literature.
This journal also frequently publ. bibls. on special topics. 13 (1979):
178-225: "Allusion Studies: An International Annotated Bibliography, 1921-77," by Carmela Perri. 14 (1980):103-26: "A Bibliography of the Colloquial as a Stylistic Term: An Introduction," by
John S. Childs, et al.

1/73 Milic, Louis T. Style and Stylistics: An Analytical Bibliography.
N. Y.: The Free Press/London: Collier-Macmillan, 1967. 199 pp.
Lists books and arts. in English, French and German. Entries annotated
with 2 to 6 "descriptors" (subject labels), seemingly taken from
the text of the study: names, periods, langs., and other aspects,
e. g., Adjectivals, Grand Style, Imagery. Indexes of the author
descriptors and of the other descriptors.

1/74 Bailey, Richard W. and Lubomír Doležel. Annotated Bibliography
of Statistical Stylistics. Ann Arbor: Dept. of Slavic Langs. and
Lits., U. of Michigan, 1968. 97 pp.
Lists books, arts., and research reports in the langs. of W. and E. Eu
rope, and diss. as found in DAI.

1/75 Shibles, Warren A. Metaphor: An Annotated Bibliography and History. Whitewater, Wisc.: Language Pr., 1971. 414 pp.
Books and arts. in English, French, German, etc., by author, pp. 23-
318. Indexes, incl. aspects of metaphor, and general terms and
names. Many annotations, sometimes lengthy.
YWMLS 72:236

1/76 "Bibliography." In Reader-Response Criticism: From Formalism to
Post-Structuralism, Jane P. Tompkins, ed., Baltimore & London:
Johns Hopkins U. Pr., 1980, pp. 233-72.
Annotated list of books and arts. in English, French and German, in 2

sections (Theoretical and Applied), by scholar.

1/77 Eschbach, Achim and Wendelin Rader. Semiotik-Bibliographie. I.
    Frankfurt am Main: Autoren- und Verlagsgesellschaft Syndikat, 1976.
    221 pp.
12 chapters on disciplines. 6: Literatur, pp. 44-64, entries 1071-1578,
    by author. Books and arts. in various langs. Index of authors.
    Index of subjects, with cross-refs.from English terms.

1/78 Language, Literature and Meaning: Current Trends in Literary Re-
    search. Amsterdam: Benjamins, 1980. (Linguistics & Literary
    Studies in Eastern Europe, vol. 1, pt. 2) 567 pp.
John Odmark, ed. Contains a bibl. of 432 entries on Czech and Slovak
    literary structuralism, incl. transls. and studies in English, etc.,
    and bibl. of Polish theory, both with classified subject indexes.

1/79 Eimermacher, Karl and Serge Shishkoff. Subject Bibliography of
    Soviet Semiotics: The Moscow-Tartu School. Ann Arbor: Dept. of
    Slavic Langs. and Lits., U. of Michigan, 1977. 153 pp.
Writings by members of this school on literature, pp. 66-93, in 4 sec-
    tions; also "Selected Writings on Soviet Semiotics and Structural-
    ism," pp. 131-40. See also Eimermacher's author bibl. Arbeiten
    sowjetischer Semiotiker der Moskauer und Tartuer Schule (Auswahl-
    bibliographie), Kronberg: Scriptor, 1974, 180 pp.
SEER 56 (1978):616-17--"very well organized"; CSP 21 (1979):94x; SEEJ
    ns 22 (1978):545-46

1/80 Shukman, Ann   "The Moscow-Tartu Semiotics School: A Bibliography
    of Works and Commentary in English." In PTL: A Journal of Descrip-
    tive Poetics and Theory of Literature, 3 (1978):593-601.

1/81 Miller, Joan M. French Structuralism: A Multi-disciplinary Bib-
    liography. N. Y. & London: Garland, 1981. 553 pp.
Lists books and arts. in English, French, German and other langs., and

diss. as found in <u>DAI</u>. Some brief annotations. Indexes of scholars and of names and other subjects. Barthes: more than 65 pp. of
his works, revs. of his works, and appr., 350 studies on him, with
many cross-refs. Also sections on Althusser, Derrida, Foucault,
Goldmann, Lacan and Lévi-Strauss.

Intended to suppl. Josué V. Harari, <u>Structuralists and Structuralisms</u>:
<u>A Selected Bibliography of French Contemporary Thought</u>, Ithaca, N.
Y.: Diacritics, 1971, 82 pp. [Not seen.] Also cites François H.
and Claire C. Lapointe, <u>Claude Lévi-Strauss and His Critics</u>: An
<u>International Bibliography of Criticism</u> (<u>1950-1976</u>), N. Y.: Gar-
land, 1977, 219 pp. Note also: John Leavey and David B. Allison,
"A Derrida Bibliography," in <u>Research in Phenomenology</u>, 8 (1978):
145-60, a list of books and arts. by and about him.

• HISTORIES •

1/82 Wimsatt, William K. and Cleanth Brooks. <u>Literary Criticism</u>: <u>A</u>
<u>Short History</u>. N. Y.: Knopf, 1957. 755 pp.
Emphasis is on Greek and Roman criticism (pp. 3-136) and on criticism--
particularly British--from the 18th c. to the 1930s (pp. 221-720).
No bibls., but footnotes. Index of names and other subjects.

1/83 Wellek, René. <u>A History of Modern Criticism</u>, <u>1750-1950</u>. New
Haven, Conn.: Yale U. Pr., 1955--.
5 vols. projected. 1): <u>The Later 18th Century</u>. 1955. 359 pp. 2): <u>The</u>
<u>Romantic Age</u>. 1955. 459 pp. 3): <u>The Age of Transition</u>. 1965.
389 pp. 4): <u>The Later 19th Century</u>. 1965. 671 pp. Covers devel-
opments in England, Germany, France, Italy, Russia and the U. S.
Each vol. contains extensive notes, a chronological table of works,
and indexes of names and of topics and terms.

• GENRES •

1/84 Ruttkowski, Wolfgang V. <u>Bibliographie der Gattungspoetik für den</u>

Studenten der Literaturwissenschaft: Ein abgekürztes Verzeichnis
von über 3000 Büchern, Dissertationen und Zeitschriftenartikeln in
Deutsch, Englisch und Französisch. München: Hueber, 1973. 246 pp.
List of studies of particular genres, pp. 61-214, by genre. Indexes of
French, English and alternative German names of genres, and of
scholars.
GRM nf 24 (1974) 365-66x

1/85 "Bibliographie zur Gattungspoetik." In Zeitschrift für französische Sprache und Literatur, 82 (1972)-85 (1975).

1) Klaus W. Hempfer. "Allgemeine Gattungstheorie (1890-1971)." 82
(1972):53-66. 220 entries.

2) Ingrid Hantsch. "Theorie der Satire (1900-1971)." 82 (1972):151-
56. 80 entries.

3) Manfred Pfister. "Theorie des Komischen, der Komödie und der Tra-
gikomödie (1943-1972)." 83 (1973):240-54. Appr. 300 entries.
Continues a bibl. by O. Rommel in Deutsche Vierteljahresschrift für
Literaturwissenschaft und Geistesgeschichte, 21 (1943):161-95.

4) Helga Gebhard. "Theorie des Tragischen und der Tragödie (1900-
1972)." 84 (1974):236-48. 247 entries.

5) Hermann Lindner. "Theorie und Geschichte der Fabel (1900-1974)."
85 (1975):247-59. 136 entries.

1/86 Hempfer, Klaus W. Gattungstheorie: Information und Synthese.
München: Fink, 1973. 312 pp.
JEGP 79 (1980):101-02--"systematically arranged review of research;"
"not concerned with individual genres"

● POETRY ●
[See also 1/19: Princeton Encyclopedia of Poetry and Poetics]

1/87 Wimsatt, William K., ed. Versification: Major Language Types:
Sixteen Essays. N. Y.: Modern Language Assn., 1972. 252 pp.
Incl. E. European and Oriental langs. Italian: 14 pp., plus notes and

a brief bibl.

1/88 Coleman, Arthur. Epic and Romance Criticism. N. Y.: Watermill,
      1973-74.
1): A Checklist of Interpretations, 1940-1970, of English and American
    Epics and Metrical Romances. 390 pp. 2): A Checklist . . . ,
    1940-1973, of Classical and Continental Epics and Metrical Roman-
    ces. 368 pp. Cites passages from certain journals and books.
LRN 1 (1976):117-21--mixed

1/89 Haymes, Edward R. A Bibliography of Studies Relating to Parry's
      and Lord's Oral Theory. Cambridge, Mass.: Harvard U., 1973. 45 pp.
ClassW 68 (1974-75):385-86; MLN 90 (1975):296-99

1/90 Hatto, Arthur T., gen. ed. Traditions of Heroic and Epic Poetry.
      London: MHRA, 1981--.
2 vols. projected. Vol. I: chapters on Greek, Sanskrit, medieval
      French, German and Spanish, and E. European, Asian and E. African
      epics. 376 pp.

1/91 Heroic Epic and Saga: An Introduction and Handbook to the World's
      Great Folk Epics. Bloomington: Indiana U. Pr., 1978. 373 pp.
Felix J. Oinas, ed. 15 chapters on ancient and medieval European poems,
      and on poems from E. Europe, the Middle East, and Africa.
SEEJ ns 24 (1980):447-48

● FICTION ●

1/92 Kearney, E. I. and L. S. Fitzgerald. The Continental Novel: A
      Checklist of Criticism in English, 1900-1966. Metuchen, N. J.:
      Scarecrow, 1968. 460 pp.
Arts. and passages from certain books and journals on W. and E. European
      novels since the Renaissance.

1/93 "Annual Bibliography of Explications of Short Fiction." In Stud-
     ies in Short Fiction, 1 (1963/64)--.
In the 3rd (Summer) issue. 17 (1980):365-95, listing books and arts. in
     English only, with specific indications of the stories discussed.

1/94 Walker, Warren S. Twentieth-Century Short Story Explication:
     Interpretations, 1900-1975, of Short Fiction since 1800. Hamden,
     Conn.: Shoestring Pr., 1977. 880 pp.
3rd ed. 1st ed. 1961. Criticism in English from certain books and
     journals.   E.T.A. Hoffmann: 4 pp., more than 40 stories, 1 to 9
     references each. Suppl., 257 pp., 1980.

● DRAMA and THEATER ●

1/95 "Bibliographie." In Revue de la société d'histoire du théâtre,
     1 (1948/49)--.
In the 4th (oct.-déc.) issue. 32 (1980), publ. 1981, covering 1979.
     Classified arrangement. Books and arts. in the langs. of W. and
     E. Europe. Sections cover the stage (incl. popular entertain-
     ments), biographical studies, and studies of dramatic literature,
     by country and playwright (1434 entries, 80 pp., with emphasis on
     W. Europe) and by other topics, incl. themes.

1/96 Palmer, Helen H. European Drama Criticism, 1900-1975. Hamden,
     Conn.: Shoestring Pr., 1977. 653 pp.
2nd ed. 1st ed. 1968. Criticism in English from certain books and
     periodicals, on playwrights from the Greeks to Beckett. Goethe:
     14 pp., incl. 10 pp. on Faust; Ionesco: 8+ pp.
ConL 10 (1969):414-15x--unfav

1/97 Coleman, Arthur and Gary R. Tyler. Drama Criticism: A Checklist
     of Interpretation since 1940. Denver: Swallow, 1966-71.
2 vols. Covers English, American and European plays. Criticism in
     English from certain books and periodicals.

1/98 Litto, Frederic M. American Dissertations on the Drama and Theater: A Bibliography. Kent, Ohio: Kent St. U. Pr., 1969. 519 pp.
List of diss., with indexes of authors, of key-words taken from the titles of the diss., and of subjects in classified order.

• HANDBOOKS •

1/99 Gassner, John and Edward G. Quinn. The Reader's Encyclopedia of World Drama. N. Y.: Crowell, 1969. 1030 pp.
Signed arts., sometimes with brief bibls., on playwrights, plays, forms, and national dramas. Büchner: 1 col., with cross-refs to Danton's Death and Woyzeck (each 1/2 col.) Mayakovsky: 1 2/3 cols., with cross-ref. to The Bathhouse. India: 9 cols., covering Sanskrit, folk and dance drama. Don Juan: 2 cols. on the theme, with other arts. on several Don Juan plays.
ETJ 26 (1974):120-24x--v fav as regards range and contents; critical of organization and accuracy; MD 16 (1973):396-401; Drama, no. 99 (Winter, 1970):64-66

1/100 McGraw-Hill Encyclopedia of World Drama. N. Y.: McGraw-Hill, 1972.
4 vols. Fairly long unsigned arts. on playwrights, with summaries of their plays. Brief arts. on some dramatic terms. Mayakovsky: 4 cols., incl. paragraphs on 4 plays, and 1 col. bibl. of plays and studies.
ETJ 26 (1974):127-31x--unfav

1/101 Hartnoll, Phyllis. The Oxford Companion to the Theatre. London & N. Y., etc.: Oxford U. Pr., 1967. 1088 pp.
3rd ed. 1st ed. 1951. Emphasis is on the stage.
Encounter 29:5 (Nov., 1967):84-86--v unfav; N&Q ns 15 (1968):480--fav, but endorses criticism of accuracy and bibls. made in Encounter.

1/102 Pavis, Patrice. Dictionnaire du théâtre: Termes et concepts de
    l'analyse théâtrale. Paris: Éd. Sociales, 1980.   482 pp.
Arts., often a page or more, on terms referring to dramatic literature
    and its presentation on the stage.

1/103 Enciclopedia dello spettacolo. Roma: Le Maschere, 1954-62.
9 vols. Suppl. vol., 1966. Often long arts. on all aspects of the
    performing arts., world-wide. Emphasis in on the stage, rather
    than on dramatic literature. Incl. actors, playwrights, etc.;
    cities and countries as centers of theatrical activity; and cer-
    tain themes and forms, e. g., Faust (7 cols. and 1/2 col. bibl.)
    and pastoral drama. Index, 1968, listing plays mentioned, incl.
    titles in original langs.

1/104 Teatral'naia éntsiklopediia. Moskva: Sovetskaia Éntsiklopediia,
    1961-67.
5 vols., and suppl., with index. Arts. from 1 to several pp. Covers
    the performing arts in W. Europe and the U. S., as well as E.
    Europe.
YWMLS 62:549

                          • HISTORIES •

1/105 Nicoll, Allardyce. World Drama from Aeschylus to Anouilh.
    London: Harrap, 1976. 965 pp.
2nd ed. 1st ed. 1949. No bibl. or notes. Index of names and titles
    (in original lang. and in English transl.) but few other subjects.

1/106 Berthold, Margot. A History of World Theater. N. Y.: Ungar,
    1972. 733 pp.
Transl. by Edith Simmons of Weltgeschichte des Theaters, Stuttgart:
    Kröner, 1968. Chapters on Near and Far Eastern theater, but em-
    phasis is on Western stage history. Index of names and other
    subjects, pp. 699-733.

● SYMBOLS ●

[See also the handbooks of symbolism in art, 11/10-11/13.]

1/107 **Bibliographie** zur **Symbolik**, **Ikonographie** und **Mythologie**: Inter-
       nationales Referateorgan. 1968--.
Annual. 12 (1979): books and arts., most publ. 1975-78, in English,
       German, French and other langs., by scholar. Abstracts. Indexes,
       incl. subjects.

1/108 Lurker, Manfred. **Bibliographie** zur **Symbolkunde**. Baden-Baden:
       Heitz, 1968. (Bibliotheca bibliographica aureliana, 12, 18 & 24)
       695 pp.
2nd ed. 1st ed. 1964. Classified arrangement, incl. sections on sym-
       bols in literature (incl. studies of specific authors and works),
       art, folklore, etc., and on traditional symbols (plants, animals,
       gods, etc.) Indexes of scholars and of subjects, incl. authors
       and symbols. Literature: pp. 170-80, entries 3609-827, and suppl.
       pp. 491-94, entries 10127-204.

1/109 Vries, Ad de. **Dictionary** of **Symbols** and **Imagery**. Amsterdam &
       London: North-Holland, 1974. 515 pp.
Many precise refs. to passages from English and classical literature and
       the Bible, esp. Forest: 9 significations, with refs. to Ovid,
       Dante, Blake and Dylan Thomas. ES 57 (1976):285-86

1/110 Lurker, Manfred, ed. **Wörterbuch** der **Symbolik**. Stuttgart: Krö-
       ner, 1979. 686 pp.
Brief signed arts. covering "general fields of symbolism and . . . rele-
       vant sciences, cultures, religions, ideas, thinkers and artists,"
       (YWMLS 79:672). Index of specific symbols, etc.

● THEMES ●

1/111 Schmitt, Franz Anselm. **Stoff-** und **Motivgeschichte** der **deutschen**

Literatur: Eine Bibliographie. (See 7/47.)

Incl. studies of themes in European literature, provided they involve German writers, but does not list studies of individual writers.

1/112 Frenzel, Elisabeth. Stoffe der Weltliteratur: Ein Lexikon dichtungsgeschichtlicher Längsschnitte. Stuttgart: Kröner, 1976. 785 pp.

4th ed. 1st ed. 1962. Covers themes associated with named characters, incl. historical figures, citing the major works in which they appear. Brief bibls. of critical studies. Faust: 8 pp.; Martin Luther: 2 1/2 pp.; Sappho: 2 3/4 pp.

1/113 Frenzel, Elisabeth. Motive der Weltliteratur: Ein Lexikon dichtungsgeschichtlicher Längsschnitte. Stuttgart: Kröner, 1980. 867 pp.

2nd ed. 1st ed. 1976. Covers themes associated with ideas, actions, circumstances, etc., with brief bibls. of studies. Arkadien: 10 pp.; Inzest: 20 pp.

1/114 Heinzel, Erwin. Lexikon historischer Ereignisse und Personen in Kunst, Literatur und Musik. Wien: Hollinek, 1956. 782 pp.

Historical figures and periods as subjects of literary works, etc. Caligula: 1/3 pp.; Martin Luther: 3 1/2 pp., with many cross-refs.; Französische Revolution, 1789-1850: 5 1/2 pp., with many crossrefs.; Empedokles: 1/4 pp., citing Matthew Arnold.

1/115 Heinzel, Erwin. Lexikon der Kulturgeschichte in Literatur, Kunst und Musik mit Bibliographie und Ikonographie. Wien: Hollinek, 1962. 492 pp.

Poets, artists, etc., as subjects of literary works, operas, etc. Faust: 4 1/2 pp. Empedokles: 1/2 p., not citing Matthew Arnold.

1/116 Koch, Willi August. Musisches Lexikon: Künstler, Kunstwerke und Motive aus Dichtung, Musik und bildender Kunst. Stuttgart:

Kröner, 1976. 1290 cols.

3rd ed. 1st ed. 1956. Brief arts. on writers, composers and artists;
on historical and mythological figures; and on statues, buildings
and other works of art. Empedokles: 2/3 col., with ref. to works
by Hölderlin; Totentanz: 1 col., as a theme in art, chiefly, but
mentioning Schubert.

[There may also be refs. to themes in the general literary handbooks
(1/18-1/29) and the handbooks to the various national literatures.
Note also the handbooks in chapter 11 on art, film, opera and
folklore, and the folklore type and motif indexes. Certain standard reference works designed chiefly for public-library use
should not be overlooked: Play Index (1/117), Fiction Catalog (1/
118), Short Story Index (1/119) and Granger's Index to Poetry (1/
120). All of these list works in English only, but incl. transl.
from many langs. All offer indexing by subject or theme. The
first 3 indicate actions and activities; settings, incl. specific
places; characteristics of the chief characters, incl. profession,
etc.; as well as entries for specific named events and historical
figures. These books are not designed for scholarly use; they are
meant to be guides for readers and they all incl. works which are
light, transitory or worthless, but they also incl. ancient and
modern masterpieces.]

1/117 Play Index, 1949-1952. N. Y.: Wilson, 1953. 239 pp.
Suppls., 1953-1960 through 1973-1977, 1963-78. Adultery: plays by Woody
Allen, John Dryden, Eugène Labiche, Philip Massinger, Luigi Piran-
dello, August Strindberg, and others.

1/118 Fiction Catalog. N. Y.: Wilson, 1976. 797 pp.
9th ed. 1st ed. 1908. Brief plot summaries.

1/119 Short Story Index. N. Y.: Wilson, 1953. 1553 pp.
Suppls., 1950-1954 through 1974-1978, 1956-79.

1/120 Granger, Edith. Granger's Index to Poetry. N. Y. & London:

Columbia U. Pr., 1973.　2223 pp.

6th ed.　1st ed. 1904.　William James Smith, ed.　Suppl., 1970-1977,
1978, 635 pp.

●　SPECIFIC THEMES　●

●　ARTHURIAN　●
[See 1/146-1/149.]

●　DON JUAN　●

1/121　Singer, Armand E.　The Don Juan Theme, Versions and Criticisms: A
Bibliography.　Morgantown: West Virginia U., 1965.　370 pp.

2nd ed.　1st ed. 1954.　Chapters incl. a list of versions, by author,
incl. music and films; of criticism of individual works, by author
of the work; and general criticism, by scholar.　Chronological
list of versions, pp. 352-70.　Some annotations, esp. in the list
of versions.　Suppls. in West Virginia U. Philological Papers, 17
(1970):102-78 and 20 (1973):66-106.

HR 36 (1968):167-69; YWMLS 74:305--"valuable"

●　FAUST　●

1/122　Henning, Hans.　Faust-Bibliographie.　Berlin & Weimar: Aufbau,
1966-76.

3 vols. in 5.　I: the Faust theme before Goethe; II: Goethe (in 3
parts); III: Faust since Goethe.　Lists eds., transl., and studies
in various langs.

GQ 45 (1972):371-72; 50 (1977):561-62

1/123　Butler, Eliza Marian.　The Fortunes of Faust.　Cambridge: The
University Pr., 1952.　365 pp.

Covers French, German and English Faust literature.

YWMLS 79:741--"a masterpiece"

1/124 Dédéyan, Charles. **Le thème de Faust dans la littèrature europé-**
      enne. Paris: Lettres modernes, 1955-66.
4 vols. in 6 parts. Covers European literature, incl. Russia.

• The PICARESQUE •
[See also 6/36-6/37.]

1/125 Bjornson, Richard. **The Picaresque Hero in European Fiction.**
      Madison & London: U. of Wisconsin Pr., 1977.   308 pp.
Covers Spanish, German, French and English works.
Monatshefte 70 (1978):430-31--v fav; YWES 77:6; FS 35(1981):201-02

1/126 Blackburn, Alexander. **The Myth of the Picaro: Continuity and**
      Transformation of the Picaresque Novel, 1554-1954. Chapel Hill:
      U. of North Carolina Pr., 1979.   267 pp.
Covers Spanish, German, French, Russian and English works.
RES ns 32(1981):213-14x

• UTOPIAS, IMAGINARY VOYAGES and TALES of the FUTURE •

1/127 Winter, Michael. **Compendium Utopiarum: Typologie und Bibliogra-**
      phie literarischer Utopien. Stuttgart: Metzler, 1978--. (Reper-
      torien zur deutschen Literaturgeschichte, 8)
1: **Von der Antike bis zur deutschen Frühaufklärung.** 287 pp. Pp. 1-100:
      Chronological list of Utopian writings, with lengthy comments.
      Pp. 202-29: charts and tables illustrating themes and other char-
      acteristics. Pp. 231-43: bibl. of secondary studies, 573 entries,
      incl. many on individual writers or texts. Indexes incl. themes
      and characteristics, characters, etc.
MLR 75 (1980):694-96; YWMLS 79:670-71

1/128 Manuel, Frank E. and Fritzie P. Manuel. **Utopian Thought in the**
      Western World. Cambridge, Mass.: Harvard U. Pr., 1979. 896 pp.
AHR 85 (1980):859; ECS 14 (1980-81):338-44; ALR 13 (1980):123-26x

1/129 Trousson, Raymond. Voyages aux pays de nulle part: Histoire
       littéraire de la pensée utopique. Bruxelles: Eds. de la U. de
       Bruxelles, 1975. (U. libre de Bruxelles, Faculté de philosophie
       et lettres, Travaux 60) 298 pp.
Bibl. of texts and criticism, pp. 263-89.
CLS 54 (1980):227-29; LR 33 (1979):95-97; PTL 4 (1979):385-89--v unfav;
       YWMLS 75:9--"distinguished chronological history;" RLC 54 (1980):
       227-29

● PLOTS and CHARACTERS ●

1/130 Magill, Frank N., ed. Masterplots. Combined Edition. Fifteen
       Hundred and Ten Plot-stories and Essay-reviews from the World's
       Fine Literature. N. Y.: Salem Pr., 1960.
6 vols. 3529 pp. This is unfortunately the largest and most wide-rang-
       ing collection of plot-summaries in English. No doubt the summa-
       ries are adequate; the critical comments are brief and inane.
       There are no bibls. The summaries in the general collections
       have also been packaged as regional and genre collections. A
       "Special Edition" in 18 vols., publ. in 1971, offers 1510 entries
       on world literature in 15 vols. and a "Survey of Contemporary
       Literature" in 3 vols., i. e., 300 summaries of recent American
       publs.

1/131 Kolar, Carol Koehmstedt. Plot Summary Index. Metuchen, N. J.:
       Scarecrow, 1981. 526 pp.
2nd ed. 1st ed. 1973. An index by author and title to some English-
       lang. collections of plot-outlines, incl. Masterplots and its
       derivatives, as well as some literary handbooks.

1/132 Kindlers Literatur-Lexikon. Zürich: Kindler, 1964-72.
7 vols. Suppl., 1974. Most entries 1 to 2 cols., arranged by title in
       the orig. lang. Not limited to literary works. Arts. incl. crit-
       ical comment and biographical or historical background. Bibls.

list eds., transls. into German (and occasionally into other
langs.), studies, and adaptations (drama, opera, film). Extensive
coverage of E. European, African and Oriental literatures. Indexes of authors, of anonymous works, and of some variant or short
titles and some titles in German transl. This is a transl. with
extensive revisions of 1/133.

Certain arts. from this set have been repackaged, unrevised, into a series of 6 vols. on French, German, English, American, Hebrew and
ancient (Greek, Latin and early Christian) literatures, arranged
by period (Hauptwerke der französischen [etc.] Literatur).

Vol 7 incl. a section of essays on the literatures of the world, which
has also been publ. separately. See 1/64.

GQ 50 (1977):87-88--"intelligent resumés," "insightful comments," with
ref. to Hauptwerke der deutschen Literatur.

1/133 Dizionario letterario Bompiani delle opere e dei personaggi di
tutti i tempi e di tutte le letterature. Milano: Bompiani, 1963-
64.

9 vols. 2 vol.suppl., 1964-66. Entries arranged by Italian title. 344
pp. section in vol. 1 on the movements of western literature, arranged alphabetically. Vol. 8: Personaggi: arts., usually less
than 1 col., arranged by first name in the Italian form (Davide
Copperfield, Achab [i. e., Ahab]). Vol. 9: indexes to titles in
the orig. lang., of authors (Chaucer, 6 titles; Baudelaire, 11
titles), incl. philosophers, historians, composers, etc. Chronological tables covering 2773 BC to 1914 AD, in columns by country.
The suppl. vols. cover 20th c. literature, with indexes but no
chronology. See 1/193. This has been transl. into German (1/132),
French (1/134 and 1/192) and other langs., but not into English.

1/134 Dictionnaire des oeuvres de tous les temps et de tous les pays:
littérature, philosophie, musique, sciences. Paris: SEDE, 1968.
5th ed. 1st ed. 1952-59. 4 vols. and index vol. (The 1st ed., with
suppl. entries in each vol.) Entries under French title. Index

of authors. See also 1/192.

1/135 Olbrich, Wilhelm, et al. Der Romanführer. Stuttgart: Hierse-
    mann, 1950-79.
16 vols. to date. Vols. 1-14: plots of European novels through the mid-
    1960s, esp. German and other W. European works. Vol. 15: index of
    novelists and of titles, incl. titles in the orig. langs. Vol.
    16: German novels through 1973.

1/136 Gregor, Joseph, et al. Der Schauspielführer. Stuttgart: Hierse-
    mann, 1953-79.
11 vols. to date. Vols. 1-7: plots of plays, worldwide, but esp. Ger-
    man, English-lang. and other W. European, through the mid-1950s.
    Vols. 8-11: plays 1956-1965 through 1974-1976, by author, 1967-79.
    Total of 2169 plays

1/137 Dictionnaire des personnages littéraires et dramatiques de tous
    les temps et tous les pays. Paris: SEDE, 1960. 666 pp.
Arts. of 1/2 col. or more, by last name of character, in the French
    form (e. g., Achab).

● PERIODS ●

● MEDIEVAL ●

• BIBLIOGRAPHIES •

1/138 International Medieval Bibliography. 1967--.
Now 2/yr. Covers the culture and society of Europe, chiefly W. Europe,
    from 500 to 1500. Lists. arts. publ. in journals and in books, in
    the langs. of W. and E. Europe, arranged in broad subject cate-
    gories. Has covered literature since 1970 only. Vol. for Jan.-
    June, 1980, publ. 1981, 3696 entries, chiefly publs. of 1979-80,
    of which appr. 700 concern literature, in 3 sections (General,

Prose and Verse) subdivided by nation or region. Author index.
Subject index, chiefly of names, places and titles, but also some
other topics, e. g., Drama, Fabliaux, Franciscan Order. This is
likely to be of more use in research on intellectual and cultural
history than in literary research.
RES ns 29 (1979):78-79; CASS 11 (1977):456

1/139 "Bibliographie." In Cahiers de civilisation médiévale: X^e-XIIe
   siècles. 1 (1958)--.
Annual, since 12 (1969), in a suppl. issue. Lists books and arts. from.
   appr. 700 journals, chiefly in French, English, German and Italian, diss., as listed in DAI, and book revs. Incl. Islamic and
   some S. Asian topics, but emphasis is on W. Europe. Alphabetical
   subject arrangement, with cross-refs. and index of scholars. 22
   (1979), publ. 1981: 160 pp., 2338 entries, most publ. 1977-80,
   but some earlier.

1/140 Williams, Harry F. Index of Mediaeval Studies Published in Festschriften, 1865-1946, with Special Reference to Romanic Material.
   Berkeley: U. of California Pr., 1951. 165 pp.
12 regional divisions, covering N. and W. Europe, subdivided by broad
   topic (section 5: literature). Index of scholars and subjects.

1/141 Farrar, Clarissa P. amd Austin P. Evans. Bibliography of English
   Translations from Medieval Sources. N. Y.: Columbia U. Pr., 1946.
   (Records of Civilization: Sources and Studies, 39) 534 pp.
Transls. publ. in books and journals. Annotated. Arranged by author
   (anonymous works by title in orig. lang.). Incl. transls. from
   Hebrew, Arabic and Persian. Index of translators, editors and
   subjects. Continued by Mary Anne Ferguson, Bibliography of English Translations from Medieval Sources, 1943-1967, N. Y.: Columbia U. Pr., 1974, (Records of Civilization: Sources and Studies,
   88), 274 pp.
GQ 49 (1976):551-52

● REVIEW of RESEARCH ●

1/142 Fisher, John H., ed. The Medieval Literature of Western Europe:
    A Review of Research, Mainly 1930-1960. N. Y.: N. Y. U. Pr., for
    the MLA, 1966. 432 pp.
Covers Latin; the Romance literatures, incl. Catalan; German, English
    and Norse, and Celtic. Index of names (subjects and scholars).
YWMLS 66:41; 67:172; YWES 66:61; 67:64-65; MLR 63 (1968):141-42

● HANDBOOKS ●

1/143 Lexikon des Mittelalters. München: Artemis, 1977--.
5 vols. in 50 fascicles projected. Arts., sometimes 10 or more cols.,
    on all aspects of medieval culture, incl. Jewish and Arabic top-
    ics. Vol. 1: Aachen bis Bettelordenskirchen, 2108 cols. Beo-
    wulf: 2 3/4 cols. of text, 1/4 col. bibl., with an additional
    brief art. on the Beowulf manuscript. Aristoteles: 13 2/3 cols.,
    in a number of sections and subsections, each separately signed
    and with a bibl., incl 4+ cols. on the translation of his works
    and his influence. Benediktiner: 23 cols. Many biographical
    arts.
MLR 74 (1979):389-90; EHR 94 (1979):440-41; YWMLS 77:609; 79:662--speaks
    of "the very high standard of scholarship and depth of coverage"
    and of the "impressive . . . prominence accorded to Oriental mate-
    rial."

1/144 Encyclopedia of the Middle Ages, Renaissance and Reformation.
    Leiden: Brill, 198 --.
Not yet publ. (Expected to begin in 1982.) Ed. by Nicholas Mann,
    Guillaume Posthumus Meyjes and Gerard Verbeke. 20 vols. projec-
    ted, to cover nearly all aspects of European culture, except art,
    incl. biographies.

• HISTORY •

1/145 Jackson, William Thomas Hobdell. The Literature of the Middle
    Ages. N. Y.: Columbia U. Pr., 1960. 432 pp.
Covers Latin, French and Provençal, Italian, Germanic (incl. Icelandic),
    Spanish, Arabic and English, but concentrates on French and Ger-
    man, and on the 12th and 13th c. Text is generally organized by
    form (the Romance, the Beast Epic). Chronology, pp. 359-68.
    Bibl., books only, classified, pp. 369-414. Index of names, ti-
    tles, and other subjects.
YWMLS 60:1; 61:156, 300

• SPECIAL TOPICS •

• ARTHURIAN •

1/146 International Arthurian Society. Bulletin bibliographique. 1
    (1949)--.
Annual. 32 (1980): 377 pp. Pt. 1: "Bibliographie," pp. 11-227, in 11
    sections, by nation of publ. (incl. Japan). Lists eds., studies
    (books, arts., diss.) and book revs. on Arthurian literature to
    the 20th c. Most entries have a brief summary, usually 1/2 p. or
    less, usually in French or English. Index of names (scholars and
    subjects) and of other subjects, incl. titles of Arthurian works.
    The rest of each issue is essays, obituaries, etc.
Romania 98 (1977):522-23

1/147 "A Bibliography of Critical Arthurian Literature for the Year."
    In Modern Language Quarterly, 1 (1940)-24 (1963).
Covers 1936/39-1962. By author. Covers Arthurian literature to the
    20th c. Unannotated. Index of names, titles and other subjects.
    Continues John J. Parry, A Bibliography of Critical Arthurian Lit-
    erature for the Years 1922-1929 [and] 1930-1935, N. Y.: MLA, 1930-

36. Total of 5328 numbered entries.

1/148 Pickford, C. E. and R. W. Last. The Arthurian Bibliography.
       Woodbridge, Suffolk: Brewer/Totowa, N. J.: Rowman & Littlefield,
       1981. 856 pp.
Cumulated author list of entries from "the standard Arthurian bibls.,"
       incl. the two above, with various subject indexes. Not seen.

1/149 Loomis, Roger Sherman, ed. Arthurian Literature of the Middle
       Ages: A Collaborative History. Oxford: Clarendon Pr., 1959. 574
       pp.
Covers Welsh, English, French and German works esp., but also Dutch,
       Scandinavian, Latin, Spanish and Portuguese. Index, chiefly of
       names and titles.
YWMLS 59:43, 200; YWES 59:66--"the bibl. is necessarily selective, but
       remarkably full," 59:93

• COURTLY LITERATURE •

1/150 "Courtly Bibliography." In Encomia, 1 (1975)--.
Irregular. 2:3 (Spring, 1980):25-149, mainly publs. of 1978, by nation
       of publ. 958 entries, with occasional brief notes, listing books,
       arts., book revs., and U. S. and British diss. Indexes of sub-
       jects, incl. names, anonymous titles and other topics, and of
       scholars.
YWMLS 77:44-45

1/151 Boase, Roger. The Origin and Meaning of Courtly Love: A Critical
       Study of European Scholarship. Manchester, Engl.: Manchester U.
       Pr./Totowa, N. J.: Rowman & Littlefield, 1977. 171 pp.
Text in 3 parts: a survey of scholarship, chronologically, pp. 5-61;
       of theories of origin, pp. 62-99; and of interpretations, pp. 100-
       16. Index of names (scholars and subjects).
YWMLS 77:45; 79:255; BHS 55 (1978):262--"immensely helpful;" Speculum 54

(1979):338-42; YES 10 (1980):241-42

• DRAMA •

1/152 Stratman, Carl J. Bibliography of Medieval Drama. N. Y.: Ungar,
    1972.
2nd ed. 1st ed. 1954. 2 vols. 1035 pp. Lists books, arts., chapters
    in books and U. S. and occasionally European diss. Covers Latin
    liturgical drama, English drama (most extensively), and Byzantine,
    French, German, Italian, Netherlandic and Spanish drama, incl.
    drama in Latin from those countries. Index of scholars and sub-
    jects, incl. playwrights, titles and themes.
YWMLS 72:53; 74:13; YWES 72:101

• EPIC •

1/153 Société Rencesvals. Bulletin bibliographique. 1 (1958)--.
12 (1979-80), publ. 1981. 161 pp. 303 entries, incl. eds., transls.,
    and critical studies of the chanson de geste and similar tradi-
    tions in the literatures of W. and N. Europe, esp. the Chanson
    de Roland and Poema de mío Cid. Abstracts in French. Indexes
    of names (scholars and subjects) and of other subjects, incl.
    titles.

1/154 "Bibliographical Note" and "Article Abstracts and Reviews." In
    Olifant, 1 (1973/74)--.
Both irregular, in several issues a year. "Bibl. Note," 7:1 (Autumn,
    1979):66-89, 266 entries, mainly publs. of 1978-79, on French,
    Spanish and German Charlemagne literature. "Art. Abstracts," 7:2
    (Winter, 1979):162-96, 18 evaluative summaries of arts. from
    journals and books.
YWMLS 76:48

• RHETORIC •

1/155 Murphy, James Jerome. Medieval Rhetoric: A Select Bibliography.
    Toronto & Buffalo: Toronto U. Pr., 1971. (Toronto Medieval Bibli-
    ographies, 3) 100 pp.
Classified arrangement. Brief annotations. Lists eds., transls., and
    studies (books and arts.) in English, French, German, etc. See
    also his Rhetoric in the Middle Ages: A History of Rhetorical The-
    ory from Saint Augustine to the Renaissance, Berkeley: U. of Cal-
    ifornia Pr., 1974, 395 pp.
SN 45 (1973):405-10

● RENAISSANCE ●

• BIBLIOGRAPHIES •

1/156 Bibliographie internationale de l'Humanisme et de la Renaissance.
    1 (1965)--.
Annual. Slow to appear. 11 (1975), publ. 1980. 708 pp. 6449 numbered
    entries. 3503 entries on individuals, alphabetically, incl. au-
    thors. Remainder arranged by subject, incl. appr. 650 entries
    on literature, by country, with cross-refs. to the entries on
    authors. Lists books and arts. Covers Petrarch through Donne.
    Index of scholars. Preceded by a "Bibliographie des articles re-
    latifs à l'histoire de l'humanisme et de la renaissance" in
    Bibliothèque d'humanisme et renaissance, 20 (1958)-27 (1965), cov-
    ering 1956-64.
BHR 42 (1980):697-98; LR 31 (1977):86; MLR 63 (1968):929-30; 68 (1973):
    607-09; 69 (1974):662

1/157 "Literature of the Renaissance." In Studies in Philology, 20
    (1923)-66 (1969).
Annotated. From 36 (1939) incl. sections on English, French, Italian,
    Spanish, Portuguese and Germanic literatures. Previously had

covered only English. Each section is in 3 divisions: General;
History, manners, customs; Authors. Covers from Petrarch through
Milton. 66 (1969): Italian Authors: 108 entries on minor figures,
270 on 25 major writers. Index of names (subjects and scholars).

● REVIEW of RESEARCH ●

1/158 The Present State of Scholarship in Sixteenth Century Literature.
Columbia & London: U. of Missouri Pr., 1978. 256 pp.
William M. Jones, ed. Covers English, French, German, Italian, Neo-
Latin and Spanish literatures. No indexes.
YWMLS 78:468; N&Q ns 28 (1981):69-70--unfav, criticizes overcompression

● HANDBOOK ●
[See 1/144: Encyclopedia of the Mid. A., Renaissance and Reformation]

● HISTORY ●

1/159 Krailsheimer, A. J., ed. The Continental Renaissance, 1500-1600.
Hassocks, Engl.: Harvester Pr./Atlantic Highlands, N. J.: Humanities Pr., 1978. 576 pp. (Pelican Guides to European Literature)
Reprint of 1971 ed. Covers Neo-Latin, Italian, French, Spanish and German literatures. Chapters cover a genre, subdivided by a literature or author. Chronological table, pp. 529-39. Index of names
and other subjects.
YWMLS 71:9, 408, 565; CL 26 (1974):95-- v fav; BHS 50 (1973):170-71--
regrets lack of an expressly comparative approach

● 17th & 18th CENTURIES ●

● BIBLIOGRAPHIES ●

1/160 The Eighteenth Century: A Current Bibliography. ns 1 (1975)--.
Annual. Lists books, book revs. and arts. in English, French, German

and other W. European langs. Covers English, French, German,
Italian, Scandinavian, Slavic, Spanish and American literatures.
Many annotations, occasionally evaluative, to 1 p. In 6 sections: Printing and Bibliographical Studies; Historical, Social
and Economic Studies; Philosophy, Science and Religion; the Fine
Arts; Literary Studies; and Individual Authors. ns 2 (1976),
publ. 1979: 448 pp.; "Individual Authors," pp. 224-411. Index of
names (scholars and subjects). No other subject index, and the
first 5 sections are not subdivided by specific subject. Continues the bibl. in Philological Quarterly (see 1/161).
YWES 78:217

1/161 "The Eighteenth Century: A Current Bibliography." In Philolog-
    ical Quarterly, 50 (1971)-54 (1975).
Similar to 1/160. Previous installments [from 5 (1926) through 49
    (1970)] had covered English literature, 1660-1800, chiefly, with
    some notice of European literature and writers, and have been
    collected in English Literature 1660-1800: A Bibliography of Mod-
    ern Studies, Princeton, N. J.: Princeton U. Pr., 1950-72, 6 vols.
YWMLS 74:97--"thorough interdisciplinary coverage," "good crit. comment"

• BAROQUE •

1/162 Carozza, Davy A. European Baroque: A Selective Bibliography.
    Norwood, Pa.: Norwood Eds., 1977. 226 pp.
1745 entries, incl. on the nations and regions of W. and E. Europe and
    Latin America. Index of scholars.
YWMLS 77:89

1/163 Skrine, Peter N. The Baroque: Literature and Culture in Seven-
    teenth Century Europe. London: Methuen/N. Y.: Holmes & Meier,
    1978. 176 pp.
8 chapters on themes in Baroque literature, illus. usually with English
    examples.

MLR 75 (1980):443-44; CL 33 (1981):202-03; YWMLS 78:94

1/164 Warnke, Frank J. Versions of Baroque: European Literature in the
    Seventeenth Century. New Haven & London: Yale U. Pr., 1972. 229
    pp.
9 chapters on aspects of the Baroque: the epic, the image of the world
    as a theater, etc.
MLR 71 (1976):165-67; YCGL 22 (1973):94-96; YWMLS 78:90

• MANNERISM •

1/165 Studing, Richard and Elizabeth Kruz. Mannerism in Art, Litera-
    ture and Music: A Bibliography. San Antonio, Texas: Trinity U. Pr.
    (Checklists in the Humanities and Education, 5) 60 pp.
Separate sections on art, literature (pp. 39-46, entries 456-565) and
    music. No indexes. Books and arts. in English and other langs.
RQ 33 (1980):769x--v unfav

• ENLIGHTENMENT •

1/166 Grimsley, Ronald, ed. The Age of Enlightenment, 1715-1789.
    Harmondsworth, Engl., etc.: Penguin, 1979. (Pelican Guides to
    European Literature) 505 pp.
Covers "almost exclusively" English, French, German and Italian litera-
    ture. Chapters on poetry, drama, the novel, "the literature of
    ideas" and aesthetics, subdivided by nation. Chronology, 1702-
    1800, pp. 424-53. Bibl. of texts and studies, nearly all books.
YWMLS 79:757

• ROMANTICISM •

• BIBLIOGRAPHIES •

1/167 The Romantic Movement: A Selective and Critical Bibliography.

1980--

Annual. Covers 1979--. Bibl. for 1979: 333 pp. Similar to 1/168. The
   Italian section which should have appeared in this vol. has been
   postponed to the 1980 vol.

1/168 "The Romantic Movement: A Selective and Critical Bibliography."
   In English Language Notes, 3 (1965/66)-17(1979).
Sections on English, French, German, Italian and Spanish Literatures.
   Annotations, sometimes lengthy and evaluative. Cites books and
   arts. in English, French, German, Italian and Spanish. Each section is in subsections for general studies (not further subdivided) and studies of authors. No indexes. Bibl. for 1977: 195
   pp. Previously in ELH: A Journal of English Literary History, 4
   (1937)-16 (1949) and Philological Quarterly 29 (1950)-43 (1964),
   but see The Romantic Movement Bibliography, 1936-1970: A Master
   Cumulation from ELH, Philological Quarterly and English Language
   Notes, Ann Arbor, Mich.: Pierian Pr., 1973, 7 vols., 3289 pp.,
   which collects (but does not cumulate) the first 35 installments
   of this bibl., with cumulated indexes, incl. scholars, and authors
   as subjects.
YWES 78:261

• HISTORIES •

1/169 Eichner, Hans, ed. "Romantic" and Its Cognates: The European
   History of a Word. Manchester, Engl.: Manchester U. Pr./Toronto
   & Buffalo: U. of Toronto Pr., 1972. 536 pp.
Covers Germany, England, France, Italy, Spain, Scandinavia and Russia.
   Quotations from German, etc. not translated. "Trends of Recent
   Research," by Henry H. H. Remak, pp. 475-500. Chronology, pp.
   501-13.
MLR 69 (1974):610-13; BHS 52 (1975):176-77; JEGP 72 (1973):407-09
   YWMLS 72:126

1/170 Furst, Lilian. <u>Romanticism</u> <u>in</u> <u>Perspective</u>: <u>A</u> <u>Comparative</u> <u>Study</u>
     <u>of</u> <u>Aspects</u> <u>of</u> <u>the</u> <u>Romantic</u> <u>Movements</u> <u>in</u> <u>England</u>, <u>France</u> <u>and</u> <u>Ger</u>-
     <u>many</u>. London, etc.: Macmillan/N. Y.: St. Martin's Pr., 1979.
     370 pp.
2nd ed. 1st ed. 1969. Text is unrevised.
Monatshefte 63 (1971):177-78--unfav; MLR 66 (1971):172-73--v unfav;
     critical of judgment and balance; YWMLS 69:122, 228-29, 566

1/171 Van Tieghem, Paul. <u>L'Ère</u> <u>romantique</u>: <u>Le</u> <u>Romantisme</u> <u>dans</u> <u>la</u> <u>lit</u>-
     <u>térature</u> <u>européenne</u>. Paris: Michel, 1948. 560 pp.
Covers E. as well as W. Europe. A survey of characteristics, themes
     and forms. Index of names and some titles. Reprinted, 1960, with
     suppl. bibl.

● MID-19th CENTURY ●

• HISTORY •

1/172 Hemmings, Frederick W. J., ed. <u>The</u> <u>Age</u> <u>of</u> <u>Realism</u>. Hassocks,
     Engl.: Harvester Pr./Atlantic Highlands, N. J.: Humanities Pr.,
     1978. 414 pp. (Pelican Guides to European Literature)
Reprint of 1974 ed. Sections on France, Russia, Germany, Spain, Portu-
     gal and Italy. Chronological table, covering 1812-1900, pp. 372-
     85. Index of names, titles and other subjects.

● 1880s and AFTER ●

• BIBLIOGRAPHIES •

1/173 "Annual Review." In <u>Journal</u> <u>of</u> <u>Modern</u> <u>Literature</u>, 1 (1970/71)--.
Currently in issue no. 4. Books (with evaluative comments, sometimes
     lengthy), arts. and diss., covering the "Modernist" period (1885-
     1950) in the literatures of W. and N. Europe and Russia chiefly.
     Occasional entries on other literatures. 7 (1979):565-882,

covering publs. of 1977-78. 11 sections, the largest (pp. 649-853) on writers, A to Z, most English, Irish or American. Other sections on themes and movements and on forms, incl. film.

1/174 "Current Bibliography." In <u>Twentieth Century Literature</u>, 1 (1955)--.

Currently irregular, in several issues a year. Alphabetical subject arrangement, usually names, but occasionally some other topic, e. g. narrative, style, Cuban novel. Annotated. 27:2 (Summer, 1981):197-206. Cumulated and suppl. through publs. of 1970 in next entry.

1/175 Pownall, David E. <u>Articles on Twentieth Century Literature: An Annotated Bibliography, 1954 to 1970</u>. N. Y.: Kraus-Thomson, 1973--.

7 vols. covering authors, A-Z. An 8th vol, expected 1982 or 83, will cover general topics and index the set. Lists arts. only, in the western langs., on writers worldwide, with abstracts. Limited strictly to **writers active this** century: incl. Strindberg but not Ibsen, yet covers Strindberg's entire career.

· HANDBOOKS ·

1/176 <u>Columbia Dictionary of Modern European Literature</u>. N. Y.: Columbia U. Pr., 1980. 895 pp.

2nd ed., rev. by Jean-Albert Bédé and William B. Edgerton. 1st ed. 1947, ed. by Horatio Smith. Covers 36 European literatures (excl. literature in English) and 1853 writers, incl. living writers and writers from the last 1/3 of the 19th c., selectively. Little biographical data; mainly descriptive and critical comments on the works. Most arts. have very brief bibls. Spanish literature: 15 1/2 cols.; Norwegian literature: 7 3/4 cols. Garcia Lorca: 2+ cols.; Brecht: 4 1/2 cols; G. Grass: 3 cols. No entries on movements, forms or technical terms.

1/177   Encyclopedia of World Literature in the 20th Century.   N. Y.:
        Ungar, 1981--.
2nd ed., Leonard S. Klein, ed.   1st ed. 1967-71, 3 vols. and suppl., ed.
        by Wolfgang B. Fleischmann.   Arts., usually 1 col. to 2 pp., on
        writers active in the 20th c., emphasizing criticism rather than
        biography.   Longer arts. on national literatures.   A few arts. on
        movements.   Brief bibls., often incl. arts. as well as books.
        Barthes: 2 1/2 cols.; Borges: 3 1/2 cols. text, 1+ col. bibl. of
        works and studies, 3 1/2 cols. quotations from critics.   Chinese
        literature: 9 cols.

1/178   Lexikon der Weltliteratur im 20. Jahrhundert.   Freiburg: Herder,
        1963-64.
3rd ed.   1st ed. 1960-61.   2 vols.   The 1st ed. of 1/177 was an "en-
        larged and updated" transl. of this.

1/179   Kunitz, Stanley J. and Howard Haycraft.   Twentieth Century Au-
        thors: A Biographical Dictionary of Modern Literature.   N. Y.:
        Wilson, 1942.   1577 pp.
Suppl., 1955, 1123 pp.   Total of appr. 2500 entries.   See 1/32 for a
        list of the arts. in this and in 1/180 (but not 1/181), as well as
        in 1/31, which covers European literature from 1000 to 1900.

1/180   Wakeman, John.   World Authors, 1950-1970.   N. Y.: Wilson, 1975.
        1594 pp.
959 entries, with emphasis on European and particularly British and
        American writers.   Incl. some figures from before 1950 omitted
        from 1/179, but does not update its entries otherwise.
JML 5 (1976/77):549

1/181   Wakeman, John.   World Authors, 1970-1975.   N. Y.: Wilson, 1980.
        894 pp.
Covers scholars, philosophers, etc., as well as literary figures.   Most
        entries 1-4 pp.

1/182 Dizionario universale della letteratura contemporanea. Milano:
       Mondadori, 1959-63.
5 vols. Mainly literature after 1870, but covers a number of early 19th
       c. writers (Balzac, Dickens). Arts. on writers and national lit-
       eratures, as well as on movements, literary journals, etc. Mo-
       dernismo: 3 cols., plus 1 1/2 col. bibl., and a separate 3 col.
       art. on Latin American modernism; Vorticism: 1/3 col.

1/183 Ivask, Ivar and Gero von Wilpert, eds. World Literature since
       1945: Critical Surveys of the Contemporary Literatures of Europe
       and the Americas. N. Y.: Ungar, 1973. 724 pp.
28 chapters. American literature: 62 pp. text, by form, and 2 pp.
       bibl., books only. Polish literature: 22 pp. Yiddish literature:
       8 pp. Also publ. in German as Moderne Weltliteratur, Stuttgart:
       Kröner, 1972.
MLR 69 (1974):837--"comprehensive and up-to-date," but faults certain
       chapters; SS 48 (1976):452-54--critical of details, esp. of crit-
       ical passages; very critical of bibls.: "virtually useless"

● HISTORY ●

1/184 Bradbury, Malcolm and James McFarlane, eds. Modernism, 1890-
       1930. Hassocks, Sussex: Harvester Pr./Atlantic Highlands, N. J.:
       Humanities Pr., 1978. 684 pp. (Pelican Guides to European Lit.)
Reprint of 1974 ed. Covers English, American, French, German, Russian,
       Italian, Austrian, Czech and Scandinavian literatures. Chronolo-
       gy, pp. 571-612. Brief biographical arts., pp. 613-40. Bibl.
       pp. 641-64.
YWMLS 75:668; YWES 78:345-46

● DRAMA ●

1/185 "Modern Drama Studies: An Annual Bibliography." In Modern Drama,
       17(1974)--.

In issue no. 2 (June).   24 (1981):146-233.   Arranged by region or lang.,
    then playwright.   Covers from Ibsen and Strindberg (with section
    on Büchner).   Cites books and arts. in English and other langs.
    Also publ. in 3 (1960/61)-11 (1968/69).
YWMLS 74:222; 75:303; YWES 78:419

1/186   Breed, Paul F. and Florence Sniderman.   Dramatic Criticism Index:
    A Bibliography of Commentaries on Playwrights from Ibsen to the
    Avant-garde.   Detroit: Gale Research, 1972.   1022 pp.
Criticism in English from "appr. 630 books and over 200" journals.
MD 16 (1973):110--v unfav, noting omission of important studies

1/187   Boyer, Robert D.   Realism in European Theatre and Drama, 1870-
    1920: A Bibliography.   Westport, Conn.: Greenwood Pr., 1979.   236
    pp.
By nation, then playwright, covering 10 nations or regions of W. and N.
    Europe and Russia.   Cites books and arts. in various langs., and
    diss., chiefly U. S.
YWMLS 79:535--unfav, with ref. to coverage of Italy

1/188   Matlaw, Myron.   Modern World Drama: An Encyclopedia.   N. Y.:
    Dutton, 1972.   960 pp.
Arts. on playwrights and plays, beginning in the latter part of the 19th
    c.   Also arts. on national dramas and other topics.   Mayakovsky:
    1 1/4 cols., with cross-refs. to arts. on Mystery-Bouffe and The
    Bedbug.   The Screens (Genet): 1/2 col.   Expressionism: 3/4 col.
    Index of characters.   Index of subjects, largely a list of the
    arts., with a few names and terms not given separate entries, and
    the orig. titles of foreign plays listed in the text under an
    English title.
MD 16 (1973):396-401--v fav; ETJ 26 (1974):124-26x--v fav

1/189   Crowell's Handbook of Contemporary Drama.   N. Y.: Crowell, 1971.
    505 pp.

Michael Anderson, et al. Arts. on playwrights, plays, movements, crit-
    ical terms, etc., since the 1940s, in the U. S. and Europe.
YWES 72:409; ETJ 26 (1974):131-32x; MD 16 (1973):396-401

1/190 Brockett, Oscar Gross and Robert B. Findlay. Century of Innova-
    tion: A History of European and American Theatre and Drama since
    1870. Englewood Cliffs, N. J.: Prentice-Hall, 1973. 826 pp.
Considerable attention to the stage, incl. theater companies, directors,
    and productions of classic and modern plays.

• THEMES •

1/191 Glaser, Hermann. Literatur des 20. Jahrhunderts in Motiven.
    München: Beck, 1978--.
I: 1870-1918, 220 pp.; II: 1918-1933, 392 pp. Arts. on literary themes
    as exemplified in the work of one or several authors. Tote
    Seelen (I:73-79): 5 writers, all Russian, chiefly Gogol and Tol-
    stoy. Frontier (I:117-28): a number of American writers, chiefly
    Dreiser and Henry James.

• PLOTS •

1/192 Dictionnaire des oeuvres contemporaines de tous les pays: Littér-
    ature, philosophie, musique, sciences. Paris: SEDE, 1967. 765
    pp.
Vol. 5 of 1/134. Covers books, incl. collections of poetry, literary
    journals, musical compositions, etc.

1/193 Dizionario letterario Bompiani delle opere e dei personaggi di
    tutti i tempi e di tutte le letterature. Appendice. Milano: Bom-
    piani, 1964-66.
2 vols. Suppl. to 1/133. Covers books, incl. collections of poetry,
    and literary journals, etc. No entries on characters. Indexes

of authors and of titles in orig. langs.

1/194 Sprinchorn, Evert. 20th Century Plays in Synopsis. N. Y.: Cro-
       well, 1965. 493 pp.
5 plays by Anouilh, 4 by J. M. Barrie, 1 by Beckett. Incl. Strindberg
       (10 plays) but not Ibsen. Entries are 2-4 pp.
Shaw R 9 (1966):117-18

1/195 Kienzle, Siegfried. Schauspielführer der Gegenwart: 714 Einzel-
       interpretationen zum Schauspiel seit 1945. Stuttgart: Kröner,
       1978. 659 pp.
3rd ed. 1st ed. 1966. Covers only plays available in German. Beckett:
       5 plays; Mrozek: 7 plays. An earlier ed. was transl. into Eng-
       lish: Modern World Theatre: A Guide to Productions in Europe and
       the United States since 1945, N. Y.: Ungar, 1970, 509 pp.

• EXPRESSIONISM •

1/196 Weisstein, Ulrich Werner, ed. Expressionism as an International
       Literary Phenomenon. Paris: Didier, 1973. (A Comparative History
       of Literature in Western Languages, 1) 360 pp.
Chapters on Expressionism in Germany, England and America, and other
       countries in W. and E. Europe, and on Expressionism in art, music
       and film. Classified bibl., pp. 329-49. Index of names only.
CLS 12 (1975):429-33; MLR 70 (1975):588-89; GQ 50 (1977):320-21x;
       Monatshefte 69 (1977):457-59; RLC 52 (1978):199-21

• SYMBOLISM •

1/197 Anderson, David L., Georgia S. Maas, and D.-M. Savoye. Symbol-
       ism: A Bibliography of Symbolism as an International and Multi-
       Disciplinary Movement. N. Y.: N. Y. U. Pr., 1975. 160 pp.
3182 numbered entries in classified order. Books and arts. in the
       langs. of W. and E. Europe, and diss. as listed in DAI.

RLC 51 (1977):109-11

• POST-SYMBOLISM •

1/198   Krawitz, Henry. A Post-Symbolist Bibliography. Metuchen, N. J.:
        Scarecrow, 1973. 284 pp.
4141 entries. Books and arts. in English, French, German, Italian and
        Spanish, chiefly, publ. 1950-70, chiefly. In 4 sections, incl.
        section covering 19 writers. Some very brief annotations. Index
        of scholars.
RLC 49 (1975):341-42--mixed; faults choice of authors given special
        coverage

II

CLASSICAL LITERATURE

OUTLINE

● ●   CLASSICAL LITERATURE   ● ●

● BIBLIOGRAPHIES ●

2/1   Dee, James H.   "A Survey of Recent Bibliographies of Classical Lit-
      erature."   In Classical World, 73 (1979/80):275-90.
Alphabetical, by author covered or other topic. Annotated. Covers
      bibls. publ. since 1945 as books or in books or journals. Lists
      the bibls. in Lustrum (2/10) through 19 (1976), in Classical World
      (2/9) through 72 (1978/79) and in Anzeiger für die Altertumswis-
      senschaft (2/11) through 31 (1978).

2/2   L'Année philologique: Bibliographie critique et analytique de l'
      antiquité gréco-latine.   1928--.
Annual. Covers from 1924. 49 (1978), publ. 1980. 12964 numbered en-
      tries, most with an abstract in French, English or German, of 1-5
      sentences. In 2 parts: I: Auteurs et textes (5130 entries); II:
      Matières et disciplines (in 10 sections, divided and subdivided,
      incl. literary history, in 10 broad subdivisions, as well as lan-
      guage, philosophy, history, etc.). Vergilius: nearly 125 entries,
      incl. cross-refs., on Vergil's works, thought and influence, by
      scholar. Covers medieval Greek and Latin to 800 AD. Cites books,
      incl. eds. and transls., book revs., and arts. in books and jour-
      nals, in various langs., and diss. as cited in DAI. Indexes
      (since 24 [1953]) of anonymous titles and general subject headings
      used in part I; ancient names (incl. gods, etc.); place names; hu-
      manists; and modern scholars. Preceded by the next 4 entries.

2/3   Marouzeau, Jules. Dix années de bibliographie classique: Biblio-
      graphie critique et analytique de l'antiquité gréco-latine pour la
      periode 1914-1924. Paris: Belles Lettres, 1927-28.
2 vols. Auteurs et textes and Matières et disciplines. Continues 2/4.

2/4   Lambrino, Scarlat. Bibliographie de l'antiquité classique, 1896-

1914. Paris: Belles Lettres, 1951.
I: Auteurs et Textes. No more publ. Continues 2/5.

2/5 Klussmann, Rudolf. Bibliotheca scriptorum classicorum et graecorum
       et latinorum: die Literatur von 1878 bis 1896 einschliesslich
       umfassend. Leipzig: Reisland, 1909-13. Continues 2/6.
2 vols. in 4

2/6 Engelmann, Wilhelm. Bibliotheca scriptorum classicorum. Leipzig:
       Engelmann, 1880-82.
8th ed., rev. by E. Preuss. 2 vols. Lists studies from 1700 to 1878.

2/7 "Bibliographische Beilage." In Gnomon: Kritische Zeitschrift für
       die gesamte klassische Altertumswissenschaft.
Usually in every other issue. 52 (1980): in issues 1, 3, 5, and 7,
       appr. 100 pp., listing publs. of 1979-80, chiefly, and in German,
       English, French and Italian, chiefly. Each installment is in 12
       sections, incl. one on studies of ancient authors.

2/8 McGuire, Martin Rawson Patrick. Introduction to Classical Scholar-
       ship: A Syllabus and Bibliographical Guide. Washington, D. C.:
       Catholic U. of America Pr., 1961. 257 pp.
New and rev. ed. 1st ed. 1957. Part II: a classified and annotated
       bibl. of books and arts. on all aspects of Greek and Roman cul-
       ture, pp. 15-144. No sections on individual writers. Index of
       scholars.
Class J 56 (1960/61):380-82--ref. to 1st ed.

● REVIEWS of RESEARCH ●

2/9 [Reviews of various topics.] In Classical World.
Irregular, 1 or 2/yr., in recent vols. Classified and annotated, with
       notes sometimes of 1 1/2 pp., covering 10 items. "Ovid's Meta-
       morphoses: A Bibliography, 1968-1978," by Alison Goddard Elliot,

73 (1979/80):385-412. "Homer Studies, 1971-1977," by James P.
Holoks, 73 (1979/80):65-150. This series of reviews began in
1953, when the journal was called Classical Weekly (vol. 47), and
have been collected in 5 subject vols., publ. in 1977. See 2/35,
2/62, and 2/87.

2/10 [Reviews on various writers.] In Lustrum: Internationale For-
schungsberichte aus dem Bereich des klassischen Altertums,
1956--.
Annual. Each vol. is entirely devoted to bibliographic essays (usually
3), in German. 19 (1976): Homer, 1971-77 (60 pp., continuing 3
previous surveys); Euripides, 1976-77; and Plautus, 1935-75 (117
pp., more than 1200 refs.). The Homer and Plautus bibls. are classified, annotated and indexed. 22 (1980) incl. a cumulative list
of the surveys in vols. 1-21, and see also 2/1.
REG 93 (1980):290-91--ref. to a bibl. on Plato in 20 (1977)

2/11 [Reviews on various writers.] In Anzeiger für die Altertums-
wissenschaft, 1 (1948)--.
Reviews of research on major writers, updated frequently. Greek tragedy: 14 installments between 1 (1948) and 30 (1977); Homer: 13
installments between 3 (1950) and 30 (1977); Ovid: 4 installments
between 11 (1958) and 26 (1973); Vergil: 5 installments between
3 (1950) and 32 (1979), and others. See the list in 2/1, through
31 (1978). Erich Thummer, "Horaz: Bericht über die Literatur,
II," 32 (1979): cols. 21-66, 825 entries in classified order, covering research of 1963-75 and continuing a survey in 15 (1962).

2/12 Fifty Years (and Twelve) of Classical Scholarship. N. Y.: Barnes
& Noble, 1968. 523 pp.
2nd ed. 1st ed. 1954. 14 chapters by various scholars, e. g. "Early
Greek Lyric Poetry," essay, pp. 50-76; notes, pp. 76-82; and ap-
pendix, pp. 83-87, covering the additional 12 years.
ClassP 64 (1969):64

2/13 <u>Jahresbericht</u> <u>über</u> <u>die</u> <u>Fortschritte</u> <u>der</u> <u>klassischen</u> <u>Altertums-</u>
      <u>wissenschaft.</u> 1873-1945.

"Gave at regular intervals critical, and in **principle exhaustive**, sur-
      veys of recent work in all the main fields of classical study."
      <u>OCD</u>, 2nd ed., p. 1151 (2/21). A suppl. was <u>Bibliotheca</u> <u>philo-</u>
      <u>logica</u> <u>classica</u>, 1875-1941, an enumerative bibliography.

· DISSERTATIONS ·

2/14 Thompson, Lawrence S. <u>A</u> <u>Bibliography</u> <u>of</u> <u>American</u> <u>Doctoral</u> <u>Disser-</u>
      <u>tations</u> <u>in</u> <u>Classical</u> <u>Studies</u> <u>and</u> <u>Related</u> <u>Fields</u>. Hamden, Conn.:
      Shoe String, 1968. 250 pp.

All aspects of classical culture, through 500 AD. A suppl., publ. 1976,
      adds American diss. 1964-72 and British diss., 1950-72.

· FESTSCHRIFTEN ·

2/15 Rounds, Dorothy. <u>Articles</u> <u>on</u> <u>Antiquity</u> <u>in</u> <u>Festschriften</u>: <u>An</u> <u>In-</u>
      <u>dex</u>. <u>The</u> <u>Ancient</u> <u>Near</u> <u>East</u>, <u>the</u> <u>Old</u> <u>Testament</u>, <u>Greece</u>, <u>Rome</u>,
      <u>Roman</u> <u>Law</u>, <u>Byzantium</u>. Cambridge, Mass.: Harvard U. Pr., 1962.
      560 pp.

Scholars and subjects, in one alphabet. Some cross-refs. Covers
      through 1954.
ClassW 56 (1962/63):216

· LITERATURE ·

2/16 Gwinup, Thomas and Fidelia Dickinson. <u>Greek</u> <u>and</u> <u>Roman</u> <u>Authors</u>: <u>A</u>
      <u>Checklist</u> <u>of</u> <u>Criticism</u>. Metuchen, N. J.: Scarecrow, 1973. 194
      pp.

Criticism in English only, from certain books and journals, on about 70
      authors, Homer to Jerome. Catullus: 4 1/2 pp., incl. 3 pp. of
      studies of 25 individual poems.

2/17 Pöschl, Viktor, Helga Gärtner and Waltraut Heyke, eds. Biblio-
       graphie zur antiken Bildersprache. Heidelberg: Winter, 1964.
       674 pp.
A list of studies of imagery. Ancient authors, pp. 53-443, with notes
       identifying in 1 word the image discussed. Images, pp. 447-594,
       as an index to the Authors list. Other indexes incl. Greek and
       Latin words, and modern scholars. Vergilius: 14+ pp., by scholar.

• TRANSLATIONS •

2/18 Parks, George B. and Ruth Z. Temple, eds. The Greek and Latin
       Literatures. N. Y.: Ungar, 1968. (The Literatures of the World
       in English Translation) 442 pp.
Incl. Classical, Byzantine and Modern Greek, and Classical, Medieval
       and Neo-Latin writings. Lists transls. publ. as or in books.

• HANDBOOKS •

2/19 Pauly, August Friedrich von. Paulys Real-Encyclopädie der class-
       ischen Altertumswissenschaft. Stuttgart: Metzler, 1894-1972.
New ed., by Georg Wissowa. 34 vols. in 46. 15 vols. of suppls., 1903-
       78, all A through Z. Signed arts., often very lengthy, on all as-
       pects of classical civilization, with bibls. citing ancient wri-
       ters and modern scholars. Vergil: 470+ cols., covering his life,
       works and influence, incl. 130+ cols. on the Aeneid, with a book-
       by-book commentary. Epigram: 40 cols. Called "Pauly-Wissowa."
       Register der Nachträge und Supplemente, 1980, 250 pp., listing the
       arts. in the suppl. vols. and the suppl. entries at the back of
       most of the orig. vols.

2/20 Daremberg, Charles and Edmund Saglio, eds. Dictionnaire des an-
       tiquités grecques et romaines, d'après les textes et les monu-
       mentes. Paris: Hachette, 1873-1919.
5 vols. in 9. Lengthy arts., with illus., on classical society, law and

culture, but not literature. No biographical entries.

2/21 <u>Oxford</u> <u>Classical</u> <u>Dictionary</u>. N. G. L. Hammond and H. H. Scullard, eds. Oxford: Clarendon Pr., 1970. 1176 pp.

2nd ed. 1st ed. 1949. Brief arts. (2 lines to several pp.), usually with bibls., on all aspects of Greek and Roman civilization to 337 AD. Virgil: 9 cols., 1/2 col. bibl. Epigram: 3 1/2 cols., 1/2 col. bibl.

ClassR ns 21 (1971):124-25; JRomSt 61 (1971):269-71

2/22 <u>Der</u> <u>kleine</u> <u>Pauly</u>: <u>Lexikon</u> <u>der</u> <u>Antike</u>. Konrad Ziegler and Walther Sontheimer, eds. Stuttgart: Druckenmüller, 1964-75.

5 vols. Brief signed arts., with bibls., incl. refs. to the arts. in Pauly-Wissowa (2/19). Vergil: 11 cols. Epigram: 2 cols.

2/23 <u>Lexikon</u> <u>der</u> <u>alten</u> <u>Welt</u>. Zürich & Stuttgart: Artemis, 1965. 3524 cols.

Brief signed arts., few longer than 1/2 col., with brief bibls.

• LITERATURE •

2/24 Harvey, Sir Paul. <u>Oxford</u> <u>Companion</u> <u>to</u> <u>Classical</u> <u>Literature</u>. Oxford: Clarendon Pr., 1937. 468 pp.

Brief entries, few more than several sentences. No bibls. Covers authors, works, characters, literary terms and allusions, incl. much not given a separate entry in <u>OCD</u> (2/21). Virgil: 1+ p.; <u>Aeneid</u>: 5 2/3 cols.; Dido: 1/4 col. Epigram: 1/3 col.

2/25 Grant, Michael. <u>Greek</u> <u>&</u> <u>Latin</u> <u>Authors,</u> <u>800</u> <u>BC-AD</u> <u>1000</u>. N. Y.: Wilson, 1980. 490 pp.

Arts. from 1 col. to 5 or more pp., with bibls. of eds., transls., and studies (books only, most in English). Plautus: 8 cols., and 2/3 col. bibl., incl. paragraphs summarizing each play. Vergil: 9 cols., and 1 1/2 cols. bibl.

TLS Aug. 8, 1980, p. 893

2/26 Feder, Lillian. Crowell's Handbook of Classical Literature. N.Y.:
       Crowell, 1964. 448 pp.
Mainly biographies (Vergil: 1 2/3 pp.) and plots (Aeneid: 11 pp.). No
       entry on the epigram as a form.
ClassJ 61 (1965/66):78-80; ClassP 60 (1965):204-07--"admirably planned
       and executed"

2/27 Kroh, Paul. Lexikon der antiken Autoren. Stuttgart: Kröner,
       1972. 675 pp.
Brief arts. on authors and anonymous works, through the 6th c. AD.

● DRAMA ●

2/28 Hathorn, Richmond Y. Crowell's Handbook of Classical Drama. N.Y.:
       Crowell, 1967. 350 pp.
Usually brief entries on playwrights, plays, characters, actors, and
       dramatic and theatrical terms. No bibls.
ClassP 63 (1968):152-53; ClassJ 63 (1967/68):92--"thoroughly useful"

2/29 Harsh, Philip Whaley. A Handbook of Classical Drama. np: Stan-
       ford U. Pr./London: H. Milford, Oxford U. Pr., 1944. 526 pp.
Lengthy plot summaries and evaluations of surviving plays.

● RHETORIC ●

2/30 Kennedy, George A. Classical Rhetoric and Its Christian and
       Secular Tradition from Ancient to Modern Times. Chapel Hill: U.
       of North Carolina Pr., 1980. 291 pp.
Covers rhetorical theory through the 18th c. in England and France, esp.
Speculum 56 (1981):218; CL 33 (1981):282-83

2/31 Lausberg, Heinrich. Handbuch der literarischen Rhetorik: Eine

Grundlegung der Literaturwissenschaft. München: Hueber, 1973.
2nd ed. 1st ed. 1960. 2 vols. 983 pp. Vol. 2 is mostly a glossary
    and index of Latin (pp. 639-845), Greek and French terms.

● INFLUENCE ●

2/32 London. University. Warburg Institute. Library. Catalog. Bos-
    ton: Hall, 1967.
11 vols. Suppl., 1971. Catalog of a library "concerned with the study
    of the survival and revival of classical antiquity in . . . Euro-
    pean civilization." (Pref.) Lists books and arts., as available
    in the Institute's library, in classified order. Vols. 6 & 7 co-
    ver Greek and Latin literature, incl. authors, themes and forms,
    and the literatures of W. Europe, esp. through the 17th c. "The
    best bibliography on the history of ideas. . . ." ClassR ns 27
    (1977):293

2/33 Higginbotham, John, ed. Greek and Latin Literature: A Comparative
    Study. London: Methuen, 1969. 399 pp.
11 essays on genres and areas of ancient writing, surveying the devel-
    opment of the genre, the influence of Greek on Latin, and of both
    on European literature.
ClassJ 66 (1970/71):262-63--"reliable"; ClassR ns 21 (1971):75-78;
    ClassW 63 (1969/70):126-27--unfav

2/34 Highet, Gilbert. The Classical Tradition: Greek and Roman Influ-
    ences on Western Literature. N. Y.: Oxford U. Pr., 1949. 763 pp.
Covers literature in English, French, German, Italian and Spanish, to
    Joyce and the Symbolists. Extensive index of names and other sub-
    jects.

● ●   GREEK   ● ●

● REVIEW of RESEARCH ●

2/35 The Classical World Bibliography of Greek Drama and Poetry.   N.Y.:
      Garland, 1978.   339 pp.
Reprints surveys from Classical World (2/9).

● HANDBOOK ●

2/36 Whibley, Leonard, ed. Companion to Greek Studies. Cambridge:
      the University Pr., 1931. 790 pp.
4th ed. 1st ed. 1905. Chapters surveying literature, philosophy, reli-
      gion and mythology, etc. Chronological chart, pp. 80-116, cover-
      ing political and literary events to 146 BC.

● HISTORIES ●

2/37 Lesky, Albin. A History of Greek Literature. London: Methuen,
      1966. 921 pp.
Transl. of 2nd, 1963, German ed. Covers through the 2nd c. AD. Lengthy
      bibls. after each section, and many footnotes. Index of names
      and other subjects, pp. 898-921. 3rd German ed., Bern & München:
      Francke, 1971, 1023 pp.
ClassR ns 17 (1967):224; ClassP 59 (1964):273-74--ref. to 2nd German ed.

2/38 Hadas, Moses. A History of Greek Literature. N. Y.: Columbia U.
      Pr., 1950. 327 pp.
Covers through Lucian and the fiction writers of the 2nd and 3rd c. AD.

2/39 Croiset, Alfred and Maurice Croiset. Histoire de la littérature
      grecque. Paris: Boccard, 1914-47.
5 large vols. No bibls., but footnotes. Index in vol. 5 (pp. 1079-96)
      of names and other subjects, covering the set. "More readable and

more stimulating [than Schmid (2/40)]," M. Hadas, (2/38).

2/40   Schmid, Wilhelm and Otto Stählin. Geschichte der griechischen
       Literatur. München: Beck, 1929-48. (Handbuch der Altertums-
       wissenschaft, 7 Abt.)
2 vols. in 7 parts. I: Die klassische Periode. In 5 parts. II: Die
       nachklassische Periode. To 530 AD. Extensive footnotes. A re-
       vision of a work by Wilhelm von Christ.

2/41   Wright, Frederick Adam. A History of Later Greek Literature from
       the Death of Alexander in 323 BC to the Death of Justinian in 565
       AD. N. Y.: Macmillan, 1932. 415 pp.
Brief bibls. no notes. Brief index of names. Touches on many minor
       figures. Many quotations, all in translation only.

● POETRY ●

2/42   Fatouros, Georgios. Index verborum zur frühgriechischen Lyrik.
       Heidelberg: Winter, 1966. 415 pp.
No contexts. Covers 42 poets.

● DRAMA ●

2/43   Ferguson, John. A Companion to Greek Tragedy. Austin: U. of
       Texas Pr., 1972. 623 pp.
Sections on the 3 surviving tragedians and on all the surviving plays.
       Classified bibl., pp. 573-604. Detailed index of names and other
       subjects.
MLJ 57 (1973):442-43--"full and useful, though unannotated, bibls."

● RHETORIC ●

2/44   Kennedy, George A. The Art of Persuasion in Greece. Princeton,
       N. J.: Princeton U. Pr., 1963. 350 pp.

Covers chiefly from the 5th to the 1st c. BC.   Footnotes, but no bibl.
   Detailed index.
ClassR ns 15 (1965):200-02; ClassW 56 (1962/63):218; MLJ 48 (1964):57-58

● AUTHORS ●

2/45 Wartelle, André. Bibliographie historique et critique d'Eschyle
      et de la tragédie grecque, 1518-1974. Paris: Belles Lettres,
      1978. 685 pp.
By year of publ. Annotated. Cites book revs. Indexes incl. scholars
      and subjects, incl. names, titles of Aeschylus' works, and other
      topics (Images, comparaisons, métaphores, symboles: 28 lines of
      citations, identified by author and year).
ClassW 73 (1979/80):276

2/46 Italie, Gabriel. Index Aeschylus. Leiden: Brill, 1955. 336 pp.
Brief definitions, in Latin. Context of a few words. See also the set
      of 7 concordances to the individual plays, by Henrik Holmboe, Co-
      penhagen: Akademiskboghandel, 1971-73.

2/47 Dunbar, Henry. A Complete Concordance to the Comedies and Frag-
      ments of Aristophanes. Hildesheim and N. Y.: Olms, 1973. 372 pp.
New ed., rev. and enl. by Benedetto Marzullo. Orig. ed. 1883. Brief
      context.

2/48 Erickson, Keith. Aristotle's Rhetoric: Five Centuries of Philo-
      logical Research. Metuchen, N. J.: Scarecrow, 1975. 187 pp.
More than 1590 entries, by author. No subject index. Occasional an-
      notations. Lists books, arts. and chapters in books, in English
      and other langs., and U. S. diss. and M. A. theses.
ClassW 73 (1979/80):277; ClassR ns 27 (1977):17-18--critical of errors

2/49 Allen, James Turney and Gabriel Italie. A Concordance to Eurip-
      ides. Berkeley: U. of California Pr., 1954. 686 pp.

A suppl. by Christhoper Collard, Groningen: Bouma, 1971, 52 pp. Brief
     context. See also the series of concordances to individual plays
     by Marianne McDonald, Irvine, Calif.: TLG Publs., 1977--.
ClassR ns 30 (1980):133-34; REG 92 (1979):246-47--both ref. to McDonald

2/50 Hofinger, M. and M. Mund-Dopchie. Lexicon Hesiodeum: cum Indice
      Inverso. Leiden: Brill, 1973-78.
4 vols. and suppl. Definitions in French. 1 or more lines of context.

2/51 Minton, William W. Concordance to the Hesiodic Corpus. Leiden:
      Brill, 1976. 313 pp.
ClassR ns 28 (1978):342

2/52 Heubeck, Alfred. Die homerische Frage: Ein Bericht über die
      Forschung der letzten Jahrzehnte. Darmstadt: Wissenschaftliche
      Buchgesellschaft, 1974. (Erträge der Forschung, 27) 326 pp.
A review of scholarship from the 1930s to 1969. Bibl., pp. 243-304, of
      about 1500 items. Various indexes, incl. subjects.
JHS 96 (1976):165; ClassW 73 (1979/80):66; ClassR ns 27 (1977):1-2

2/53 Packard, David W. and Tania Meyers. A Bibliography of Homeric
      Scholarship: Preliminary Edition, 1930-1970. Malibu, Calif.: Un-
      dena Pr., 1974. 183 pp.
A cumulation of the references and cross-refs. under Homer in L'Année
      philologique (2/2), omitting the annotations. 3,840 entries, by
      scholar, with subject indexes.
ClassR ns 27 (1977):1-2; ClassW 73 (1979/80):66

2/54 Wace, Alan J. B. and Frank H. Stubbings, eds. A Companion to Ho-
      mer. London: Macmillan/N. Y.: St. Martin's Pr., 1962. 595 pp.
Sections on the poems (incl. meter, style, and transmission of the
      texts) and their background. No bibl., and few notes. Homeric
      quotations in Greek only.
ClassR ns 13 (1963):133-36; ClassW 56 (1962/63):285; G&R ns 10 (1963):81

2/55   Prendergast, Guy Lushington. A Complete Concordance to the Iliad
         of Homer. Hildesheim: Olms, 1962. 427 pp.
New ed., rev. and enl. by Benedetto Marzullo. Orig. ed. 1875.

2/56   Dunbar, Henry. A Complete Concordance to the Odyssey of Homer.
         Hildesheim: Olms, 1962. 398 pp.
New ed., rev. and enl. by Benedetto Marzullo. Orig. ed. 1883.

2/57   Gerber, Douglas E. A Bibliography of Pindar, 1513-1966. Cleve-
         land: Case Western Reserve U. Pr., 1969. 160 pp.
Publ. for the American Philological Assn. Much of the book lists stud-
         ies of particular poems. Other sections on "Style and Imagery"
         and "Relationships to Other Writers," etc.
ClassR ns 21 (1971):16-17--v fav

2/58   Slater, William J. Lexicon to Pindar. Berlin: de Gruyter, 1969.
         563 pp.
Brief definitions in English. Context sometimes lengthy.
ClassJ 68 (1972/73):79

2/59   Ellendt, Friedrich Theodor. Lexicon Sophocleum. Berolini: Born-
         traeger, 1872. 812 pp.
Ed. corrected by Hermannus Genthe. Definitions in Latin. Brief con-
         text.

● ● LATIN ● ●

● BIBLIOGRAPHIES ●

2/60   "Rassegna delle riviste" and "Notiziario bibliografico." In Boll-
         ettino di studi latini, 2 (1972)--.
In each issue (2/yr.). The "Rassegna" is a list of the contents of re-
         cent journals, with abstracts. 10 (1980):135-89, covering about
         50 journals, most from 1978 or 1979. The "Notiziario" is a list

of books, book revs. and arts. on Latin authors or general topics
(in alternating issues).   10 (1980):190-224, on Latin authors.   15
entries on Petronius, most of which are abstracted in the Rassegna
of this or the previous or following issue.
Most issues also contain one or more reviews of research.   9 (1979):281-
315, L. Perelli, "Rassegna di studi terenziani (1968-1978)."

2/61   Herescu, Niculae I.   Bibliographie de la littérature latine.
Paris: Belles Lettres, 1943.   426 pp.
Lists eds., transls., bibls. and concordances, and studies (books, arts.
and diss.) in various W. European langs., **by period and author.**

● REVIEW of RESEARCH ●

2/62   The Classical World Bibliography of Roman Drama and Poetry and
Ancient Fiction.   N. Y.: Garland, 1978.   387 pp.
Reprints surveys of scholarship from Classical World (2/9).

● HANDBOOK ●

2/63   Sandys, Sir John Edwin, ed.   Companion to Latin Studies.   Cambridge: the University Pr., 1925.   891 pp.
Chapters on literature, art, philosophy, etc.   Chronological tables,
largely of civil events through 565 AD, pp. 114-48.

● HISTORIES ●

2/64   Duff, John Wight.   Literary History of Rome from the Origins to
the Close of the Golden Age.   London: Benn, 1953.   535 pp.
3rd ed., ed. by A. M. Duff.   1st ed. 1909.   Many quotations, some in
English only, others in Latin only.

2/65   Duff, John Wight.   Literary History of Rome in the Silver Age,
from Tiberius to Hadrian.   London: Benn, 1964.   599 pp.

3rd ed., ed. by A. M. Duff. 1st ed. 1927. Covers first 2 centuries AD.

2/66 Hadas, Moses. A History of Latin Literature. N. Y.: Columbia U.
       Pr., 1952. 474 pp.
Covers through the mid 6th c. AD (to Boethius and Cassiodorus), but con-
       centrates on the period through Tacitus. Index of names and other
       subjects.

2/67 Schanz, Martin von. Geschichte der römischen Literatur bis zum
       Gesetzgebungswerk des Kaisers Justinian. München: Beck, 1911-27.
       (Handbuch der klassischen Altertumswissenschaft, Abt. 8)
4th ed., rev. by Carl Hosius. 4 vols. in 6. Dense with facts and bib-
       liographical refs. Index of names and other subjects in vol. 4.

2/68 Rostagni, Augusto. Storia della letteratura latina. Torino:
       UTET, 1964.
3rd ed., rev. and expanded by Italo Lana. 1st ed. 1949-52. 3 vols.
       Covers through the 5th C. Vol. 3 contains an index to the set,
       chiefly of names.

● POETRY ●

2/69 Swanson, Donald C. The Names in Roman Verse: A Lexicon and Re-
       verse Index of All Proper Names of History, Mythology and Geog-
       raphy Found in the Classical Roman Poets. Madison: U. of Wiscon-
       sin Pr., 1967. 425 pp.
Covers 35 poets or anonymous works and 2 collections of fragments.
       Brief identifying notes.

● RHETORIC ●

2/70 Kennedy, George A. The Art of Rhetoric in the Roman World, 300
       BC-AD 300. Princeton, N. J.: Princeton U. Pr., 1972. 658 pp.
Bulk of the book covers Cicero and the Augustan period. No bibls., but

many notes. Index of names and other subjects.
ClassR ns 25 (1975):64-66--v fav; ClassW 67 (1973/74):304-06; JHI 35
(1974):351-52x

● AUTHORS ●

2/71 Harrauer, Hermann. A Bibliography to Catullus. Hildesheim: Ger-
      stenberg, 1979. (Bibliography to the Augustan Poetry, 3) 206 pp.
Books and arts., since 1500. Classified arrangement. Indexes incl. individual poems as subjects (pp. 147-70) and names and other topics (pp. 171-84).

2/72 McCarren, V. P. A Critical Concordance to Catullus. Leiden:
      Brill, 1977. 210 pp
Context of up to several lines of verse.
JRomS 68 (1978):230-31--unfav

2/73 Cooper, Lane. A Concordance to the Works of Horace. Washington:
      Carnegie Inst., 1916. 593 pp.
Line or more of context.

2/74 Bo, Domenico. Lexicon Horatianum. Hildesheim: Olms, 1965-66.
2 vols. Definitions in Latin. Brief contexts.
ClassR 16 (1966):325-27; ClassP 62 (1967):270-71

2/75 Deferrari, Roy J., Maria W. Fanning and Anne S. Sullivan. A Con-
      cordance of Lucan. Washington: Catholic U. of Amer. Pr., 1940.
      602 pp.

2/76 Roberts, Louis. A Concordance of Lucretius. N. Y. & London: Gar-
      land, 1977. 359 pp.
2nd ed. 1st ed. 1968.

2/77 Deferrari, Roy J., et al. A Concordance of Ovid. Washington:

Catholic U. of Amer. Pr., 1939. 2220 pp.
Context of up to several lines of verse.

2/78 Schmeling, Gareth L. and Johanna H. Stuckey. A Bibliography of
      Petronius. Leiden: Brill, 1977. (Supplementum Mnemosyne, 39)
      239 pp.
Secondary materials: entries 743-2044, by author. A few brief notes.
ClassR ns 29 (1979):153-54--mixed; ClassW 72 (1978/79):55-57--v unfav

2/79 Hughes, J. David. A Bibliography of Scholarship on Plautus. Am-
      sterdam: Hakkert, 1975. 154 pp.
2328 entries, listing books and arts. in English and other langs., and
      diss., incl. some from Europe. Classified arrangement, incl. 60
      pp. (more than 1000 entries) on the plays. Cross-refs. Index of
      scholars.

2/80 Lodge, Gonzalez. Lexicon Plautinum. Lipsiae: Teubnerus, 1924-33.
      2 vols.

2/81 Harrauer, Hermann. A Bibliography to Propertius. Hildesheim:
      Gerstenberg, 1973. (Bibliography to the Augustan Poetry, 2) 219
      pp.
Chapters on themes, style and influence.
ClassW 69 (1975/76):471-72

2/82 Busa, Roberto, S. J., and A. Zampolli. Concordantiae Senecanae.
      Hildesheim & N. Y.: Olms, 1975. 1473+ pp.

2/83 Deferrari, Roy J. and M. Clement Egan. A Concordance of Statius.
      Hildesheim: Olms, 1966. 926 pp.
Reprint of the 1943 ed.

2/84 McGlynn, Patrick. Lexicon Terentianum. London: Blackie, 1963-67.
      2 vols.

ClassR ns 15 (1965):47-49; JRomS 54 (1964):241

2/85 Harrauer, Hermann. A Bibliography to the Corpus Tibullianum.
        Hildesheim: Gerstenberg, 1971. (Bibliography to the Augustan
        Poetry, 1) 90 pp.
Books and arts., most since 1900. Classified arrangement, incl. sec-
        tions on themes and influence.
ClassP 68 (1973):313-14--praises indexes and accuracy; critical of ar-
        rangement; ClassR ns 24 (1974):138--praises arrangement; critical
        of accuracy; ClassW 66 (1972/72):106-07

2/86 "Vergilian Bibliography." In Vergilius, 9 (1963)--.
Annual. 25 (1979):46-50. Classified arrangement, with sections on
        Vergil's works, style and influence. Annotations, often evalu-
        ative.

2/87 The Classical World Bibliography of Vergil. N. Y.: Garland, 1977.
        176 pp.
Reprints reviews of scholarship from Classical World (2/9).

2/88 Warwick, Henrietta Holm. A Vergil Concordance. Minneapolis: U.
        of Minnesota Pr., 1975. 962 pp.
ClassJ 72 (1976/77):371-72; ClassW 70 (1976/77):345-46

2/89 Merguet, Hugo and Hans Frisch. Lexikon zu Vergilius. Hildesheim:
        Olms, 1960. 786 pp.
Reprint of the 1909-12 ed. Brief definitions in German.

● ● MEDIEVAL and MODERN GREEK ● ●

● BIBLIOGRAPHY ●

2/90 Dimaras, C. Th., et al. Modern Greek Culture: A Selected Bibliog-
        raphy in English, French, German, Italian. Athens: National Hel-

lenic Committee of the International Assoc. for South Eastern
   European Studies, 1974.   119 pp.
4th ed.   1st ed. 1966. Lists books and arts., incl. more than 30 pp.
   of transls. and studies of literature. (Note based on 3rd, 1970,
   ed.)

● HISTORIES ●

2/91 Politis, Linos. A History of Modern Greek Literature.   N. Y.:
      Oxford U. Pr., 1973.   338 pp.
Bibl. of texts and criticism. Chronological table, from the 9th c.   In-
      dex of names and other subjects, incl. titles (in English trans.)
MLR 69 (1974):959-60--v fav; ClassW 68 (1974/75):475-76--v fav

2/92 Dimaras, C. Th. History of Modern Greek Literature. Albany:
      State U. of New York Pr., 1972.   539 pp.
From the 9th c., but concentrates on the period from 1820 to 1940.
ClassW 68 (1974/75):475-76--v fav as regards contents; v unfav as re-
      gards transl. and printing

● ● MEDIEVAL LATIN ● ●

● BIBLIOGRAPHIES ●

2/93 McGuire, Martin Rawson Patrick and Hermigild Dressler. Intro-
      duction to Medieval Latin Studies: A Syllabus and Bibliographical
      Guide. Washington, D. C.: Catholic U. of America Pr., 1977.   406
      pp.
2nd ed.   1st ed. 1964. Covers from 200 AD through 1100, primarily.
      Syllabus in 16 chapters, some lengthy, mainly bibl. refs. inter-
      spersed with highly condensed commentary. Select Bibls., in 21
      sections. Indexes of ancient and medieval authors, of modern
      scholars, and of subjects.
SCN 36 (1978):29; LR 33 (1979):213-14

2/94 Medioevo latino: Bollettino bibliografico della cultura europea
      dal secolo VI al XIII. 1980--.
Covers from 1978. Annual. 2 (1979), publ. 1981: 659 pp., 4691 entries.
      In 4 sections, incl. Autori e testi, pp. 5-307, entries 1-2251,
      and Argomenti e discipline, pp. 353-572, in 24 sections. Covers
      eds., transls., and studies of literature in Latin, as well as
      religion, liturgy, music, philosophy, etc., but not art or social
      or political history. Lists books, arts., and chapters in books.
      Most entries annotated briefly. Cites book revs.
Speculum 56 (1981):673

● HISTORIES ●

2/95 Brunhölzl, Franz. Geschichte der lateinischen Literatur des Mit-
      telalters. München: Fink, 1975--.
4 vols. projected. I: Von Cassiodor bis zum Ausklang der karolingischen
      Erneuerung, 594 pp., incl. a lengthy bibl.
YWMLS 76:16; MLR 72 (1977):876-78--v fav; Scriptorium 34 (1980):152-53

2/96 Manitius, Maximilianus. Geschichte der lateinischen Literatur des
      Mittelalters. München: Beck, 1911-31. (Handbuch der klassischen
      Altertumswissenschaft, 9. Bd., 2. Abt.)
3 vols. From Justinian to the end of the 12th c. Very detailed.

2/97 Wright, Frederick Adam and Thomas Alan Sinclair. History of Later
      Latin Literature from the Middle of the Fourth to the End of the
      Seventeenth Century. N. Y.: Macmillan, 1931. 417 pp.
Covers W. Europe. Quotations in Latin or English.

2/98 Curtius, Ernst Robert. European Literature and the Latin Middle
      Ages. N. Y.: Pantheon, 1953. 662 pp.
Transl. from the 1948 German ed. by Willard R. Trask. The influence of
      medieval Latin literature and its classical and Biblical sources
      on the vernacular literatures, as shown by the use of specific

images, themes, etc., e. g. The Goddess Natura.

YWMLS 79:671--"much of the contents have never been superseded"

● POETRY ●

2/99 Raby, Frederic James Edward. History of Secular Latin Poetry in
the Middle Ages. Oxford: Clarendon Pr., 1957.

2 vols. 2nd ed. 1st ed. 1934. Through the end of the 12th c. Lengthy
quotations in Latin. Classified bibl. and index of names, titles
and other subjects in vol. 2.

2/100 Raby, Frederic James Edward. A History of Christian Latin Poetry
from the Beginnings to the Close of the Middle Ages. Oxford: Clarendon Pr., 1953. 494 pp.

2nd ed. 1st ed. 1927. Through the end of the 14th c. Classified bibl.
and index of names, titles and other subjects.

2/101 Szövérffy, Josef. Weltliche Dichtungen des lateinischen Mittelalters: Ein Handbuch. Berlin: Schmidt, 1970--.

4 vols. projected. I: Von den Anfängen bis zum Ende der Karolingerzeit.
771 pp. Indexes of first lines and of names and other subjects.

2/102 Schaller, Dieter and Ewald Könsgen. Initia carminum latinorum
saeculo undecimo antiquiorum: Bibliographisches Repertorium für
die lateinische Dichtung der Antike und des früheren Mittelalters.
Göttingen: Vanderhoeck & Ruprecht, 1977. 785 pp.

A listing by first line of classical and medieval poems through about
1000 AD. Notes commentaries on and interpretations of poems from
the latter part of this period. No author index. Meant to precede Hans Walther, Initia carminum ac versuum medii aevi poster-
ioris latinorum. Alphabetisches Verzeichnis der Versänfange mit-
tellateinischer Dichtungen, 2nd ed., Göttingen: Vanderhoeck &
Ruprecht, 1969, 1377 pp., which does not give citations to scholarship, but which does have an index to names and subjects.

● ● NEO-LATIN ● ●

● BIBLIOGRAPHIES ●

2/103 IJsewijn, Jozef. Companion to Neo-Latin Studies. Amsterdam,
       etc.: North Holland, 1977. 370 pp.
Bibliographic essays. The longest, "A Historical Survey" (pp. 14-205)
       is divided and subdivided: section 3, "The Flourishing and De-
       cline;" subsection "The German World," pp. 123-43, incl. a 7+ pp.
       historical survey and a bibl. of reference works and general stud-
       ies and eds. and studies of individual authors. Other chapters on
       language and style, prosody and metrics, forms and genres, etc.
YWMLS 77:21--"indispensible; ClioI 7 (1978):523-24; SCN 36 (1978):29;
       Moreana 61 (1979):39-41

2/104 "Instrumentum bibliographicum." In Humanistica Lovaniensia 24
       (1974)--.
Annual. 27 (1978):340-58. Classified, in broad categories. Some brief
       notes, sometimes evaluative.

● HISTORY ●

2/105 Van Tieghem, Paul. La Littérature latine de la renaissance. Ge-
       nève: Slatkine, 1966. 254 pp.
Reprint of an essay first publ. in Bibliothéque d'humanisme et renais-
       sance, Travaux et documents, IV (Volume A. Lefranc), Paris: Droz,
       1944, pp. 177-418. Chapters on poetry, drama and prose, with em-
       phasis on the early 15th through the early 17th cs.

● AUTHORS ●

2/106 Margolin, Jean-Claude. Quatorze années de bibliographie eras-
       mienne, 1936-1949. Paris: Vrin, 1969. 431 pp.

2/107 Margolin, Jean-Claude. <u>Douze</u> <u>années</u> <u>de</u> <u>bibliographie</u> <u>eras-</u>
<u>mienne,</u> <u>1950-1961</u>. Paris: Vrin, 1963. 204 pp.

2/108 Margolin, Jean-Claude. <u>Neuf</u> <u>années</u> <u>de</u> <u>bibliographie</u> <u>eras-</u>
<u>mienne,</u> <u>1962-1970</u>. Paris: Vrin/Toronto & Buffalo: U. of Toronto
Pr., 1977. 850 pp.
All vols. arranged by year of publ. Lengthy annotations. All vols.
have index of scholars. "Quatorze" and "neuf" also have several
subject indexes.
YWMLS 78:22; MLR 74 (1979):393-94; Ren&R ns 4 (1980):122-23--praises
completeness and index.

2/109 Coppens, J. "Bibliographia erasmiana." In <u>Scrinium</u> <u>erasmianum</u>:
<u>Mélanges</u> <u>historiques</u> <u>publiés</u> <u>sous</u> <u>le</u> <u>patronage</u> <u>de</u> <u>l'Université</u> <u>de</u>
<u>Louvain</u> <u>à</u> <u>l'occasion</u> <u>du</u> <u>cinquième</u> <u>centenaire</u> <u>de</u> <u>la</u> <u>naissance</u> <u>d'</u>
<u>Erasme</u>. Leiden: Brill, 1969.
In vol. 2, pp. 621-78. Books and arts., 1536-1969, in chronological
order.

2/110 Bolchazy, Ladislaus J. et al. <u>A</u> <u>Concordance</u> <u>to</u> <u>the</u> <u>Utopia</u> <u>of</u> St.
<u>Thomas</u> <u>More</u> <u>and</u> <u>a</u> <u>Frequency</u> <u>Word</u> <u>List</u>. Hildesheim & N. Y.: Olms,
1978. 332 + 56 pp.
Moreana 65/66 (1980):125-27

III

ROMANCE LITERATURES

OUTLINE

● ROMANCE LITERATURES ●

● BIBLIOGRAPHIES ●

3/1 Romanische Bibliographie. Bibliographie romane. Romance Bibliog-
     raphy. 1878--.
Irregular, ideally every other year. Covers 1961/62--. In 3 vols.: I:
     list of periodicals and other sources, and indexes, incl. names as
     subjects; II: linguistics and the Romance langs.; and III: the
     Romance literatures. Vols. for 1971/72, publ. 1980. III:
     Literaturwissenschaft, 416 pp., entries 6505-15051. Covers all
     the Romance literatures except French (which had been covered in
     all previous installments). Lists books, book revs., and arts.
     in books and journals, in English, German and the Romance langs.
     Does not cite diss. Italian literature: pp. 131-260, entries
     9255-12019, by period and author.
This is usually described as the "most comprehensive" bibl. of Romance
     studies. In fact, recently both this bibl. and the MLA Bibl.
     (1/9) list certain categories of publs. not in the other. This
     lists scholarly eds. and book revs. of eds. and studies. The MLA
     lists U. S. diss., as listed in DAI, and research in Russian and
     a number of other langs. In addition to these differences, each
     bibl. may list arts. within the scope of the other, but omitted
     from it. RB 1971/72 lists vol. 2 (1971) of Studi goldoniani in a
     single entry; the MLA lists 14 arts. from it separately, as well
     as a number of scattered entries in other sections not in RB. On
     the other hand, this has a significant number of entries not in
     the MLA through 1974. Earlier vols. of this, particularly those
     from the 1950s and earlier, will have an even clearer advantage
     over the MLA. The arrangement of the two bibls. is essentially
     similar; neither offers much advantage in this respect. The sub-
     ject index to RB lists names only. Previously pub. as a suppl. to
     Zeitschrift für romanische Philologie 1 (1875/76)-72/76 (1956/60).
FS 31 (1977):102-03; LR 29 (1975):247-48

3/2 Hatzfeld, Helmut. A Critical Bibliography of the New Stylistics
     Applied to the Romance Literatures, 1900-1952. Chapel Hill: n.
     p., 1953. (U. of North Carolina Studies in Comparative Litera-
     ture, 5)   302 pp.

3/3 Hatzfeld, Helmut. Bibliografía crítica de la nueva estilística,
     aplicada a las literaturas románicas. Madrid: Gredos, 1955.
     (Biblioteca románica hispanica)   660 pp.
A bibliographical essay, revising and expanding 3/2.

3/4 Hatzfeld, Helmut. Essai de bibliographie critique de stylistique
     français et romane (1955-1960). Paris: PUF, 1961.   312 pp.
Suppl. to 3/3.

3/5 Hatzfeld, Helmut. A Critical Bibliography of the New Stylistics
     Applied to the Romance Literatures, 1953-1965. Chapel Hill: n.
     p., 1965. (U. of North Carolina Studies in Comparative Litera-
     ture, 37)   184 pp.
Suppl. to 3/2. Annotated. Classified arrangement. Chapter V: Style
     and Structure of Literary Works. Other chapters cover theory,
     translation, grammatical and rhetorical topics, rhythm and melody,
     etc. Chapter III contains 22 entries, compared with 12 in 3/4,
     but of those 12, 2 are omitted altogether from this version, and
     3 are transferred to another chapter.
RPh 22 (1968/69):67-69; Symposium 23 (1969):179-80

3/6 Flasche, Hans. Die Sprachen und Literaturen der Romanen im Spiegel
     der deutschen Universitätsschriften, 1885-1950: Eine Biblio-
     graphie. Bonn: Bouvier, 1958.   299 pp.
Literaturwissenschaft: pp. 102-249, by literature, period and subject,
     incl. authors. Based on entries in Jahresverzeichnis der deut-
     schen Hochschulschriften. Indexes of scholars and of subjects.

3/7 "Romantische Habilitationsschriften und Dissertationen." In

Romantisches Jahrbuch, 5 (1952)--.

German and Austrian diss., completed and in progress, by university,
   from 1947. 30 (1979):7-16.

3/8 Parks, George Bruner. The Romance Literatures. N. Y.: Ungar,
       1970. (The Literatures of the World in English Translation)
2 vols. Vol. 2 covers French literature; vol. 1 covers all other Romance literatures. Lists transls. publ. as books and in books
   and journals.

● HANDBOOKS ●

3/9 Grundriss der romanischen Literaturen des Mittelalters. Heidel-
       berg: Winter, 1968--.

13 vols. projected. Hans Robert Jauss and Erich Köhler, general eds.

1:   Généralités. 1 vol. 1972. 742 pp.

YWMLS 73:200; 74:362; FS 31 (1977):437-38

Première partie: Genèse et developpement des traditions littéraires
   romanes (genres et formes) jusqu'à le fin du XIIIe siècle.

2:   Les Genres lyriques. 1979--.

3:   Les Épopées romanes.

4:   Le Roman. 1978--.

YWMLS 79:50--"of major importance"; Speculum 56 (1981):132-33

5:   Les Formes narratives brèves.

6:   La Littérature didactique, allégorique et satirique. 1968-70. 2
     vols.

FS 25 (1971):55-56; 28 (1974):177-78; YWMLS 69:372; 72:287

Deuxième partie: Traditions et tendences nouvelles aux XIVe et XVe
   siècles.

7-12: vols. on Italian, French and Iberian literatures, and on history-
     writing and the drama.

13:   Synthèses---Chronologie---Index.

Chapters in German, English or a Romance lang. on authors, works, forms,
   themes and other topics, with extensive notes. Vol. 2 of 3/9/6

has an extensive descriptive list of texts and manuscripts.

3/10 Curley, Dorothy Nyren and Arthur Curley. <u>Modern Romance Litera-</u>
<u>tures</u>. N. Y.: Ungar, 1967. (Library of Literary Criticism) 510
pp.
Passages from criticism of 20th c. French, Spanish and Italian writers,
incl. transls. from French criticism. Gives exact citations to
original sources.

IV

FRENCH LITERATURE

OUTLINE

Seventeenth Century
    Bibliographies 4/35-4/36
    Histories 4/37-4/38
    Drama 4/39
    Authors
        Corneille 4/40
        Molière 4/41-4/44
        Racine 4/45
Eighteenth Century
    Bibliography 4/46
    Authors
        Diderot 4/47
        Marivaux 4/48
        Rousseau 4/49-4/51
        Voltaire 4/52
Nineteenth Century
    Bibliographies 4/53-4/56
    History 4/57
    Authors
        Balzac 4/58
        Baudelaire 4/59-4/62
        Flaubert 4/63
        Stendhal 4/64
        Zola 4/65-4/66
Late Nineteenth Century and After
    Bibliographies 4/67-4/69
    Handbooks 4/70-4/72
    Histories 4/73-4/75
    Special Topics
        Dadaism 4/76
        Surrealism 4/77-4/78
        Symbolism 4/79-4/80
        Periodicals 4/81-4/82

Authors

    Apollinaire 4/83

    Beckett 4/84

    Camus 4/85-4/87

    Gide 4/88-4/89

    Ionesco 4/90

    Mallarmé 4/91

    St. John Perse 4/92-4/93

    Proust 4/94-4/95

    Rimbaud 4/96-4/97

    Sartre 4/98-4/99

● FRENCH LITERATURE ●

● BIBLIOGRAPHIES ●

4/1   Kempton, Richard. French Literature: An Annotated Guide to
       Selected Bibliographies. N. Y.: MLA, 1981. 42 pp.
94 numbered entries, of which less than 1/2 deal with French literature
       and its periods. The remainder cover general and related topics.
       Evaluative and comparative notes. No entries on writers.

4/2   Bibliographie de la littérature française du moyen âge à nos
       jours. 1963--.
Annual. Covers from 1962. 1979 (publ. 1980): 7202 numbered entries,
       1/3 on the 20th c. Cites books and book revs., arts. in journals,
       books, literary encyclopedias, etc., and U. S. diss., as listed in
       DAI, and French diss. A few brief annotations. Indexes of au-
       thors as subjects and of other subjects, but no index of scholars.
       Covers literature in French from outside France, incl. Canada,
       Africa, etc. Vols. for 1962-65 did not cover the medieval period.
       Sometimes referred to by the name of its compiler, René Rancoeur.
       Updated by the brief lists in each issue of Revue d'histoire litt-
       éraire de la France [80 (1980): 6 installments of 10 pp. each,
       covering publs. of 1979].
LR 29 (1975):248; 30 (1976):320; 35 (1981):263-64

4/3   Klapp, Otto. Bibliographie der französischen Literaturwissen-
       schaft. 1960--.
Now an annual. Covers from 1956. Vol 17 (1979), publ. 1980: 722 pp.,
       9919 numbered entries, 1/3 on the 20th c. Lists books, arts. in
       journals and books, U. S. diss. as listed in DAI, and French and
       occasionally other diss. Covers literature in French from outside
       France. Indexes of subjects (authors and other topics) and of
       scholars. All index terms and section headings are in French.
There are some items in this which will not be found in BLF (4/2), al-

though many of them will be eds. or book revs. A few items not in
this will be found in BLF. Each may also list items a year earlier or later than the other. Both offer a number of refs. (in
addition to the book revs. and foreign diss.) not in the MLA Bibl.
(1/9), incl. sections on authors not covered by the MLA, yet there
will be occasional studies found in the MLA not in these, esp.
studies from American specialized or local journals. The overall
arrangement of these bibls. and the MLA is similar, being by period and author, but the general sections in BLF (4/2) are more
carefully subdivided: the general section at the front of the 18th
c. section of the 1978 vol. of BLF is in 55 subject divisions, as
compared with 10 in this and 10 in the 1978 MLA. Both this and
BLF offer subject indexing for studies on themes, forms, influences, etc., which is similar in principle, but the choice of
items indexed may differ. Someone interested in such a topic
would do well to start with BLF, for its superior arrangement,
then if thorough coverage is wanted, check its index and the index
in this. BLF and the MLA give cross-refs. by entry number only,
so that one must follow up all refs. to know which are of use;
this gives author and title and one follows up the cross-ref. for
publ. details only.
YWMLS 71:69--"more general and less systematic" than BLF

4/4 "Rassegna bibliografica." In Studi francesi, 1957--.
3/yr. 24:3 (sett-dic, 1980): 529-614, by period, with arts. on an au-
       thor grouped together, but otherwise the period sections are not
       arranged by any obvious system. Lengthy signed notes, often eval-
       uative.

4/5 Osburn, Charles B. Research and Reference Guide to French Studies.
       Metuchen, N. J., & London: Scarecrow Pr., 1981. 532 pp.
2nd ed. 1st ed. 1968. Classified annotated list of books, arts. and
       diss. as found in DAI. Cites mainly bibls. (of studies and of
       eds.), revs. of research, concordances, handbooks, surveys of

themes, movements, etc. Indexes of scholars and of subjects.
FS 25 (1971):245-46; 29 (1975):498-500

4/6 Entry cancelled.

4/7 Bassan, Fernande, et al. An Annotated Bibliography of French Lan-
     guage and Literature. N. Y.: Garland, 1976. 306 pp.
No entries on individual authors.
FR 51 (1977/78):109-10--v fav; FS 33 (1979):949-50; MLJ 62 (1978):201

4/8 Cabeen, David Clark, ed. A Critical Bibliography of French Liter-
     ature. Syracuse, N. Y.: Syracuse U. Pr., 1947--.
1:   Holmes, Urban T. The Mediaeval Period. 1947. 256 pp. 2588 en-
     tries.
2:   Schutz, Alexander H. The Sixteenth Century. 1956. 365 pp.
     2897+ entries.
3:   Edelman, Nathan. The Seventeenth Century. 1961. 638 pp. 4750
     entries.
4:   Havens, George R. and Donald F. Bond. The Eighteenth Century.
     1951. 411 pp. Suppl., 1968, 283 pp. Total of 5962 entries.
FS 24 (1970):398-99; MLR 65 (1970):424-25
5:   not yet publ.
6:   Alden, Douglas W. and Richard A. Brooks. The Twentieth Century.
     1980. 3 vols. 2073 pp. 17,939 entries.
LR 34 (1980):294-96--v fav
All vols. list books, arts. and parts of books in French, English, and
     German, sometimes in other W. and E. European langs., as well as
     book revs. Nearly all entries briefly annotated. Classified ar-
     rangement. Subject index. Vol. 6: Valéry: 80 pp., 570+ entries
     in classified order, incl. nearly 180 on his poetry.

4/9 Lanson, Gustave. Manuel bibliographique de la littérature fran-
     çaise moderne: XVIe, XVIIe, XVIIIe et XIXe siècles. Paris: Ha-
     chette, 1931. 1820 pp.

New (i. e., 4th) ed. 1st ed. 1913. Lists eds. and studies. Journal
    arts. are cited without page refs.

4/10 Giraud, Jeanne. Manuel de bibliographie littéraire pour les XVIe,
    XVIIe et XVIIIe siècles français, 1921-1935. Paris: Vrin, 1958.
    304 pp.
2nd ed. 1st ed. 1939. This, and its continuations for 1936-1945 (1956,
    270 pp.) and 1946-1955 (1970, 493 pp.), are meant to be suppls. to
    Lanson. Cites books and arts., chiefly in French, but also in
    English, German and Italian. Index of subject sections.
RLC 46 (1972):136-37; FS 27 (1973):190; FR 45 (1971/72):286-87

•   DISSERTATIONS   •

4/11 "Dissertations in Progress." In French Review.
Annual. In issue no. 1 (October). Mainly U. S. diss. 55 (1981/82):99-
    108.

4/12 Taylor, Alan Carey. Bibliography of Unpublished Theses on French
    Subjects Deposited in University Libraries of the United King-
    dom, 1905-1950. Oxford: Blackwell, 1964. 45 pp.

•   FESTSCHRIFTEN   •

4/13 Modern French Literature and Language: A Bibliography of Homage
    Studies. Madison: U. of Wisconsin Pr., 1976. (Distributed by
    Ann Arbor: UMI) 175 pp.
Lloyd W. Griffin, et al. Subject list, in classified order, of arts. on
    literature since 1500, in Festschriften. "Literary and Intellec-
    tual Relations between France and Other Countries," pp. 110-25,
    entries 2533-3027. Index of names (subjects and scholars). Re-
    places a bibl. of the same title by H. H. Golden and S. O. Sim-
    ches.

● HANDBOOKS ●

4/14 Dictionnaire des lettres françaises. Paris: Fayard, 1951--.
Cardinal Georges Grente, gen. ed., with Albert Pauphilet, et al. 5
      vols. in 7 parts, to date. I: Moyen âge. 1964. 766 pp. II:
      Seizième siècle. 1951. 718 pp. III: Dix-septième siècle. 1954.
      1031 pp. IV: Dix-huitième siècle. 1960. 2 vols. V: Dix-neu-
      vième siècle. 1971. 2 vols. Mainly biographical arts., usually
      1 paragraph to 1 page, often signed. Vol V: Balzac: 17+ cols. on
      his life, 25 cols. on his works, 2 cols. bibl. Stendhal: 11 cols.
      on his life, 7 2/3 cols. on his works, 1 2/3 col. bibl., almost
      entirely books in French. Angleterre (Relations littéraires avec
      l'): 5 cols. and 1/3 col. bibl. Symbolisme français: 4+ cols.
      and 1/2 col. bibl.

4/15 Harvey, Sir Paul and Janet E. Heseltine. The Oxford Companion to
      French Literature. Oxford: Clarendon Pr., 1959. 771 pp.
Brief entries without bibls. on writers and historical figures, liter-
      ary works and movements, forms, themes, characters, etc. Ronsard:
      2 3/4 cols. Stendhal: 2 2/3 cols. and separate arts. on 5 of his
      works, incl. 1 col. on Le Rouge et le noir. Symbolisme: 1 1/3
      col. Limited coverage of literature since 1939.
MLR 55 (1960):115-16--v fav

4/16 Reid, Joyce M. H. The Concise Oxford Dictionary of French Liter-
      ature. Oxford: Clarendon Pr., 1976. 669 pp.
Revises, condenses and combines arts. from OCFL (4/15). Adds a number of
      entries on literature since 1939 and omits French-Canadian liter-
      ature (see 8/182). Stendhal: 2 1/2 cols., and arts. on 5 of his
      works, incl. 1 col. on Le Rouge et le noir, omitting little of
      the substance of the arts. in OCFL.
FMLS 13 (1977):86; FS 31 (1977):308-09

4/17 Simone, Franco, ed. Dizionario critico della letteratura francese.

Torino: UTET, 1972.

2 vols. 1322 pp. Mostly lengthy arts. on writers (few less than 1
   col.) Also anonymous works, movements and periods. Ronsard: 12+
   cols., and 2/3 col. bibl. Stendhal: 8 cols. and 1 1/4 col. bibl.,
   chiefly listing books, in French, Italian and English. Symbolisme: 7+ cols. and 1/2 col. bibl.

YWMLS 73:83; FS 27 (1973):491-95; MLR 69 (1974):163-64

● HISTORIES ●

4/18 Littérature française. Paris: Arthaud, 1968-78.
Claude Pichois, director. 16 vols. in 6 divisions.

1:   Payen, J. C. Le Moyen âge. I: Des origines à 1300. 1970. 356
        pp.
YWMLS 71:57

2:   Poirion, D. Le Moyen âge. II: 1300-1480. 1971. 342 pp.
YWMLS 71:69--"an invaluable reference book;" LR 33 (1979):214-15

3:   Giraud, Y. and M.-R. Jung. La Renaissance. I: 1480-1548. 1972.
        365 pp.
FS 28 (1974):57-58

4:   Balmas, E. La Renaissance. II: 1548-1570. 1974. 296 pp.
YWMLS 74:64; FS 29 (1975):74

5:   Morel, J. La Renaissance. III: 1570-1624. 1973. 307 pp.
FS 29 (1975):74; YWMLS 73:64--"superficial"

6:   Adam, A. L'Âge classique. I: 1624-1660. 1968. 367 pp.
YWMLS 68:80

7:   Clarac, Pierre. L'Âge classique. II: 1660-1680. 1969. 324 pp.

8:   Pomeau, R. L'Âge classique. III: 1680-1720. 1971. 288 pp.
YWMLS 71:99, 107

9:   Ehrard, J. Le XVIIIe siècle. I: 1720-1750. 1974. 337 pp.
YWMLS 74:97-98--v fav

10: Mauzi, R. and S. Menant. Le XVIIIe siècle. II: 1750-1778. 1977.
        289 pp.
YWMLS 77:113; FS 32 (1978):74-75

11:    Didier, B. Le XVIIIe siècle. III: 1778-1820. 1976. 383 pp.
YWMLS 76:121, 175; FS 34 (1980):205-06

12:    Milner, M. Le Romantisme. I: 1820-1843. 1973. 405 pp.

13:    Pichois, C. Le Romantisme. II: 1843-1869. 1979. 565 pp.
FS 33 (1979):459-60; YWMLS 79:173

14:    Pouilliart, R. Le Romantisme. III: 1869-1896. 1968. 336 pp.
FS 24 (1970):185-86; YWMLS 68:137

15:    Walzer, P.-O. Le XXe siècle. I: 1896-1920. 1975. 456 pp.
FS 30 (1976):482-83; LR 31 (1977):264-67; YWMLS 75:169

16:    Brée, G. Le XXe siècle. II: 1920-1970. 1978. 429 pp.
RR 70 (1979):317-19

All vols. are illustrated. Most have a dictionary of authors, sometimes
    incl. bibl. refs.; a bibl., sometimes in the form of a review
    essay; and a chronology in 6 cols., giving personal dates, his-
    torical and scientific events, and landmarks of French and foreign
    (chiefly W. European) literatures and the arts.

4/19   Manuel d'histoire littéraire de la France. Paris: Eds. Sociales,
    1965--.

Pierre Abraham and Roland Desné, gen. eds. 6 vols. projected.

1:     Payen, J. C. and H. Weber, eds. Des origines à 1600. 1971. 659
    pp.

2:     Ubersfeld, A. and R. Desné, eds. De 1600 à 1715. 1975. 492 pp.

3:     Duchet, M. and M. Goulemot, eds. De 1715 à 1789. 1974. 624 pp.

4:     Barbéris, P. and C. Duchet, eds. De 1789 à 1848. 1972-73. 2
    vols.

5:     Duchet, C., ed. De 1848 à 1913. 1977. 814 pp.
YWMLS 77:185; LR 28 (1974):407-09

Many collaborators. Each vol. has an index of names, a detailed table
    of contents, a chronology and an extensive bibl. of books and
    arts., chiefly in French, paralleling the text.

4/20   Littérature française. Paris: Larousse, 1967-68.
Ed. by Antoine Adam, Georges Lerminier and Édouard Morot-Sir. 2 vols.

I: <u>Des origines à la fin</u> du XVIII<u>e siècle</u>. 399 pp. II: <u>XIXe et
<u>XXe siècle</u>. 416 pp. Covers through 1965. Brief chapters on Bel-
gian, Swiss, Canadian and other literatures in French. Heavily
illus. Index of names and some titles in vol. 2. Brief bibls.,
chiefly of books, paralleling text, in each vol. This is meant to
be a new ed. of the history by J. Bédier and P. Hazard, rev. ed.
by P. Martino, 1948.

FR 42 (1968/69):786-88; YWMLS 68:102--"Authoritative; well-presented and
indexed"

4/21 The <u>Literary History of France</u>. London: Benn/N. Y.: Barnes &
      Noble, 1967-74.
1:    Fox, J. <u>The Middle Ages</u>. 1974. 380 pp.
FS 29 (1975):177-78--v fav; MLR 72 (1977):169-71; YWMLS 74:43
2:    McFarlane, I. D. <u>Renaissance France, 1470-1589</u>. 1974. 557 pp.
FS 29 (1975):184; MLR 71 (1976):658-59; YWMLS 74:64
3:    Yarrow, P. J. <u>The Seventeenth Century, 1600-1715</u>. 1967. 432 pp.
FS 22 (1968):149-51; MLR 63 (1968):478-80
4:    Niklaus, R. <u>The Eighteenth Century, 1715-1789</u>. 1970. 434 pp.
YWMLS 70:108; FS 25 (1971):80-81
5:    Charvet, P. E. <u>The Nineteenth Century, 1789-1870</u>. 1967. 395 pp.
FS 22 (1968):254-56; MLR 63 (1968):713-14
6:    Charvet, P. E. <u>The Nineteenth and Twentieth Centuries, 1870-1940</u>.
      1967. 315 pp.
FS 22 (1968):254-56
Brief classified bibls., of books only. Indexes of names, titles and
      other topics. Quotations in French only, except for medieval vol.

4/22 Charlton, D. G., ed. <u>France</u>: <u>A Companion to French Studies</u>. Lon-
      don: Methuen, 1979. 690 pp.
2nd ed. 1st ed. 1972. Chapters on literature, by period, and on art,
      music, and social and intellectual history. Index of names and
      other subjects.
FS 34 (1980):367-68--v fav; YWMLS 72:63-64, 95, 126, 164

• CHRONOLOGY •
[See also 1/69.]

4/23 Chassang, Arsène and Charles Senninger. Les Grandes dates de la
        littérature française. Paris: PUF, 1973. 127 pp.
2nd ed. 1st ed. 1969. More than half the book is on the period 1801-
        1972. Literary events only (births, deaths and publications).

● MEDIEVAL ●

• BIBLIOGRAPHY •
[See also 4/8/1.]

4/24 Bossuat, Robert. Manuel bibliographique de la littérature fran-
        çaise du moyen âge. Melun: Librairie d'Argences, 1951. 638 pp.
Suppls. cover 1949-1953 (1955) and 1954-1960 (1961). Total of more than
        8000 entries, some containing several refs. Annotated. The orig.
        vol. also had many descriptive headnotes on authors and works.
        Indexes of authors and anonymous works; of scholars; and of sub-
        jects.

● CHRONOLOGY ●

4/25 Levy, Raphael. Chronologie approximative de la littérature fran-
        çaise du moyen âge. Tübingen: Niemeyer, 1957. (Beihefte zur
        Zeitschrift für romanische Philologie: Heft 98) 59 pp.
Main section of text lists only events datable to a precise year. Works
        datable only to a period are listed alphabetically, after the in-
        dex.

● AUTHORS and WORKS ●

4/26 Duggan, Joseph J. A Guide to Studies on the Chanson de Roland.
        London: Grant & Cutler, 1976. (Research Bibls. and Checklists,

15) 133 pp.

Covers studies from 1956 to 1974, chiefly. Lists books and arts., mainly in English, French and German, U.S. diss., as found in DAI, and
European diss. Chapter 5, on the poetry, divided and subdivided,
incl. sections on the characters, on themes, and on comparative
studies. See also a bibl. by Albert Junker in Germanisch-Roman-
ische Monatsschrift 37 (1956):97-144, reviewing publs. of the
1940s and early 50s, chiefly.

MLR 74 (1979):446-47; FS 34 (1980):316-17; RPh 34 (1980/81):136-37

4/27 Duggan, Joseph J. A Concordance of the Chanson de Roland. n. p.:
Ohio St. U. Pr., 1969. 420 pp.

Speculum 47 (1972):303-04; FS 26 (1972):181-84--unfav; FR 44 (1970/71):
814-15

4/28 Kelly, Douglas. Chrétien de Troyes: An Analytic Bibliography.
London: Grant & Cutler, 1976. (Research Bibls. and Checklists,
17) 153 pp.

Classified arrangement, incl. 4 sections on various aspects of his style
and technique, each subdivided, and sections on influence, the
Grail, etc. Lists books, arts. and chapters in books in various
langs. Occasional brief notes.

YWMLS 76:51; MLR 74(1979):446-48; FS 33 (1979):537-39; FR 52 (1978/79):
634

4/29 Burgess, Glyn Sheridan. Marie de France: An Analytical Bibliography. London: Grant & Cutler, 1977. (Research Bibls. and
Checklists, 21) 133 pp.

529 entries, incl. eds. and transls., annotated. Lists books, arts.
and passages in books in English, French, German and Italian, and
U.S., British and European diss. Indexes of scholars, of Marie's
works and of names and other titles as subjects.

MLR 75 (1980):881-82--"reliable and thorough;" FS 34 (1980):437-38;
YWMLS 77:48; RPh 34 (1980/81):349-50

● 16th CENTURY ●

• BIBLIOGRAPHY •
[See also 4/8/2.]

4/30 Cioranescu, Alexandre. Bibliographie de la littérature française
    du seizième siècle. Paris: Klincksieck, 1959. 745 pp.
Lists studies to 1950. 22,106 entries, in classified order. Most of
    book (nearly 20,000 entries) is devoted to authors. Clement
    Marot: about 250 entries, incl. early and modern eds., and studies
    in 15 sections, incl. individual works. Also sections on intel-
    lectual history, themes, forms, and other topics. Index of names,
    anonymous titles and other subjects, but without ref. to sections
    specifically devoted to those topics, for which see the table of
    contents.

• AUTHORS •

4/31 Wells, Margaret Brady. Du Bellay: A Bibliography. London: Grant
    & Cutler, 1974. (Research Bibls. and Checklists, 9) 113 pp.
Entries arranged by form of publ. (books, arts., diss. [U. S. and Euro-
    pean], etc.). Indexes of scholars and of Du Bellay's works.
YWMLS 74:63-64; FS 33 (1979):628-29--"useful rather than authoritative"

4/32 Marcu, Eva. Répertoire des idées de Montaigne. Genève: Droz,
    1965. 1429 pp.
Extracts arranged under about 200 headings: Famille; Guerre; Moi et "les
    autres"; Stupidité, with cross-refs.
FR 40 (1966/67):144-46; FS 21 (1967):341-42; MLR 63 (1968):477-78--crit-
    ical of arrangement

4/33 Creore, Alvin Emerson. A Word Index to the Poetic Works of Ron-
    sard. Leeds: Maney, 1972. (Compendia)
2 vols. 1652 pp. No context.

FS 30 (1976):197-98

4/34   Nash, Jerry C. Maurice Scève: Concordance de la Délie. Chapel
       Hill: Dept. of Romance Langs., U. of North Carolina, 1976. (UNC
       Studies in the Romance Langs. and Lits., 174)
2 vols. 820 pp.
FS 33 (1979):69-70; FR 50 (1976/77):921

● 17th CENTURY ●

● BIBLIOGRAPHIES ●
[See also 4/8/3.]

4/35   Modern Language Association of America. French Group III. Bib-
       liography of French Seventeenth Century Studies. 1953--.
Covers 1952/53--. Annual. 28 (1980), 116 pp., citing publs. of 1979
       and 1980, chiefly, incl. book revs. and diss. from DAI.

4/36   Cioranescu, Alexandre. Bibliographie de la littérature française
       du dix-septième siècle. Paris: CNRS, 1965-67.
3 vols. 2231 pp. 67,472 entries, in classified order, listing books
       and arts. publ. to about 1960. Most of the entries (more than
       60,000) devoted to authors. The longer author sections are sub-
       divided, incl. sections on individual works. Molière: pp. 1429-
       1477, entries 47798-49780, incl. more than 500 entries on his
       works, and sections on his sources, subdivided by nation or cul-
       ture, then by specific writer, and on his influence.
FS 22 (1968):151-52; SCN 25 (1967):17

● HISTORIES ●

4/37   Adam, Antoine. Histoire de la littérature française au XVIIe
       siècle. Paris: Domat, 1948-56.
5 vols. Index of names only, in each vol.

4/38 Peyre, Henri Maurice. <u>Qu'est-ce que le classicisme</u>? Paris:
      Nizet, 1967. 313 pp.
Rev. ed. 1st ed. 1933. Annotated bibl., pp. 267-313, with subject in-
      dex. No index to text.
FR 39 (1965/66):801-02; FS 20 (1966):184-86

• DRAMA •

4/39 Guiraud, Pierre, et al., eds. <u>Index du vocabulaire du théâtre</u>
      <u>classique</u>. Paris: Klincksieck, 1955-65.
19 vols., covering 4 plays by Corneille, 11 by Racine, 2 by Rotrou and
      1 by Regnard. No context.

• AUTHORS •

4/40 Besançon, France. Université. Centre d'étude du vocabulaire
      française. <u>P. Corneille</u>, "<u>Le Cid</u>:" <u>Concordances, index et relevés</u>
      <u>statistiques</u>. Paris: Larousse, 1966. 134 pp.
This center has also produced concordances to <u>Cinna</u> (1971) and <u>Polyeucte</u>
      (1967).
FS 22 (1968): 247; 24 (1970):289-90

4/41 Saintonge, Paul. "Thirty Years of Molière Studies: A Bibliog-
      raphy, 1942-71." In <u>Molière and the Commonwealth of Letters</u>: <u>Pat-</u>
      <u>rimony and Posterity</u>, pp. 747-826. Ed. by Roger Johnson, Jr., E.
      S. Neumann and G. T. Trail. Jackson: U. Pr. of Mississippi, 1975.
Lists books (incl. eds.), arts., diss., incl. European diss., etc., in
      various langs. Incl. revs. of performances and book revs. Index
      of names, incl. scholars, characters from Molière's works and
      other characters, literary and historical figures and titles of
      Molière's works and other works. 1363 entries, in classified
      order. 570+ entries on individual plays; also a section on his
      influence on French and foreign writers.
Preceded by a survey art. "The Present State of Molière Studies" by H.

Gaston Hall, pp. 728-46.
YWMLS 76:113

4/42 Saintonge, Paul and Robert Wilson Christ. Fifty Years of Molière
      Studies: A Bibliography, 1892-1941. Baltimore: Johns Hopkins Pr.,
      1942. (Johns Hopkins Studies in Romance Lit. and Langs., Extra
      Vol. 19) 313 pp.
3316 entries. Suppl. in Modern Language Notes 59 (1944):282-85. Con-
      tinued by 4/41.

4/43 Livet, Charles Louis. Lexique de la langue de Molière, comparée
      à celle des écrivains de son temps. Paris: Imprimerie nationale,
      1895-97.
3 vols. Words and phrases, cited by play and scene only, from Molière,
      Scarron, LaFontaine, Malherbe, and others.

4/44 Desfeuilles, Arthur and Paul Desfeuilles. Lexique de la langue de
      Molière. N. Y.:B. Franklin, 1973.
Reprint of the orig. ed., 1900, vols. 12-13 of the Oeuvres in the Grands
      écrivains de la France series. 2 vols. Cites more words than
      Livet, and gives exact vol. and page refs. to the ed. of which it
      was a part, but does not give comparative quotations from other
      writers.

4/45 Freeman, Bryant C. Concordance du théâtre et des poésies de Jean
      Racine. Ithaca: Cornell U. Pr., 1968.
2 vols. 1481 pp. See also the concordances to Andromaque (1970) and
      Phédre (1966) from the Université de Besançon.
FR 42 (1968/69):775-76; MLJ 53 (1969):522

● 18th CENTURY ●

● BIBLIOGRAPHY ●
[See also 4/8/4.]

4/46 Cioranescu, Alexandre. Bibliographie de la littérature française
      du dix-huitième siècle. Paris: CNRS, 1969.
3 vols. 2137 pp. 67,912 entries for books and arts., publ to 1960.
      Most entries (more than 60,000) devoted to authors. Classified
      arrangement. General section is in 10 divisions, all further
      divided and subdivided. Voltaire: appr. 3800 entries, incl. eds.,
      subdivided by subject. Indexes incl. an index of names and other
      subjects.
DHS 4 (1972):379-80; 3 (1971):361-70--commentary by Cioranescu

● AUTHORS ●

4/47 Spear, Frederick A. Bibliographie de Diderot: Répertoire analy-
      tique international. Genève: Droz, 1980. 902 pp.
3967 entries, in 10 sections, most divided and subdivided. Section 6:
      Rapports et influences intellectuels, pp. 195-338, appr. 625 en-
      tries, by country and author; France: appr. 320 entries, 48 au-
      thors, incl. his predecessors and successors.
MLR 76 (1981):704; LR 34 (1980):296-97

4/48 Spinelli, Donald C. A Concordance to Marivaux's Comedies in
      Prose. Chapel Hill: Dept. of Romance Langs., U. of North Caro-
      lina, 1979. (Distr. by Ann Arbor: UMI) (UNC Studies in the
      Romance Langs. and Lits., 218)
4 vols. 2762 pp.

4/49 "Bibliographie des années [years] et complement à la bibliographie
      des 1963-[year]." In Annales de la Société J.-J. Rousseau, 1

(1905)--.

Very irregular. A group of review essays, in French, noting books,
    arts., chapters in books and diss., by country of publ. Also a
    "Chronique," unannotated, by subject. There seems to be no dupli-
    cation between these two features, which in 38 (1969-71), publ.
    1974, took up nearly 170 pp.

4/50 Trousson, Raymond. "Quinze années d'études rousseauistes." In
    Dix-huitième siècle, 9 (1977):343-86.
See also his Rousseau et sa fortune littéraire, Paris: Nizet, 1977, 263
    pp., (a reprint of the 1971 ed., with a brief suppl.)
YWMLS 71:118; 77:143

4/51 Launay, Léo. Le Vocabulaire littéraire de Jean-Jacques Rousseau.
    Genène: Slatkine, 1979. (Études rousseauistes et index des
    oeuvres de J.-J. Rousseau. Sér. A: Champs sémantiques) 750 pp.
More than 250 entries. Auteur: 18 pp., mostly a work-by-work list of
    occurences, with a phrase of context. Launay has also compiled
    a guide to Rousseau's political vocabulary.

4/52 Barr, Mary-Margaret H. and Frederick A. Spear. Quarante années
    d'études voltairiennes: Bibliographie analytique des livres et
    articles sur Voltaire, 1926-1965. Paris: Colin, 1968. 208 pp.
In 10 sections. 4: Rapports et influences intellectuels: 38 pp., 585
    entries, divided and subdivided. Some brief annotations. Index
    of names (scholars and subjects), of titles of Voltaire's works,
    and of other subjects. Continues a bibl. by Barr publ. in 1929.
RHLF 70 (1970):131-32

● 19th CENTURY ●

● BIBLIOGRAPHIES ●

4/53 Thieme, Hugo Paul. Bibliographie de la littérature française de

1800 à 1930. Genève: Droz, 1933.
3 vols. Vols. 1 and 2 (1061 & 1041 pp.): books and arts. by and about
    French writers. Vol. 3 (216 pp.): La Civilisation, in 7 sections,
    all divided and subdivided, incl. Genres littéraires and Écoles
    littéraires, as well as general topics such as La Femme et la
    féminisme. No indexes.

4/54   Dreher, S. and M. Rolli. Bibliographie de la littérature fran-
       çaise, 1930-1939. Lille: Giard, 1948. 438 pp.

4/55   Drevet, Marguerite L. Bibliographie de la littérature française,
       1940-1949. Genève: Droz, 1954. 644 pp.
This and the entry above are meant to be continuations of Thieme (4/53),
    but neither has a section on general topics to correspond to vol.
    3 of Thieme. Valéry: 2 1/3 cols. of books and arts. by Valéry;
    11 cols. of studies of him, by year of publ., with arts. listed
    separately from books (incl. passages in books). Often does not
    give exact page refs.

4/56   Talvart, Hector and Joseph Place. Bibliographie des auteurs mo-
       dernes de langue française (1801-1927). Paris: Chronique des
       lettres française, 1928--.
22 vols. to date, through Claude Morgan, listing books and arts., by and
    about. Vol 22 covers 1801-1975.

●   HISTORY   ●

4/57   Peyre, Henri Maurice. Qu'est-ce que le romantisme? Paris: PUF,
       1971. 307 pp.
Bibl., pp. 289-94. English transl.: What is Romanticism? Transl. by
    Roda P. Roberts, University: U. of Alabama Pr., 1977, 214 pp.,
    with unrevised bibl.
LR 28 (1974):187-91; FS 27 (1973):74-75; MLR 69 (1974):877-78--compares
    unfav with works by Phillippe van Tieghem and P. Moreau.

●   AUTHORS   ●

4/58 "Bibliographie balzacienne." In L'Année balzacienne, 1961--.
N. s. 1 (1980), for 1979, pp. 335-45, entries 1402-1521, by subject.
    Incl. French and U. S. diss. Also "Balzac à l'étranger," noting
    diss. and other studies in progress, as well as publ. books and
    arts., by country. Note a cumulative index to the arts. in
    L'Année from 1961, by subject and scholar, in 1979:289-361.

4/59 "Recensement bibliographique." In Bulletin baudelairien, 1
        (1965)--.
Covers from 1963. 15 (1980), suppl. issue, covering 1978, 30 pp., 323
    entries, by author.
YWMLS 78:177--"exhaustive"

4/60 Cargo, Robert T. Baudelaire Criticism, 1950-1967: A Bibliography
        with Critical Commentary. University: U. of Alabama Pr., 1968.
        171 pp.
More than 1200 books and arts., in various langs., by author, with
    subject index. Meant to suppl. the bibl. by Henri Peyre in Con-
    naissance de Baudelaire, Paris: Corti, 1951.
FS 24 (1970):191-92

4/61 Besançon, France. Université. Centre d'étude du vocabulaire
        français. Baudelaire: Les Fleurs du mal. Concordances, index et
        relevés statistiques. Paris: Larousse, 1970. 246 pp.
MLN 81 (1966):358-60

4/62 Cargo, Robert T. Concordance to Baudelaire's Petits poèmes en
        prose, with Complete Text of the Poems. University: U. of Ala-
        bama Pr., 1971. 470 pp.
See also his Concordance to Les Fleurs du mal, Chapel Hill: U. of North
    Carolina Pr., 1965, 417 pp.
FS 27 (1973):87-88

4/63 Carlut, Charles, Pierre H. Dubé and J. Raymond Dugan. A Concor-
      dance to Flaubert's Madame Bovary. N. Y.: Garland, 1978.
2 vols. See also their concordances to L'Éducation sentimental (1978),
      Salammbô (1979) and La Tentation de Saint Antoine (1979). Phrase
      (to several lines of very small print) of context.
FS 33 (1979):467; 34 (1980):214; 34 (1980):353; CHum 15 (1981/82):37-39
      --unfav

4/64 "Bibliographie stendhalienne." In Stendhal-club, 1 (1958/59)--.
Covers from 1957. In issue no. 1. 23 (1980/81):99-112, entries 10065-
      225. Index of scholars and of Stendhal's works and other sub-
      jects. Also occasional bibls. on special topics, e. g., Christa
      Riehn, "Stendhal en Allemagne," 20 (1977/78):82-96, covering 1972-
      76 and continuing a series of 5 previous bibls.
The bibls. have been collected in groups of 3 or so and publ. sepa-
      rately, continuing V. del Litto, Bibliographie stendhalienne,
      1938-1943, Grenoble: Arthaud, 1945, 30 pp., etc.

4/65 "Bibliographie." In Cahiers naturalistes, 1 (1955)--.
From 1940, but covers esp. 1952--. Brief bibls. on Zola and French
      naturalism, and their influence abroad. 25 (1979):201-12, publs.
      of 1976-78, incl. French, Australian and other diss. Also occa-
      sional bibls. on special topics, e. g., English criticism of Zola,
      1877-1970, in 1972:105-23.

4/66 Baguley, David. Bibliographie de la critique sur Émile Zola,
      1864-1970. Toronto & Buffalo: U. of Toronto Pr., 1976. 689 pp.
Cites books and book revs., and arts. in the langs. of W. and E. Europe,
      Japanese, etc. Detailed indexes of names (scholars and subjects)
      and of other subjects, but citing entry no. only.
FS 31 (1977):353-54--v fav; MLR 73 (1978):432; YWMLS 76:209

● LATE 19th CENTURY and AFTER ●

● BIBLIOGRAPHIES ●
[See also 4/8/6 and 4/53-4/56.]

4/67 French XX Bibliography: Critical and Biographical References for
the Study of French Literature since 1885. 1949--
Covers from 1940. Now an annual. Formerly known as French VII. 32
(publ. 1980): nearly 350 pp., 7413 entries, chiefly publs. of
1979. Lists books, arts., and parts of books, chiefly in the
major W. European langs. Occasional very brief notes, usually
identifying the work particularly studied. Most entries concern
authors (Proust: 101 entries); general subjects are listed in 10
sections, some subdivided, e. g., Literary Genres; Esthetics,
Stylistics, Themes; Symbolism. There is a section on film,
listing general studies and studies of actors, directors, etc.:
an important feature since vol. 7 Many cross-refs., but no indexes.

4/68 "Carnet bibliographique," or "Bibliographie." In Revue des lettres modernes.
In each issue. Each issue is devoted to a different French writer.
(Occasional issues of the 1950s and 60s were devoted to an American writer.) André Malraux 4 (No. 537-42 [1978]): bibl., pp. 151-
97, covering 1973-75.

4/69 "Calepins de bibliographie." Paris: Minard, 1969--.
A series of bibls. of eds. and criticism in French and English of certain modern French writers: Camus, Céline, Green, Bernanos, etc.
Camus II: criticism, 1937-67, a fairly thick book, but unpaginated and with many blank and half-blank pages. Arranged chronologically; no indexes. Camus I covers criticism 1937-62.

•   HANDBOOKS   •

4/70 Bonnefoy, Claude, et al. Dictionnaire de littérature française
      contemporaine. Paris: Delarge, 1977. 411 pp.
1-2 pp. entries on writers in French (incl. African, etc.) who were
      alive in January, 1976. The arts. are more concerned with criti-
      cism than biography.

4/71 Boisdeffre, Pierre de, et al. Dictionnaire de littérature con-
      temporaine. Paris: Eds. Universitaires, 1966. 700 pp.
3rd ed. 1st ed. 1962. Brief signed critical arts.

4/72 Popkin, Debra and Michael Popkin. Modern French Literature: A
      Library of Literary Criticism. N. Y.: Ungar, 1977.
2 vols. Critical passages with full refs. to original sources, some
      transl. from French. Incl. writers from Africa, Canada, etc.
FR 51 (1977-78):441-42; FS 33 (1979):935-36

•   HISTORIES   •

4/73 Clouard, Henri. Histoire de la littérature française du sym-
      bolisme à nos jours. Paris: Michel, 1947-62.
2 vols. De 1885 à 1914. 668 pp. De 1915 à 1960. (New ed.; 1st ed.
      1949.) 678 pp. Index of names.

4/74 Boisdeffre, Pierre de. Une Histoire vivante de la littérature
      d'aujourd'hui: 1939-1960. Paris: Le Livre contemporaine, 1960.
      802 pp.
3rd ed. 1st ed. 1958. Chronological section and sections on forms
      (novel, poetry, theater, essay), subdivided by school, theme,
      etc. Index of names.
YWMLS 58:149--"outstanding"

4/75 Brenner, Jacques. Histoire de la littérature française de 1940 à

nos jours. N. p.: Fayard, 1978. 585 pp.
Chronology, 1940-1978, pp. 557-65. Index of names.

•   DADAISM   •

4/76 Hugnet, Georges. Dictionnaire du dadaïsme, 1916-1922. Paris:
      Simoën, 1976. 365 pp.
Brief entries on writers, artists, publications (journals, manifestos,
      etc.), events and other topics. Montage, ou Photomontage: 3 pp.;
      Tzara: 1 1/3 pp.; Maintenant (a journal, 1912-15): 15+ pp.,
      illus., many quotations, and summaries of each issue.

•   SURREALISM   •

4/77 Recherches sur le surréalisme: Revue bibliographique. 1976--.
Covers from 1969. Now an annual. 4 (1979), covering publs. of 1977
      chiefly, some earlier, a few from 1978, on Surrealism in France
      and Belgium. 115 entries, with annotations, sometimes lengthy.
      Detailed index of titles and other subjects, pp. 59-104; index of
      names (subjects and scholars), pp. 105-08.
LR 33 (1979):188

4/78 Gershman, Herbert S. Bibliography of the Surrealist Movement in
      France. Ann Arbor: U. of Michigan Pr., 1969. 57 pp.
See also his The Surrealist Revolution in France, Ann Arbor: U. of
      Michigan Pr., 1969, 255 pp.
FS 25 (1971):351-53

•   SYMBOLISM   •

4/79 Guiraud, Pierre. Index du vocabulaire du symbolisme. Paris:
      Klincksieck, 1953-62.
7 vols., covering Alcools of Apollinaire, Poésies of Valery and Mal-
      larmé, Cinq grandes odes of Claudel, Illuminations and Une Saison

en enfer of Rimbaud and *Fêtes galantes* and other works by Ver-
laine.

4/80 Peyre, Henri Maurice. *Qu'est-ce que le symbolisme?* Paris: PUF,
      1974. 262 pp.
Bibl. essay, pp. 245-54. Index of names. Transl. by Emmett Parker,
      What is Symbolism?, University: U. of Alabama Pr., 1980, 176 pp.
YWMLS 76:190; 74:156-57; FS 32 (1978):211; LR 31 (1977):260-64

•   PERIODICALS   •

4/81 Place, Jean-Michel and André Vasseur. *Bibliographie des revues
      et journaux des XIXe et XXe siècles.* Paris: Chronique des lettres
      françaises, 1973--.
Tables of contents, editorial history and index of authors. 3 vols. to
      date, covering journals since the 1840s, but most from the 1880s
      and after.
YWMLS 73:165

4/82 Admussen, Richard L. *Les Petites revues littéraires (1914-1939):
      Répertoire descriptif.* St. Louis, Mo.: Washington U. Pr./Paris:
      Nizet, 1970. 158 pp.
FS 27 (1973):108-09

•   AUTHORS   •

4/83 Besançon, France. Université. Centre d'études du vocabulaire
      français. *G. Apollinaire: Calligrammes: Concordances, index et
      relevés statistiques.* Paris: Larousse, 1967. 179 pp.
FS 25 (1971):483

4/84 Federman, Raymond and John Fletcher. *Samuel Beckett: His Works and
      His Critics, an Essay in Bibliography.* Berkeley: U. of California
      Pr., 1970. 383 pp.

Indexes incl. subjects and Beckett's works.
JJQ 8 (1970/71):413-20

4/85 Di Pilla, Francesco. Albert Camus e la critica: Bibliografia
      internazionale, 1937-71, con un saggio introduttivo. Lecce:
      Milella, 1973. 341 pp.
With a separately paged introduction of nearly 120 pp. 4800+ entries
      for books, arts. and chapters in books, chronologically. Index
      of scholars only.

4/86 Roeming, Robert F. Camus: A Bibliography. Madison, etc.: U. of
      Wisconsin Pr., 1968. 298 pp.
Nearly 2700 books and arts., by author. No subject index.
FS 25 (1971):112-13; CLS 6 (1969):359; JML 1 (1970/71):737-38x

4/87 Gay-Crosier, Raymond. Camus. Darmstadt: Wissenschaftliche Buch-
      gesellschaft, 1976. 258 pp.
A review of research, in German. L'Étranger: pp. 30-56, incl. sections
      on structure, style, Meursault, etc., with 93 notes.
YWMLS 77:243--"invaluable"

4/88 "Chronique bibliographique: Livres, revues et journaux." In
      Bulletin des Amis d'André Gide.
In each issue (4/yr.)
YWMLS 77:221

4/89 Cunningham, Joyce I. and W. D. Wilson. A Concordance of André
      Gide's La Symphonie pastorale. N. Y.: Garland, 1978. 316 pp.
A phrase of context.
FS 35 (1981):357x

4/90 Leiner, Wolfgang, et al. Bibliographie et index thématique des
      études sur Eugène Ionesco. N. p.: Éds. universitaires Fribourg
      suisse, 1980. 192 pp.

1667 entries, by scholar, listing books, arts., passages in books in
    English, French, German, etc., U. S. diss., as found in DAI, and
    European diss. Classified subject index.

4/91 Morris, Drewry Hampton. Stéphane Mallarmé: Twentieth Century
    Criticism, 1901-1977. University, Miss.: Romance Monographs,
    1977. (Romance Monographs, 25) 208 pp.
Rev. and enl. ed. 1st ed. 1975. 1077 numbered entries, many annotated
    with 1 word to several sentences. Chronological arrangement.
    Indexes of scholars and of names, titles and other subjects.
MLR 73 (1978):921--v fav; YWMLS 77:191

4/92 "Bibliographie sélective." In Cahiers St.-John Perse, 1 (1978)--.
Annual. Covers from 1976. 3 (1980):135-39, for 1978. Lists books,
    arts. and parts of books, in French, English and German, and
    diss., incl. French diss.
YWMLS 78:215

4/93 Little, Roger. Saint-John Perse: A Bibliography for Students of
    His Poetry. London: Grant & Cutler, 1971. (Research Bibls. and
    Checklists) 76 pp.
Suppl. no. 1, Grant & Cutler, 1976, 88 pp. See also his Word Index of
    the Complete Poetry and Prose of Saint-John Perse, n. p., 1967,
    290 leaves and Suppl. A, n. p., n. d., 42 leaves. No context.
FS 30 (1976):236; YWMLS 71:199; 77:225; MLR 62 (1967):134-35

4/94 Bulletin d'informations proustiennes. 1975--.
2/yr. Contents varies. May incl. a bibl. of recent publs., annotated;
    bibls. on special topics (10 [Aut., 1979]: brief bibl. of studies
    of Proust's notebooks and mss.); inventories of his mss.; lists
    of work in progress. Also publ. studies.
The bibls. in Études proustiennes (a subseries of Cahiers Marcel Proust:
    CMP ns. 6=Études 1) duplicate the material in BLF (4/2), with a
    delay of several years. The bibls. in Proust Research Assn. News-

letter, 1969--, (in each issue, but irregular) offer a few notes, but seem otherwise useless.

4/95 Graham, Victor E. Bibliographie des études sur Marcel Proust et son oeuvres. Genève: Droz, 1976. 237 pp.

2274 entries, through 1972, by author, listing books and arts. in various langs. Subject index, citing entry numbers only (Style: 70+ citations).

FS 31 (1977):356-57; FR 51 (1977/78):124; RR 68 (1977):158-59

4/96 "Bibliographie rimbaldienne." In Rimbaud vivant, 1973--
Irregular. No. 16 (1979):45-53.

4/97 Carter, William C. A Concordance to the Oeuvres complètes of Arthur Rimbaud. Athens: Ohio U. Pr., 1978. 810 pp.

YWMLS 78:181-82

4/98 Lapointe, François and Claire Lapointe. Jean-Paul Sartre and His Critics. Bowling Green, Ohio: Philosophy Documentation Center, Bowling Green U., 1981. 697 pp.

2nd ed. 1st ed. 1975. Lengthy section on studies of individual works. Some brief annotations.

4/99 Wilcocks, Robert. Jean-Paul Sartre: A Bibliography of International Criticism. Edmonton: U. of Alberta Pr., 1975. 767 pp.

Mainly studies of Sartre's works. Sections on Fiction; Drama and Cinema; Literary Criticism; etc., subdivided by work. Index of scholars. Annotations, occasionally evaluative, occasionally with a quotation from the study.

YWMLS 75:204

V

ITALIAN LITERATURE

OUTLINE

Bibliographies 5/1-5/9
Reviews of Research 5/10-5/15
Special Bibliographies
    Dissertations 5/16
    Festschriften 5/17
Handbooks 5/18-5/21
Histories 5/22-5/29
Periods
    Through 1400
        Dolce Stil Novo 5/30-5/31
        Sicilian School 5/32
        Authors
            Boccaccio 5/33-5/35
            Dante 5/36-5/46
            Petrarca 5/47
    1400-1800
        Authors
            Ariosto 5/48-5/49
            Boiardo 5/50
            Goldoni 5/51-5/52
            Tasso 5/53-5/54

● ITALIAN LITERATURE ●

● BIBLIOGRAPHIES ●

5/1 "Schedario." In _Italianistica_, 1 (1972)--.
In issue no. 3 (sett.-dic.). Schedario 1979, in 9 (1980):510-52. Lists
     arts., books and parts of books, chiefly in Italian, arranged by
     period and author, through the 19th c., but excluding Dante. This
     is much less complete than the Italian section of the _MLA Bibl._
     (1/9), yet it will cite studies not to be found there.

5/2 "Rassegna bibliografica." In _La Rassegna della letteratura itali-
     ana_.
In each issue (irregular, usually 2/yr.). Summarizes or reviews books
     and arts., incl. arts. from specialist encyclopedias, and cites
     book revs. Entries from 1 sentence to 10 pp. Items cited in
     each issue were publ. that year or during the preceding 2 years,
     and sometime earlier. 84 (1980): issue 1/2, pp. 269-422; issue
     3, pp. 601-710, incl. 12 pp. on the Cinquecento, covering 26
     studies, grouped by subject.
YWMLS 76:464

5/3 "Spogli dalle riviste." In _Studi e problemi di critica testuale_,
     1 (1970)--.
In each issue (2/yr,). 21 (oct., 1980): 293-340. By nation of publ.
     Italia: pp. 302-37, by period. Evaluative annotations, up to 4 or
     5 sentences. Also an unannotated list by scholar of arts. and
     book revs. publ. in the U. S.
YWMLS 74:467--"useful summaries"

5/4 _Annuario bibliografico di italianistica_. 1978--.
Noticed by R. Frattarolo, _Materiali per uno studio_ (5/56), p. 2, but I
     have been unable to confirm its existence elsewhere.

5/5 "Bibliography of Italian Studies in North America." In _Italica_.
Irregular, but in most issues. Books and arts. from major journals.
      Lists book revs., but not diss.

5/6 "Works of Italian Interest Published in Great Britain." In _Italian_
      Studies.
Annual. Books and arts.

5/7 Prezzolini, Giuseppe. _Repertorio bibliografico della storia e_
      della critica della letteratura italiana. Roma: Ed. Roma, 1937-
      48.
4 vols. _1902-1932_, 2 vols., 1099 pp. _1932-1942_, 2 vols., 331 & 358 pp.
      A-Z by subject, mostly authors, but some general topics, move-
      ments, etc. See the list of these headings in vol. 2 of 1902-32
      set, pp. 1069-70. Index in vol. 2 of each set, of names, anony-
      mous titles and a few other subjects. Lists books and arts.,
      mostly in Italian. Many annotations.

5/8 _Repertorio bibliografico della letteratura italiana_. Firenze: San-
      soni, 1951--.
Umberto Bosco, dir. _1943-1947_, publ. 1969, 138 pp.; _1948-1949_, 1951,
      90 pp.; _1950-1953_, n. d., 295 pp. No more publ. Arranged by
      scholar. Detailed but difficult to use subject indexes. Index
      to 1950-53 vol. has appr. 230 refs. under Pavese, by entry number
      only; Petrarca: 1 full col. of refs., by entry number, but many
      with a qualifying phrase, "e Boiardo," "e la Francia," etc. Sys-
      tem of adding qualifying phrase is used somewhat more freely in
      the 1943-47 vol. A few brief annotations in the 1943-47 vol.
GSLI 147 (1970):477-78

5/9 Fucilla, Joseph Guerin. _Saggistica letteraria italiana: Biblio-_
      grafia per soggetti, 1938-1952. Firenze: Sansoni, 1956. (Biblio-
      teca bibliografica italiana, 12) 281 pp.
Lists names only, as subjects. Covers 533 collections of essays by

Italian scholars. Covers Italian and foreign literature, art,
history, etc. Continues his Universal Author Repertoire of Italian Essay Literature, N. Y.: Vanni, 1941, 534 pp., which covered
1697 vols., publ. between 1821 and 1938.

● REVIEWS of RESEARCH ●

5/10 "Rassegne bibliografiche." In Critica letteraria, 1 (1973)--.
In each issue (4/yr.). E. g., C. del Giudici, "Rassegna di studi cri-
    tici sul Carducci (1957-1977)," 6 (1978):339-64, with 101 notes.
YWMLS 78:507--"exemplary," with ref. to del Giudici

5/11 [Surveys of various subjects.] In Lettere italiane. 1 (1949)--.
In each issue (4/yr.). G. Santato, "Rassegna alfieriana (1972-1977),"
    30 (1978):388-410, continuing a survey in 25 (1973); G. Chiecchi,
    "Rassegna boccacciana: per un centenario (1971-1977), 31 (1979):
    241-81.
YWMLS 78:495--ref. to Santato; 79:467--"a very useful comprehensive
    critical survey and analysis of the main critical trends," ref.
    to Chiecchi.

5/12 Puppo, Mario. Manuale critico-bibliografico per lo studio della
    letteratura italiana. Torino: Soc. ed. internazionale, 1972.
    437 pp.
12th ed. 1st ed. 1954. Chapters on reference sources, methods, lan-
    guage and style, 7 periods, 21 major authors (Ariosto: appr. 9
    pp.), and on the relations of Italian and the other literatures of
    Europe. Chapters usually have an intro. essay on the history of
    the study of the subject and a classified bibl., with comments.
    Cites some studies in English, French and German.

5/13 Beccaro, Felice del. Guida allo studio della letteratura itali-
    ana. Milano: Mursia, 1975. 350 pp.
Quattrocento: 16 pp., in 5 sections, incl. Pulci, Boiardo, Poliziano and

Lorenzo di Medici. Novecento: 95 pp., in 14 sections, incl. sections on Croce, Svevo and Pirandello, and one on film.

5/14 Mazzamuto, Pietro. Rassegna bibliografica-critica della letteratura italiana. Firenze: Le Monnier, 1956. 673 pp.
3rd ed. 1st ed. 1952. 17 chapters, most on major writers. Cites
studies in English, German and French, as well as Italian.

5/15 Frattarolo, Renzo. Bibliografia speciale della letteratura italiana. Milano: Marzorati, 1959. (Problemi ed orientamenti critici, vol. 1, pt. 2 [5/21]) 554 pp.
2nd ed. A survey of eds. and criticism, by period, with chapters on
major writers. Ariosto: appr. 8 pp. 15 chapters (appr. 130 pp.)
on the 1800s, incl. 10 major writers. No indexes.

• DISSERTATIONS •

5/16 Cervigni, Dino. "Survey of American and Canadian Dissertations in
Italian and Italian-related Subjects." In Italica 55 (1978):36-
67.
Suppl. in Italica 56 (1979):322. Diss. in progress or completed, by
subject or period. Previously (work in progress only) in 46
(1969):89-97 and 48 (1971):542-49.

• FESTSCHRIFTEN •

5/17 Golden, Herbert Herschel and Seymour O. Simches. Modern Italian
Language and Literature: A Bibliography of Homage Studies. Cam-
bridge: Harvard U. Pr., 1959. 207 pp.
Appr. 1500 entries under Literature, in classified order.

• HANDBOOKS •

5/18 Dizionario enciclopedico della letteratura italiana. Bari:

Laterza, 1966-70.

6 vols. Giuseppe Petronio, dir. Unsigned arts. on writers, artists,
   historical figures, etc.; forms and genres; literary movements,
   groups and journals, etc. Alfieri: 17 cols., plus 3 cols. bibl.;
   Leopardi: 18 cols. and 1 3/4 cols. bibl; neorealismo: 2 cols., 3/4
   col. bibl.; alienazione: 2/3 col.; canzone a ballo: 2 cols., incl.
   bibl. Vol 6 incl. indexes of titles (pp.23-383) and of names (pp.
   385-549).

5/19 Dizionario critico della letteratura italiana. Torino: UTET,
      1973.

3 vols. Vittore Branca, ed. Signed arts. on writers, movements, literary journals, etc. Alfieri: 10 cols., plus 3 cols. bibl.; Leopardi: 37+ cols., plus 9 1/2 cols. bibl.; neorealismo: 10 cols.,
   plus 1+ cols. bibl. Illustrated. Index of names and other subjects in vol. 3.

5/20 Bondanella, Peter and Julia Conaway Bondanella. Dictionary of
      Italian Literature. Westport, Conn.: Greenwood Pr., 1979. 621
      pp.

400+ signed arts. on writers, forms, movements, etc. Brief bibls.
   Chronological tables, pp. 554-93, incl. Italian literature, European literature, philosophy, science and the arts.
YWMLS 79:447, 462, 472, 512 ("admirably fulfilling its purpose as a
   short ref. guide, though of necessarily limited value to the
   specialist"), 533, 548; IQ 22 (no. 84 [Spring, 1981]):108-09

5/21 Momigliano, Attilio, ed. Problemi ed orientamenti critici di
      lingua e di letteratura italiana. Milano: Marzorati, 1949-65.
5 vols. in 10.
1:    Notizie introduttive e sussidi bibliografici. Pt. 1, 3rd ed.,
      1965, 477 pp.; pt. 2, 2nd ed., 1959, 554 pp. (see 5/15); pt. 3,
      2nd ed., 1960, 392 pp.
2:    Tecnica e teoria letteraria. 2nd ed., 1951. 357 pp. Incl. a

history of the theory of literary genres from Aristotle to Croce by Mario Fubini, 80+ pp., etc.

3: Questioni e correnti di storia letteraria. 1949. 965 pp. Essays by various scholars on the periods of Italian literature, incl. chapters on Dante, Boccaccio and Petrarch and Petrarchism (100+ pp., incl. a 60 pp. classified annotated bibl.)

4: Letterature comparate. 1948. 382 pp. Chapters by various scholars on the Troubadours and on English, French, Spanish, German, Scandinavian and Classical literatures in relation to Italian.

5: Movementi e problemi di storia dell'estetica. 4 vols. 1959-61. 2017 pp.

● HISTORIES ●

5/22 Storia letteraria d'Italia. Milano: Vallardi, 1973.

1: Viscardi, Antonio. Le Origini. 1973. 840 pp. 5th ed. 1st ed. 1939.

2: Bertoni, Giulio. Il Duecento. 1973. 495 pp. 7th reprinting of 3rd, 1939, ed., with bibl. suppl. for 1940-71.

3: Vallone, Aldo. Dante. 1973. 628 pp. Replaces Mario Apollonio, Dante, 3rd ed., 2 vols., 1964.

4: Sapengo, Natalino. Il Trecento. 1973. 626 pp. Reprinting of 3rd, 1966, ed., with bibl. suppl. 1st ed. 1933.

5: Rossi, Vittorio. Il Quattrocento. 1973. 582 pp. 9th reprinting of 1st, 1933 ed., with bibl. suppl.

6: Toffanin, Giuseppe. Il Cinquecento. 1973. 760 pp. Reprinting of 7th, 1965, ed., with bibl. suppl. 1st ed. 1927.

7: Jannaco, Carmine and Martino Capucci. Il Seicento. 1973. 775 pp. Reprinting of 2nd., 1966 ed. 1st ed. 1963.

8: Natali, Giulio. Il Settecento. 2 vols. 1973. Reprinting of 6th, 1964 ed., with bibl. suppl. 1st ed. 1929.

9: Mazzoni, Guido. L'Ottocento. 2 vols. 1973. 9th reprinting of 2nd, 1934 ed., with bibl. suppl. 1st ed. 1913.

10: Galletti, Alfredo. Il Novecento. 1973. 812 pp. 5th reprinting of 3rd, 1951 ed., with bibl. suppl. 1st ed. 1935.

These vols. represent the 2nd ed. of this set. 1st ed. 1898-1926. The
bibl. suppls. are by Aldo Vallone and fill 15-30 pp. or more,
depending on the interval since the last revision. Other notes
or bibl. with each chapter of text. Index of names only.

5/23 Letteratura italiana: I Maggiori. Milano: Marzorati, 1956.
(Orientamenti culturali)

2 vols. 1361 pp. Covers 19 writers, Dante to D'Annunzio. Petrarca,
by Umberto Bosco, pp. 111-83, incl. a list of works, with comments, and a classified bibl. of criticism, pp. 178-83. Index
of names. Detailed table of contents. The 1967 ed. seems to be
identical with that of 1956.

5/24 Letteratura italiana: I Minori. Milano: Marzorati, 1961.
(Orientamenti culturali)

4 vols. 3506 pp. Covers through the end of the 19th c. Vico: appr.
30 pp., incl. 5 pp. of bibl., but which seems to list nothing
publ. after the late 1940s. Index of names in vol 4. Detailed
tables of contents in each vol.

5/25 Letteratura italiana: Le Correnti. Milano: Marzorati, 1956.
(Orientamenti culturali)

2 vols. 1222 pp. 7 chapters on the periods of Italian literature
(Dal Romanticismo al Decadentismo: 230+ pp.); one on the history
of criticism since de Sanctis; and one on the relations of Italian
literature with European literature (130+ pp.) Bibls. with each
chapter. Index of names. Detailed table of contents.

5/26 Wilkins, Ernest Hatch. A History of Italian Literature. Cambridge, Mass.: Harvard U. Pr., 1974. 570 pp.

Rev. by Thomas G. Bergin. Orig. ed. 1954. Revisions consist of a new
chapter on post-war literature and of additions to the limited
bibl. Chronological chart, pp. 549-59. Index of names and other

subjects.
RPh 31 (1977/78):174-76; IS 10 (1955):76-77

5/27 Whitfield, John Humphreys. A Short History of Italian Literature.
      Harmondsworth, Middlesex: Penguin, 1960. 303 pp.
9 chapters (176 pp.) through the 1500s; 6 chapters (112 pp.) from the
      1600s. 20th c.: 16 pp., mainly on Pirandello. Index of names,
      chiefly.
MLR 56 (1961):150; Italica 37 (1960):294-96; IS 15 (1960):65-66

5/28 Carsaniga, Giovanni. Geschichte der italienischen Literatur von
      der Renaissance bis zur Gegenwart. Stuttgart: Kohlhammer, 1970.
      356 pp.
MLR 67 (1972):432-33--v fav; IS 27 (1972):132-34--v fav; RLC 46 (1972):
      462-64--v unfav

5/29 Friedrich, Hugo. Epoche della lirica italiana. Milano: Mursia,
      1974-76.
3 vols. I: Dalle origini al quattrocento. 1974. 281 pp. Most of
      book deals with major figures, to Poliziano. Bibl., mostly books,
      paralleling text. Indexes of first lines and of names. II: Il
      Cinquecento. 1975. 204 pp. III: Il Seicento. 1976. 194 pp.
      Transl. of Epochen der italienischen Lyrik, Frankfurt am Main:
      Klostermann, 1964. 784 pp., by Luigi Banfi and Gabriella Cacchi.
YWMLS 76:443--"useful synthesis for students;" 77;483

●   THROUGH 1400   ●

5/30 Centuori, Walter J. A Concordance to the Poets of the Dolce Stil
      Novo. Lincoln: U. of Nebraska Pr., 1977. (Distr. by Ann Arbor,
      Mich.: U. M. I.)
5 vols. 2800 pp. Covers 6 poets, incl. Guinizelli and Cavalcanti,
      each poet concorded separately. Context of several lines of verse.
YWMLS 78:451

5/31   Savona, Eugenio. Repertorio tematico del dolce stil nuovo. Bari:
        Adriatica, 1973. 517 pp.
Passages from Guinizelli, Cavalcanti and 4 others, illustrating themes.
YWMLS 73:411--"an excellent tool;" RPh 29 (1975/76):575-76

5/32   Pagani, Walter. Repertorio tematico della scuola poetica sici-
        liana. Bari: Adriatica, 1968. 541 pp.
Passages from the poets, illustrating themes.
MLR 67 (1972):665-67

5/33   "Bollettino bibliografico." In Studi sul Boccaccio 1 (1963)--.
Annual. Covers from 1938. Contents vary: some installments incl. lists
        of eds. and of transls. into various langs., but every installment
        incl. a list of critical studies, by author. 10 (1977-78):353-80:
        eds., transls. and studies, 1975-76; 11 (1979):445-71: additional
        studies, 1975-76. Some brief annotations.

5/34   Esposito, Enzo. Boccacciana: Bibliografia delle edizioni e degli
        scritti critici (1939-1974). Ravenna: Longo, 1976. 150 pp.
1614 numbered entries, listing books and arts., by year of publ. Var-
        ious indexes, incl. subjects (names, Boccaccio's works, and other
        subjects), citing item numbers only. Continues a bibl. publ. in
        1939 by Vittore Branca (as does 5/33) and other earlier bibls.
Alighieri 17 (1976):99-100; YWMLS 77:466;   GSLI 154 (1977):477

5/35   Barbina, Alfredo. Concordanze del Decameron. Firenze: C/E Giunti
        G. Einaudi, 1969.
2 vols. 2187 pp. Context of a phrase.
GSLI 148 (1971):416-17; YWMLS 71:405

5/36   "Rassegna bibliografica dantesca" and "Repertorio bibliografico."
        In Alighieri: Rassegna bibliografica dantesca, 1960--.
Repertorio: 21:1 (gen.-giugno, 1980):60-67, for 1979. A list of books,
        arts., and chapters in books. Rassegna: (usually in each issue)

21:2 (luglio-dic., 1980):57-62. 9 entries, **books, arts. and chapters in books**, also noted in the Repertorio, with commentary.

5/37 "Bibliografia dantesca ragionata." In Studi danteschi, 36 (1959)--. Annual. Covers from 1956. 50 (1973):219-81, listing books and arts. publ. from 1965 to 1972, with evaluative comments, 1 sentence to 1 page, from 100+ journals and series, arranged by year of publ. No **indexes**. Slow to appear and missing from the last 2 vols. Perhaps discontinued. Most vols. before vol. 36 had contained alphabetical bibls. of books and arts., sometimes annotated.

5/38 "American Dante Bibliography." In Dante Studies, 84 (1966)--. Annual. Gives abstracts. Previously in Dante Society of America, Annual Reports, 68-72 (1954)-83 (1965), covering from 1953.

5/39 Vallone, Aldo. Gli Studi danteschi dal 1940 al 1949. Firenze: Olschki, 1950. 138 pp.

5/40 Esposito, Enzo. Gli Studi danteschi dal 1950 al 1964. Roma: Centro ed. internazionale, 1965. 537 pp.
In 9 **sections**, incl. 4 on La Divina Commedia (a general section and 1 for each book, but not further subdivided) and 1 on Fortuna e rapporti: storia della critica. Annotated, 1 sentence to 1/2 p.

5/41 Cardillo, Angelo. "Bibliografia dantesca (1965-1974)." In Misure critiche 4:1 (gen.-giugno, 1974):3-16 and 4:2 (luglio-dic., 1974): 17-32. Not seen.

5/42 Enciclopedia dantesca. Roma: Ist. della Enciclopedia Italiana, 1970-78.
Umberto Bosco, dir. 5 vols. and suppl. Arts. on names and terms associated with Dante, his works, his times and his later reputation. Beatrice: 18 cols. and a 1 1/4 col. bibl.; Vita Nuova: 17 2/3 cols., and 3 cols. bibl.; "Voi donne, che pietoso atto mostrati:"

1 col., incl. bibl. The suppl. incl. a classified bibl. of studies,
pp. 538-618. The orig. Enciclopedia dantesca was in 3 vols., 1896-
1905.
YWMLS 71:390; 79:447; GSLI 148 (1971):413-16; 149 (1972):601-07; 152
(1975):439-42; 155 (1978):289-95

5/43 Toynbee, Paget. A Dictionary of Proper Names and Notable Matters
in the Works of Dante. Oxford: Clarendon Pr., 1968. 722 pp.
Rev. by Charles Singleton. Orig. ed. 1898. Beatrice: 3+ cols.; Vita
Nuova: 1 1/2 cols. Gives quotations in Italian and Latin.
RR 61 (1970):43; MAE 38 (1969):77-80; IS 24 (1969):116-18--praises
handling of names, critical of handling of "notable matters"

5/44 Lovera, Luciano, et al. Concordanza della Commedia di Dante Alighieri. Torino: Einaudi, 1975.
3 vols. of concordance; 4th vol. is the text, with an index of rimes.
YWMLS 75:389

5/45 Wilkins, Ernest Hatch and Thomas Goddard Bergin. A Concordance to
the Divine Comedy of Dante Alighieri. Cambridge, Mass.: Harvard
U. Pr., 1965. 636 pp.
MLR 63 (1968):266-67x; MAE 35 (1966):146-49

5/46 Sheldon, Edward Stevens and A. C. White. Concordanza delle opere
italiane in prosa e del Canzoniere di Dante Alighieri. Oxford:
Stamperia dell'Università, 1905. 740 pp.
Brief context. The 1969 reprint (N. Y.: Russell & Russell) incl. a concordance to the minor Italian works by Lewis H. Gordon, orig.
publ. in 1936.

5/47 Accademia della Crusca, Florence. Opera del Vocabolario. Concordanze del Canzoniere di Francesco Petrarca. Firenze: n. p., 1971.
2 vols. 2110 pp. Context of a line or more.

● 1400-1800 ●

● AUTHORS ●

5/48 Fatini, Giuseppe. Bibliografia della critica ariostea, 1510-1956.
        Firenze: Le Monnier, 1958. 722 pp.
By year of publ. Inadequate indexes, listing by entry number only 1)
        studies of Ariosto and his works, in 13 sections, incl. IV: Or-
        lando Furioso, studies by 1200 scholars, unsubdivided and unqual-
        ified; and 2) names, both subjects and scholars, incl. 7 lines of
        entries on Bradamente.
YWMLS 58:263

5/49 Medici, D. "La Bibliografia della critica ariostesca dal 'Fatini'
        ad oggi." In Bollettino storico reggiano 27 (1974):63-150.
360 entries, 1956-74, by year of publ. Annotated. Index of subjects,
        incl. Ariosto's works, and index of names, incl. subjects. A
        chronological unannotated suppl. of 170 entries, by R. Cremante,
        is in Studi e problemi di critica testuale, 18 (1979):237-44. The
        bibl. by Medici is part of a conference on Ariosto publ. over 5
        issues of the Bollettino (nos. 25-29) and also publ. separately
        under the title Lodovico Ariosto: Il suo tempo, la sua terra, la
        sua gente, Reggio Emilia: Poligrafici, 1974.
SPCT 18 (1979):237-44--"hasty"

5/50 Medici, D. "La Critica boiardesca dal 1800 al 1976: Bibliografia
        ragionata." In Bollettino storico reggiano 34 (1977):7-133.
645 entries for books and arts., by year of publ. Brief annotations.
        Index of names, incl. subjects.

5/51 "Bibliografia goldoniana." In Studi goldoniani, 1 (1968)--.
Irregular. 1 (1968):170-98 and 2 (1970):235-80, 844 entries listing
        scholarship and revs. of productions, 1958-67. 5 (1979):182-213,
        covering 1968-77. Some brief notes.

YWMLS 71:434

5/52 Mangini, Nicola. Bibliografia goldoniana, 1908-1957. Venezia &
      Roma: Ist. per la collaborazione culturale, 1961. (Civiltà vene-
      ziana, 10) 465 pp.
Eds., transls. and studies. Index of scholars and some subjects (incl.
      Goldoni's works, s. v. Commedie, Intermezzi and Melodrammi).

5/53 "Rassegna bibliografici dei recenti studi tassiani." In Studi
      tassiani, 2 (1952)--.
Covers from 1946. 27 (1979):127-40, for 1976. Some notes, usually
      brief. Quotations from book revs., often lengthy. This also
      publ. a separately paged "Bibliografia tassiana (studi sul Tasso)"
      which lists works from the 16th through the mid-20th c., by
      scholar: 27 (1979):2045-2140, entries 7923-8305, to Tescari.

5/54 Tortoreto, Alessandro and Joseph G. Fucilla. Bibliografia anali-
      tica tassiana (1896-1930). Milano: Bolaffio, 1935. 167 pp.
Suppl., "Nuovi studi su Torquato Tasso (1931-1945)," in Aevum 20 (1946):
      14-72, by Tortoreto.

● 1800 and AFTER ●

• BIBLIOGRAPHIES •

5/55 "Schede bibliografico." In Otto/Novecento, 1 (1977)--.
Currently irregular. 4:5/6 (sett.-dic., 1980):433-63, listing books,
      book revs. and arts. in journals and books, chiefly publ. 1978-80,
      mostly in Italian. Critical works are listed by scholar, with
      cross-refs. from the author studied. (There are few headings for
      general topics.) Also lists literary works, (books only) by
      author.
This offers many fewer entries than the MLA Bibl. (1/9); indeed, the MLA
      probably lists some Italian studies not found here. Other than

the book revs., this seems to list little not to be found in the
MLA, but often lists studies a year or more before they will be
found there. Did not appear in 5:1 or 5:2 (1981).

5/56   Frattarolo, Renzo and Marco Santoro. Materiali per uno studio
       della letteratura italiana del novecento. Napoli: Soc. ed. napo-
       letana, 1979. 160 pp.
Books and some arts. (cited without page refs.), in Italian. Lists gen-
       eral studies only; no sections on individual writers.

•   HANDBOOKS   •

5/57   Dizionario della letteratura italiana contemporanea. Firenze:
       Vallecchi, 1973.
2 vols. E. Ronconi, ed. I: mainly biographies, with bibls. Moravia:
       6 cols. biography, 3/4 col. listing works and 12 studies in Ital-
       ian. II: plot summaries and commentary on works by 50 writers.
       Pirandello: appr. 13 pp., on 7 novels, no plays.

5/58   Novecento: Gli Scrittori e la cultura letteraria nella società
       italiana. Milano: Marzorati, 1980.
10 vols. 10,277 pp. Gianni Grana, director. Essays by various schol-
       ars on writers, movements, periodicals and other topics. Bibls.
       with each chapter. Part I: vols. 1-3, covering the first decades
       of the century. Part II: vols. 4-6, covering the fascist period.
       Part III: vol. 7-10, covering post-war period. Calvino: VII:6848-
       6884, incl. 4 1/2 pp. bibl., of which 3 pp. list critical studies
       (books, arts. and chapters in books, in Italian). Il Futurismo
       italiano: II:1673-1935, incl. arts. on Marinetti and other writers
       and on Futurist theater and art, with bibls. Index, vol. 10,
       pp. 10215-277, of names and other subjects, and of contributors.
YWMLS 79:548--"indispensible"

5/59   Letteratura italiana: I Contemporanei. Milano: Marzorati, 1963-77.

(Orientamenti culturali)

6 vols.   Index of names in vols. 2, 3 and 6.   Italo Calvino: VI:1471-
    1507, incl. a bibl. which has been reprinted with a few additions
    in the preceding entry; the texts, however, are completely differ-
    ent.

5/60   Russo, Luigi.   I Narratori (1850-1957).   Milano & Messina: Prin-
       cipato, 1958.   488 pp.
3rd ed.   1st ed. 1923.   Arranged into 4 period sections.   Brief entries,
    few more than 1 p., giving barest biographical facts, a list of
    works (books only), sometimes a critical comment and sometimes a
    list of studies (books and arts., in Italian).   Pavese: 17 pp. of
    text (2 lines of biography), 1 p. bibl., incl. appr. 17 studies.

5/61   Amici, Gualtiero.   Narratori italiani da Verga alla neo-avan-
       guardia: Profili critico-bibliografici.   Bologna: Ponte Nuovo,
       1973.   219 pp.
Brief entries, few more than 1 p.   Minimal biographical or bibliograph-
    ical detail.   Bibl. of books in Italian only, pp. 211-14.
YWMLS 74:489

•   HISTORIES   •

5/62   Paparelli, Gioacchino and Claudio Scibilia.   Letteratura italiana
       del novecento.   Napoli: Conte, 1978.   716 pp.
Bibl., paralleling text, of literary works (books only) and critical
    studies (books and arts., in Italian only).   Index of names.
YWMLS 78:517

5/63   Jones, Frederic J.   La Poesia italiana contemporanea (da Gozzano a
       Quasimodo).   Messina & Firenze: D'Anna, 1975.   473 pp.
Covers 1900-1945 and focusses on 11 poets.
MLR 72 (1977):464-66; IS 31 (1976):127-28--v fav

5/64   Manacorda, Giuliano. Storia della letteratura italiana contem-
       poranea, 1940-1975. Roma: Riuniti, 1977. 538 pp.
4th ed. 1st ed. 1967. 50 pp. on the 1970s.
YWMLS 67:378

●   FUTURISM   ●

5/65   Baldazzi, Anna, ed. Contributo a una bibliografia del futurismo
       letterario italiano. Roma: Cooperativa scrittori, 1977. 629 pp.
Incl. a lengthy section on Futurist periodicals and their contents. See
       also Enrico Falqui, Bibliografia e iconografia del futurismo,
       Firenze: Sansoni, 1959 (Biblioteca bibliografia italiana, 21),
       239 pp.
YWMLS 78:517

●   AUTHORS   ●

5/66   Frattarolo, Renzo. Studi foscoliani: Bibliografia della critica
       (1921-1952). Firenze: Sansoni, 1954-56.
2 vols. 671 entries, books and arts., in Italian, English or French,
       by scholar. Brief annotations. Subject index under 19 broad
       headings, incl. Foscolo's works (by specific title or by form).

5/67   Tortoreto, A. and C. Rotundi. Bibliografia analitica leopardiana
       (1961-1970). Firenze: Olschki, 1973. 222 pp.
Classified arrangement. Index of scholars. 5th of a series. Previous
       vols.: G. Mazzatinti, Bibliografia leopardiana, 1932 (covering
       through 1898); G. Natali, Bibliografia leopardiana, 1932 and 1953
       (covering 1898-1930 and 1931-51); and A. Tortoreto, Bibliografia
       analitica leopardiana, 1963 (covering 1952-60).
YWMLS 74:492

5/68   Bufano, Antonietta. Concordanze dei Canti del Leopardi. Firenze:
       Le Monnier, 1969. 448 pp.

Brief context.
GSLI 147 (1970):465-67

5/69 Brusamolino Isella, Silvia and Simonetta Usuelli Castellani.
Bibliografia manzoniana, 1949-1973. Milano: Il Polifilio, 1974.
111 pp.
Sections covering criticism of 1949-63 and 1964-73, each by scholar. No
indexes.

5/70 Felcini, Furio. Bibliografia della critica pascoliana, 1887-1954,
con un saggio introduttivo. Firenze: Le Monnier, 1957. 197 pp.
Books and arts. in Italian, by year of publ. Survey of research, pp.
v-xlix. Index of scholars only.

5/71 Barbina, Alfredo. Bibliografia della critica pirandelliana, 1889-
1961. Firenze: Le Monnier, 1967. (Publ. dell'Istituto di studi
pirandelliani, 3) 331 pp.
Books and arts. in Italian and other langs., by year of publ. Classified subject index, incl. sections on Pirandello's works, citing
entry number only.

5/72 Chierici, Enrico and E. Paradisi. Concordanze dell'Allegria di
Giuseppe Ungaretti. Roma: Bulzoni, 1977. 175 pp.
YWMLS 77:523

5/73 Raya, Gino. Bibliografia verghiana (1840-1971). Roma: Ciranna,
1972. 690 pp.
Rev. ed. Orig, ed. 1960. Chronological arrangement. Annotated. Index of Verga's works and of some other subjects. Notes movies,
productions of operas.
MLR 70 (1975):649-50; YWMLS 72:415-16

VI

HISPANIC LITERATURES

OUTLINE

GENERAL (Spanish, Portuguese, Spanish-American and Brazilian)
    Bibliography 6/1
        Dissertations 6/2-6/5
        Festschriften 6/6

SPANISH (Some entries also cover Portuguese or Spanish-American Literature, as noted)
    Bibliography of Bibliographies 6/7
    Bibliographies 6/8-6/14
        Translations 6/15-6/16
    Handbooks 6/17-6/19
    Histories 6/20-6/26
    Drama 6/27
    Periods
        Medieval
            Bibliography 6/28
            History 6/29
            Authors and Works
                Poema de Mío Cid 6/30-6/32
                Juan Manuel 6/33

Sixteenth-Seventeenth Centuries
    Comedia 6/34-6/35
    Picaresque 6/36-6/37
    Authors and Works
        Calderón 6/38-6/40
        La Celestina 6/41-6/43
        Cervantes 6/44-6/50
        Garcilaso de la Vega 6/51
        Lope de Vega 6/52-6/53
        Quevedo 6/54
        Tirso de Molina 6/55
Eighteenth-Nineteenth Centuries
    Bibliographies 6/56-6/57
    History 6/58
    Fiction 6/59
    Authors
        Béquer 6/60
        Galdós 6/61-6/62
Twentieth Century
    Bibliography of Bibliographies 6/63
    History 6/64
    Modernism 6/65
    Novel 6/66-6/68
    Drama 6/69
    Authors
        Lorca 6/70-6/73
        Machado 6/74
        Miró 6/75
        Panero 6/76
        Sender 6/77
        Unamuno 6/78
        Valle-Inclán 6/79

PORTUGUESE (Some of the works cited in the Spanish section also cover
        Portuguese literature, as noted. See the Index.)
        Bibliography of Bibliographies 6/80
        Bibliography 6/81
        Handbooks 6/82-6/84
        History 6/85
        Authors
                Camoẽs 6/86
                Pessoa 6/87

LATIN AMERICAN (Spanish-American and Brazilian)
        Bibliographies of Bibliographies 6/88-6/92
        Bibliographies 6/93-6/98
                Translations 6/99-6/102
        Handbooks 6/103-6/105
        History 6/106
        Theater 6/107

SPANISH-AMERICAN (Some of the entries in the Spanish section cover Span-
        ish-American literature, as noted. See the Index; see also the
        Hispanic section.)
        Bibliographies 6/107-6/110
        Handbook 6/111
        Histories 6/112-6/114
        Modernism 6/115-6/116
        Novel 6/117-6/121
        Periodicals 6/122
        Authors
                Borges 6/123
                Darío 6/124-6/125
                Florit 6/126
                García Márquez 6/127
                Hernández 6/128
                Neruda 6/129

BRAZILIAN (Some of the entries under Portuguese also cover Brazilian,
        as noted. See the Index.)
        Bibliographies of Bibliographies 6/130-6/131
        Bibliography 6/132
             Translations 6/133
        Handbooks 6/134-6/135
        Histories 6/136-6/138
        Fiction 6/139
        Authors
             Coelho Netto 6/140
             Euclides da Cunha 6/141

● ● HISPANIC LITERATURES ● ●

● BIBLIOGRAPHY ●

6/1 "Review of Reviews" and "Review of Miscellanies." In <u>Bulletin</u> <u>of</u>
     <u>Hispanic</u> <u>Studies</u>, 23 (1946)--.
Alternately. Incl. Luso-Brazilian publications. "Review of Reviews"
     lists the contents of journals in Spanish, English, Portuguese,
     German, etc., on Hispanic culture and history, by journal, incl.
     single arts. from journals not otherwise devoted to Hispanic stud-
     ies. 58:4 (Oct., 1981):357-76, covering appr. 100 journals, incl.
     a few not in the <u>MLA</u> <u>Bibl.</u> (1/9), and listing arts. from others
     sometimes a year before they will appear in the <u>MLA</u>. "Review of
     Miscellanies," 58:3 (July, 1981):280-81, lists the contents of 6
     books. Called <u>Bulletin</u> <u>of</u> <u>Spanish</u> <u>Studies</u> before 26 (1949).

● DISSERTATIONS ●

6/2 "Dissertations in the Hispanic Languages and Literatures." In
     <u>Hispania</u>, 18 (1935)--.
Annual. In issue no. 2 (May). By author. Lists U. S. and Canadian
     diss., completed and in progress.

6/3 Chatham, James R. and Enrique Ruiz-Fornells. <u>Dissertations</u> <u>in</u> <u>His-</u>
     <u>panic</u> <u>Languages</u> <u>and</u> <u>Literatures</u>: <u>An</u> <u>Index</u> <u>of</u> <u>Dissertations</u> <u>Com-</u>
     <u>pleted</u> <u>in</u> <u>the</u> <u>United</u> <u>States</u> <u>and</u> <u>Canada</u>, <u>1876</u>-<u>1966</u>. Lexington:
     U. Pr. of Kentucky, 1970. 120 pp.
Classified arrangement. Indexes of subjects and scholars. Vol. 2, 1967-
     77, 1981, 162 pp.

6/4 "Theses in Hispanic Studies Approved for Higher Degrees by British
     Universities to 1971." In <u>Bulletin</u> <u>of</u> <u>Hispanic</u> <u>Studies</u> 49 (1972):
     325-54.
Continued in 52 (1975):325-44 and 56 (1979):283-304.

6/5 Rodriguez Richart, J. "'Habilitationsschriften' y tesis de docto-
     rado realizadas en las universidads de Austria, de la República
     Democrática Alemanna y de la República Federal de Alemania sobre
     temas de lengua y literatura española y portuguesa (1945-1974)."
     In Iberoromania 3 (1975):205-34.
By year. Indexes of scholars and of subjects.
YWMLS 76:289

                        •   FESTSCHRIFTEN   •

6/6 Golden, Herbert Hershel and Seymour O. Simches. Modern Iberian
     Language and Literature: A Bibliography of Homage Studies. Cam-
     bridge, Mass.: Harvard U. Pr., 1958. 184 pp.
Covers chiefly 1500 and after. Incl. Latin American literatures. Sec-
     tion III: Literature and Folklore, pp. 83-154: appr. 1120 entries,
     in classified order. Index of names (subjects and scholars) and
     anonymous titles.
Suppl. by David S. Zubatsky, "Hispanic Studies in Festschriften: An
     Annotated Bibliography (1957-75)," in Hispania 60 (1977):656-717.

                  • • SPANISH LITERATURE • •

                      •   BIBLIOGRAPHIES   •

6/7 Foster, David William and Virginia Ramos Foster. Manual of His-
     panic Bibliography. N. Y.: Garland, 1977. 329 pp.
2nd ed. 1st ed. 1970. 1050 annotated entries for bibls., esp. on
     Spanish and Spanish-American literatures.
BHS 56 (1979):272--"this book has many faults;" HR 40 (1972):216--fav

6/8 "Bibliografía." In Revista de filología española, 1 (1914)--.
Annual. Slow to appear. Covers general and Hispanic literature and
     linguistics. 58 (1976), publ. 1978: Hispanic literatures, pp.
     378-412, entries 66062-66586. "Siglo de oro:" appr. 175 entries;

18th, 19th and 20th centuries: total of 63 entries. Cites book
revs. and European diss., but otherwise there is now likely to be
little found in this not also to be found in the MLA Bibl.(1/9),
which is more comprehensive, as well. This will be most valuable
for the years before the 1960s.

6/9 "Bibliografía." In Nueva revista de filología hispánica.
2/yr. Covers Spanish literature, with some entries on Portuguese. 28:2
       (1979): more than 2000 entries, incl. appr. 1500 on literature.
       Sections on poetry, drama and fiction, subdivided into ancient,
       modern and contemporary periods. Cites book revs.
Also likely to offer little not to be found in the MLA Bibl. (1/9),
       other than the book revs., but the arrangement by genre, then by
       period may on occasion be useful.

6/10 "Literatura castellana." In Revista de literatura.
2/yr. Very irregular, of late. 40:1 & 2 (julio-dic., 1978):257-304,
       covering publs. of 1976-78, chiefly. Vols. 37-38, dated 1970, but
       publ. in 1976 as 1 vol.; the bibl. listed publs. of 1973-74.

6/11 Simón Díaz, José. Bibliografía de la literatura hispánica.
       Madrid: Consejo Superior de Investigaciones Científicas, 1950--.
The earlier vols. have appeared in a 2nd ed., 1960--. 11 vols. to date,
       the latest (publ. 1976) covering Golden Age authors, Gongora
       through Hurtado de Alcocer. Garcilaso de la Vega: vol. 10, pp.
       553-79: appr. 300 entries, incl. mss., eds., transls., and appr.
       200 critical studies, publ. 1573-1971, books and arts., in clas-
       sified order. Indexes incl. names, first lines of poems, and sub-
       jects.
BHS 49 (1972):299-301--ref. to vol. 7; 401-03--ref. to vol. 8: critical;
       careless, not reliable

6/12 Simón Díaz, José. Manual de bibliografía de la literatura espa-
       ñola. Madrid: Gredos, 1980. 1156 pp.

3rd ed.   26924 **numbered** entries, in classified order.   Siglos de Oro:
      pp. 186-528, entries 4437-13850; Garcilaso de la Vega: nearly 130
      entries, listing eds. and studies, in classified order, incl. sec-
      tions on his sources, themes, and on his works, by form, with sub-
      sections on the Églogas and the Canciones, etc.   Siglo XX: more
      than 7250 entries.   Lists books and arts. in Spanish, English,
      etc.   Index of names (subjects and scholars) and of other sub-
      jects, incl. themes, movements, places, etc.

6/13   Paci, Anna Maria.   Manual de bibliografía española.   Pisa: Univer-
       sità, 1970.   828 pp.
Lists arts. from about 100 journals from Europe, Latin America and the
       U. S., to 1968.   Garcilaso de la Vega: appr. 50 entries, mostly
       from the 1950s and 60s.   Incl. Catalan.
BHS 54 (1977):84-85--notes errors

6/14   Serís, Homero.   Manual de bibliografía de la literatura española.
       Syracuse, N. Y.: Centro de Estudios Hispánicos, Syracuse U., 1948-
       54.
Part I: Obras generales, 2 vols., 1086 pp., 8779 numbered entries,
       occasionally annotated.   "Influencias y relaciones literarias,"
       pp. 38-72, entries 329-745, by country and author.   Index of
       scholars and subjects, incl. authors, places, forms, etc.   No more
       publ.   See also his Guía de nuevos temas de literatura española,
       Madrid: Castalia, 1973, 324 pp., a survey of insufficiently stud-
       ied topics.
HR 44 (1976):179-80; BHS 52 (1975):315; YWMLS 73:219, 288

                          •   TRANSLATIONS   •

6/15   Rudder, Robert S.   The Literature of Spain in English Translation:
       A Bibliography.   N. Y.: Ungar, 1975.   637 pp.
Transls. publ. in books and journals, incl. individual poems, etc.
LRN 4 (1979):131; BHS 54 (1977):233

6/16 Pane, Remigio Ugo. English Translations from the Spanish, 1484–
      1943: A Bibliography. New Brunswick, N. J.: Rutgers U. Pr., 1944.
      218 pp.
List of corrections and additions in Hispanic Review 13 (1945):174-77.

● HANDBOOKS ●

6/17 Diccionario de literatura española. Madrid: Ed. de la Revista de
      Occidente, 1972. 1191 pp.
4th ed. 1st ed. 1949. Ed. by Germán Bleiberg and Julián Marías.
      Covers biographies, movements, genres, themes, critical terms,
      etc. Incl. Spanish-American literature. Garcilaso de la Vega: 6
      cols.; Borges: 2/3 col.; Cantar de Mío Cid: 4 1/2 cols., plus 1
      1/2 cols. bibl.; Don Juan, Mito literario de: 2+ cols. Chronol-
      ogy, through 1971, pp. 1099-1175. Index of titles, pp. 959-1097.

6/18 Sáinz de Robles, F. C. Ensayo de un diccionario de la literatura.
      (See 1/28)
Vol. 2: Escritores españoles e hispanoamericanos. 4th ed. 1973. 1338 pp.

6/19 Ward, Philip, ed. The Oxford Companion to Spanish Literature.
      Oxford: Clarendon Pr., 1978. 629 pp.
Incl. Spanish-American literature and Catalan literature. The major
      arts. have very brief bibls. Garcilaso de la Vega: 2 cols.;
      Borges: 2 1/4 cols.; Cid, Cantar: 2 2/3 cols., incl bibl. of
      transls. and 2 critical books; Don Juan: 1/2 col., with cross-
      refs. to arts. on 7 authors and 2 works.
MLR 74 (1979):719--"truly comprehensive"; YWMLS 79:323; LR 35 (1981):
      179; AUMLA no. 55 (May, 1981):129-32--critical of accuracy and
      bibls.

● HISTORIES ●

6/20 Valbuena Prat, Ángel. Historia de la literatura española.

Barcelona: Gili, 1968.

8th ed. 1st ed. 1937. 4 vols. Index of names and titles in vol. 4. Detailed tables of contents. See 6/113 for a companion vol. on Spanish-American literature.

1:   Época medieval; Los Siglos de Oro. 861 pp.

2:   Los Siglos de Oro. 774 pp.

3:   Época moderna o de la Ilustración al Vanguardismo. 638 pp.

4:   Época contemporánea, o del Vanguardismo al Existencialismo. pp. 639-1304.

6/21 Díaz-Plaja, Guillermo, ed. Historia general de las literaturas hispánicas. Barcelona: Barna, 1949-58.

5 vols. in 6. Incl. Spanish-American and Catalan literatures. Bibls. or notes with each chapter. No indexes.

1:   Desde los orígenes hasta 1400. 1949. 779 pp.

2:   Pre-renacimiento y renacimiento. 1951. 866 pp.

3:   Renacimiento y barroco. 1953. 1036 pp.

4:   Siglos XVIII y XIX. 1956-57. 2 vols. 606 & 619 pp.

5:   Post-romanticismo y modernismo. 1958. 533 pp.

6:   Literatura contemporánea. 1967. 800 pp.

6/22 Alborg, Juan Luis. Historia de la literatura española. Madrid: Gredos, 1966--.

No bibls., but many footnotes. Detailed index of names, incl. scholars cited in notes as well as authors and their works discussed in the text.

1:   Edad media y renacimiento. Rev. ed. 1970. 1082 pp. 1st ed. 1966.

2:   Época barroca. 2nd ed. 1970. 995 pp. 1st ed. 1967.

3:   Siglo XVIII. 1972. 979 pp.

4:   El Romanticismo. 1980. 934 pp.

YWMLS 66:183--"up-to-date bibls. but an old-fashioned text;" 71:239-- "expanded and vastly improved," both ref. to vol. 1; 73:261; HR 36 (1968):271-73

6/23 <u>Historia</u> y <u>crítica</u> <u>de</u> <u>la</u> <u>literatura</u> <u>española</u>. Barcelona: Crítica,
      1980--.

Francisco Rico, ed. 8 vols. projected. Chapters by various scholars,
      with brief bibls. of books and arts. Index of names (subjects
      and cited scholars) and other subjects.

1:    Deyermond, Alan, ed. <u>Edad</u> <u>media</u>. 1980. 570 pp

6:    Mainer, José-Carlos, ed. <u>Modernismo</u> y <u>98</u>. 1980. 493 pp.

6/24 <u>A</u> <u>Literary</u> <u>History</u> <u>of</u> <u>Spain</u>. London: Benn/N. Y.: Barnes & Noble,
      1971-73.

8 vols. Bibls., chiefly of books, in Spanish and English. Notes with
      each chapter, sometimes extensive. Index of names, titles and
      other subjects. Quotations given in Spanish only.

1:    Deyermond, A. D. <u>The</u> <u>Middle</u> <u>Ages</u>. 1971. 244 pp.
MLR 67 (1972):670-71; YWMLS 71:239--"**intelligent, critical, balanced**"

2:    Jones, Royston Oscar. <u>The</u> <u>Golden</u> <u>Age</u>: <u>Poetry</u> <u>and</u> <u>Prose</u>, <u>the</u> <u>Six</u>-
      <u>teenth</u> <u>and</u> <u>Seventeenth</u> <u>Centuries</u>. 1971. 233 pp.
MLR 67 (1972):925-26; YWMLS 71:254--"clear, thorough, sound"

3:    Wilson, Edward Meryon and Duncan Moir. <u>The</u> <u>Golden</u> <u>Age</u>: <u>Drama</u>,
      <u>1492-1700</u>. 1971. 171 pp.
YWMLS 71:254

4:    Glendinning, Nigel. <u>The</u> <u>Eighteenth</u> <u>Century</u>. 1972. 160 pp.
YWMLS 71:267; BHS 51 (1974):177-79; MLR 68 (1973):677-78

5:    Shaw, Donald L. <u>The</u> <u>Nineteenth</u> <u>Century</u>. 1972. 200 pp.
YWMLS 72:237; BHS 51 (1974):299-301

6:    Brown, G. G. <u>The</u> <u>Twentieth</u> <u>Century</u>. 1972. 176 pp. Covers
      through the early 1960s.
BHS 51 (1974):396-99--v fav; YWMLS 72:237, 261

7:    Franco, Jean. <u>Spanish</u> <u>American</u> <u>Literature</u> <u>since</u> <u>Independence</u>.
      1973. 306 pp. 140 pp. on the 20th c.
YWMLS 73:359; BHS 52 (1975):190-92--v fav

8:    Terry, Arthur. <u>Catalan</u> <u>Literature</u>. 1972. 136 pp.
BHS 52 (1975):102-04

There is a Spanish transl. with revised text: Barcelona: Ariel, 1973-74.

BHS 53 (1976):85--bibls. are "extended and Hispanicized where appropriate"

6/25 Russell, Peter Edward. <u>Spain</u>: <u>A</u> <u>Companion</u> <u>to</u> <u>Spanish</u> <u>Studies</u>. London: Methuen, 1977. 592 pp.

Reprinted with revs. 1st publ. 1973. Incl. 3 chapters on the history of Spanish literature and chapters on Spanish-American and Catalan literatures. Other chapters are on art, music, language and history. Replaces a work edited by E. Allison Peers.

YWMLS 73:217, 281, 291, 315, 325 (Catalan), 355 (colonial Sp.-Am.:unfav); BHS 52 (1975):79-82; MLR 69 (1974):893-95

6/26 Flasche, Hans. <u>Geschichte</u> <u>der</u> <u>spanischen</u> <u>Literatur</u>. Bern & München: Francke, 1977--.

1: <u>Von</u> <u>den</u> <u>Anfängen</u> <u>bis</u> <u>zur</u> <u>Ausgabe</u> <u>des</u> <u>fünfzehnten</u> <u>Jahrhunderts</u>. 487 pp.

MLR 75 (1980):676-77; BHS 57 (1980):239; CLS 17 (1980):341-42--praises its comparative approach

● DRAMA ●

6/27 Ruiz Ramón, Francisco. <u>Historia</u> <u>del</u> <u>teatro</u> <u>español</u>. Madrid: Alianza, 1967-71.

2 vols. I: <u>Desde</u> <u>los</u> <u>orígenes</u> <u>hasta</u> <u>1900</u>. 503 pp. II: <u>Siglo</u> <u>XX</u>. 544 pp. A 3rd ed., 1977-79, 391 and 584 pp., and 4th ed., vol. 2, 1980, not seen.

YWMLS 68:221; 72:259--"surpasses all previous treatments; reflects current critical thinking"; BHS 51 (1974):101-03; HR 38 (1970):328-39; 42 (1974):470-73

● MEDIEVAL ●

● BIBLIOGRAPHY ●

6/28 Sáez, Emilio and Mercè Rossell. Repertorio de medievalismo hi-
      spánico (1955-1973). Barcelona: El Albir, 1976--.
5 vols. projected. Covers Spain and Portugal. 2 vols. to date, listing
      books and arts. in Spanish, English, French, etc., by 3674 schol-
      ars, through Myers. Vol. 5 will incl. a subject index.
YWMLS 77:276

● HISTORY ●

6/29 López Estrada, Francisco. Introducción a la literatura medieval
      española. Madrid: Gredos, 1979. (Biblioteca románica hispánica,
      III, Manuales, 4) 606 pp.
4th ed. 1st ed. 1952. Index of names, works and other subjects.
BHS 57 (1980):266--"massive and up-to-date bibl. in the footnotes"; BH
      82 (1980):488-

● AUTHORS and WORKS ●

6/30 Magnotta, Miguel. Historia y bibliografía de la crítica sobre el
      Poema de Mío Cid (1750-1971). Chapel Hill: Dept. of Romance Langs.
      U. of North Carolina, 1976. (UNC Studies in the Romance Langs. and
      Lits., 145) 300 pp.
Bibl., pp. 261-85, listing books and arts. Index of names and subjects.
MLR 73 (1978):666-68

6/31 Deyermond, A. D. "Tendencies in Mío Cid Scholarship, 1943-1973."
      In Mío Cid Studies, A. D. Deyermond, ed., London: Támesis, 1977,
      pp. 13-47.
Rev. of research with a bibl. of 126 items, most in Spanish or English.

6/32 Waltman, Franklin M. Concordance to Poema de Mío Cid. University
      Park & London: Penn. St. U. Pr., 1972. 465 pp.

6/33 Devoto, Daniel. Introducción al estudio de Don Juan Manuel, y en
      particular de El Conde Lucanor: Una Bibliografía. Madrid: Casta-
      lia, 1971. 503 pp.
Books and arts. in Spanish, English, German and other langs., with anno-
      tations, often long and evaluative. Section I: general studies;
      II: studies of Don Juan Manuel, in 12 chapters; III: studies of
      El Conde Lucanor, incl. chapters on each tale.
YWMLS 72:201; BHS 52 (1975):90-91; HR 43 (1975):412-18--critical of
      inaccuracy in matters of detail, but praises thoroughness; MLR 69
      (1974):671-77

● 16th and 17th CENTURIES ●

• COMEDIA •

6/34 "Bibliography of Publications on the Comedia." In Bulletin of the
      Comediantes, 1 (1951)--.
In issue no. 2 (Fall). 32 (1980), for 1979-80, listing books and arts.
      publ. 1978-80. 435 entries. Lope: 56 entries; Don Juan theme: 22
      entries, on all aspects of the theme, incl. general studies and
      studies on its use in later literatures.
YWMLS 79:301

6/35 McCready, Warren T. Bibliografía temática de estudios sobre el
      teatro español antiguo. Toronto: U. Toronto Pr., 1966. 445 pp.
Books, book revs. and arts., 1850-1950. Classified arrangement. Calde-
      ron: pp. 214-59, entries 1841-2340, listing studies of general
      topics, alphabetically by topic, and eds. and studies of the
      plays, by play. Index of scholars. Many cross-refs.
HR 37 (1969):414-17--v fav

• PICARESQUE •

6/36   Laurenti, Joseph L.   Bibliografía de la literatura picaresca:
       desde sus orígenes hasta el presente.   Metuchen, N. J.: Scarecrow,
       1973.   262 pp.
2439 entries on 19 Spanish works, 1554-1743, listing eds., transls., and
       studies in books and journals.   Some brief notes.   Index of names
       only.   Suppl., N. Y.: AMS, 1981, 163 pp., 1009 entries.   An ear-
       lier version was publ. by Madrid: CSIC, 1968.
BHS 47 (1970):153--critical of completeness and accuracy

6/37   Ricapito, Joseph V.   Bibliografía razonada y anotada de las obras
       maestras de la picaresca española.   Madrid: Castalia, 1980.   613
       pp.
Covers Lazarillo, Quevedo and Alémán particularly.
JHP 5 (1980/81):69-71

• AUTHORS and WORKS •

6/38   Calderón de la Barca Studies, 1951-69: A Critical Survey and Anno-
       tated Bibliography.   Toronto: U. of Toronto Pr., 1971.   247 pp.
Jack H. Parker and Arthur M. Fox, gen. ed.   Classified arrangement.   Some
       brief annotations.   Index of scholars.
YWMLS 71:276; MLN 87 (1972):364-66

6/39   Reichenberger, Kurt and Roswitha Reichenberger.   Bibliographisches
       Handbuch der Calderón-Forschung.   Manual bibliográfico calderon-
       iano.   Kessel: Thiele and Schwarz, 1979--.
3 vols. projected.   I: Die Calderón-Texte und ihre Überlieferung.   831
       pp.   III: Bibliographische Beschreibung.   838 pp.   Vol. II, a
       bibl. of research, is not yet publ.
BCom 32 (1980):146-49; JHP 5 (1980/81):75-77

6/40   Flasche, Hans and Gerd Hofman.   Konkordanz zu Calderón.

Hildesheim & N. Y.: Olms, 1980--.

I: <u>Autos</u> <u>sacramentals</u>: Vol. 1: A-Ch, 1234 pp.

YWMLS 79:312; BCom 33 (1981):85-86

6/41   "La Celestina: Documento bibliográfico."   In <u>Celestinesca</u>: <u>Boletín</u>
       <u>informativo</u> <u>internacional</u>, 1 (1977)--.

In each issue (2/yr.) 4:2 (nov., 1980):51-58, entries S342-84. Books,
       arts. and U. S. and European diss. Annotated.

YWMLS 78:275; HR 46 (1978):278-79

6/42   Mandel, Adrienne S.   "<u>La Celestina</u>" <u>Studies</u>: <u>A Thematic Survey and
       Bibliography</u>, <u>1824-1970</u>. Metuchen, N. J.: Scarecrow, 1971.   261
       pp.

7 sections, incl. influence studies and criticism.

YWMLS 74:271; BHS 51 (1974):170-72--fav as regards the bibl., unfav as
       regards the survey

6/43   Snow, Joseph, James Schneider and Cecelia Lee.   "Un cuarto de siglo
       de interes en 'La Celestina,' 1949-75: Documento bibliográfico."
       In <u>Hispania</u> 59 (1976):610-60.

Classified and annotated. Incl. Spanish theses, as well as book revs.
       See also G. Siebenmann, "Estado presente de los estudos celesti-
       nescas (1959-1974)," in <u>Vox</u> <u>Romanica</u> 34 (1975):160-212, in 12 sec-
       tions, incl. sources, critical studies and influence, with a bibl.
       of more than 250 books, arts. and theses.

YWMLS 76:256

6/44   "Bibliografía cervantina." In <u>Anales</u> <u>cervantinos</u>, 1 (1951)--.

Covers 1945--. 18 (1979/80), publ. 1980, 44 pp., covering books and
       arts. in Spanish, English, etc., chiefly publ. 1978-79. Annota-
       tions to 1 p., occasionally longer.

6/45   Murillo, Luis Andrés. <u>Don</u> <u>Quijote</u> <u>de</u> <u>la</u> <u>Mancha</u>. (<u>Bibliografía</u>
       <u>fundamental</u>). Madrid: Clásicos Castalia, 1978.   141 pp.

Classified arrangement, incl. sections on characters (Sancho Panza: 16
     entries) and episodes, and on influence (Kafka: 3 entries).   Index
     of scholars. This is vol. 3 of his edition of Don Quixote.
BHS 57 (1980):348x--"reasonably full, fundamental and up-to-date"

6/46 Drake, Dana B. Don Quijote, 1894-1970: A Selective Annotated Bib-
      liography. Chapel Hill: Dept. of Romance Langs., U. of North
      Carolina, 1974. (UNC Studies in the Romance Langs. and Lits.,
      138) 267 pp.
A suppl. was publ. in 1978 by Miami: Universal, 269 pp., incl. 339 anno-
     tated entries and a cumulated index of names and other subjects.
Hispania 64 (1981):153

6/47 Drake, Dana B. Don Quijote in World Literature: A Selective Anno-
      tated Bibliography. N. Y. & London: Garland, 1980. 272 pp.
518 entries. Cites books, arts. and diss. as found in DAI. Chapters on
     the reception and influence of Don Quixote in Spain, England,
     France, Russia, etc. Index of names and other subjects.

6/48 Drake, Dana B. Cervantes' Novelas Ejemplares: A Selective Annota-
      ted Bibliography. N. Y.: Garland, 1981. 218 pp.
The novelas, pp. 105-201, entries 281-554, briefly annotated. Indexes.

6/49 Ruiz-Fornells, Enrique. Las Concordancias de el ingenioso hidalgo
      Don Quijote de la Mancha. Madrid: Cultura Hispánica, 1976--.
2 fascicles to date, through Ch.

6/50 Fernández Gómez, Carlos. Vocabulario de Cervantes. Madrid: Real
      Academia Español, 1962. 1136 pp.
A concordance, giving a sentence of context.
YWMLS 62:191

6/51 Sarmiento, Edward. Concordancias de las obras poéticas en caste-
      llano de Garcilaso de la Vega. Columbia: Ohio St. U. Pr., 1970.

581 pp.

BHS 49 (1972):185-86; HR 40 (1972):319; MLR 69 (1974):435-37

6/52 Lope de Vega Studies, 1937-1962: A Critical Survey and Annotated
      Bibliography. Toronto: U. of Toronto Pr., 1964. 210 pp.
Jack H. Parker and Arthur M. Fox, gen. eds. Some brief annotations.
      Classified arrangement. No indexes. Continues a bibl. by L.
      Fichter in Hispania 20 (1937):327-52
YWMLS 64:213; HR 34 (1966):370-73

6/53 Fernández Gómez, Carlos. Vocabulario completo de Lope de Vega.
      Madrid: Real Academia Española, 1971.
3 vols. 3028 pp. Lengthy context.
YWMLS 71:268

6/54 Crosby, James O. Guía bibliográfica para el estudio crítico de
      Quevedo. London: Grant & Cutler, 1976. (Research Bibls. and
      Checklists) 140 pp.
Books, book revs., arts. and U. S. and European diss. Some very brief
      annotations. Indexes incl. Quevedo's works and names as subjects.
BHS 55 (1978):160-61--v fav; YWMLS 77:295

6/55 An Annotated Analytical Bibliography of Tirso de Molina Studies,
      1627-1977. Columbia & London: U. Missouri Pr., 1979. 238 pp.
By author. Thematic index, pp. 227-38. Vern G. Williamsen, gen. ed.
BHS 57 (1980):245-46; Hispania 64 (1981):153-54; BCom 32 (1980):83-87;
      YWMLS 79:306--"cleverly devised thematic index"

● 18th and 19th CENTURIES ●

• BIBLIOGRAPHIES •

6/56 "Bibliografía dieciochista hispánica." In Boletín del Centro de
      Estudios del Siglo XVIII, 1 (1973)--.

6 (1978):107-230, publ. 1979. Annotated. Literature: appr. 13 pp.
YWMLS 75:273--"admirably complete"; 79:318

6/57 Aguilar Piñal, Francisco. Bibliografía fundamental de la litera-
      tura española: Siglo XVIII. Madrid: Soc. General Española de
      Librería, 1976. 304 pp.
2204 entries for books and arts., mainly in Spanish, but also in English,
      French, etc.; about 1650 on writers, listing eds. and studies.
HR 46 (1978):498-500; YWMLS 76:273-74

· HISTORY ·

6/58 Peers, Edgar Allison. A History of the Romantic Movement in
      Spain. Cambridge: The University Pr., 1940.
2 vols. An abridged ed. was publ. in 1949. A Spanish transl. of the
      full version was publ. in 1954.

· FICTION ·

6/59 Montesinos, José F. Introduccíon a una historia de la novela en
      España en el siglo XIX. N. p.: Castalia, 1973. 297 pp.
3rd ed. 1st ed. 1955. Incl. a bibl. of Spanish transls. of foreign
      novels, 1800-1850, pp. 149-269.

· AUTHORS ·

6/60 Ruiz-Fornells, Enrique. A Concordance to the Poetry of Gustavo
      Adolfo Bécquer. University: U. of Alabama Pr., 1970. 207 pp.

6/61 Woodbridge, Hensley C. Benito Pérez Galdós: A Selective Annotated
      Bibliography. Metuchen, N. J.: Scarecrow, 1975. 321 pp.
See also his "A Selective Annotated Bibliography of Doña Perfecta," in
      Anales galdosianos 11 (1976):91-100.
AGald 11 (1976):131-33

6/62   Sackett, Theodore A.   Pérez Galdós: An Annotated Bibliography.
       Albuquerque: U. of New Mexico Pr., 1968.   130 pp.
By scholar.   No subject index.   Annotations of 1-4 sentences.

●   20th CENTURY   ●

•   BIBLIOGRAPHY   •

6/63   Zubatsky, David S.   "An Annotated Bibliography of Twentieth Cen-
       tury Catalan and Spanish Author Bibliographies."   In Hispania 61
       (1978):654-79
Lists books, arts. and parts of books.

•   HISTORY   •

6/64   Torrente Ballester, Gonzalo.   Panorama de la literatura española
       contemporánea.   Madrid: Guadarrama, 1961.
2nd ed.   1st ed. 1956.   2 vols.   1078 pp.   Bibl., pp. 915-1078, by Jorge
       Campos, paralleling text, listing eds. and studies, mostly books,
       mostly in Spanish.   Vol. 2 is an anthology.

•   MODERNISM   •

6/65   Fretes, Hilda Gladys and Esther Barbará de Bittar.   Bibliografía
       anotada del modernismo.   Mendoza, Arg.: Biblioteca Central, Univ.
       Nacional de Cuyo, 1970.   (Cuadernos de la biblioteca, 5) 138 pp.
245+ entries, incl. sections on the characteristics of Spanish and
       Spanish-American modernism, and on the principal writers.

•   NOVEL   •

6/66   "Annual Bibliography of Post-Civil War Spanish Fiction."   In Ana-
       les de la narrativa española contemporánea, 4 (1979)--.
Lists novels and criticism, incl. book revs.   4 (1979):139-63, for 1978.

6/67   Nora, Eugenio de. <u>La</u> <u>Novela</u> <u>española</u> <u>contemporánea</u>. Madrid:
       <u>Gredos</u>, 1968-70.
2nd ed. 1st ed. 1958-62. 3 vols. Covers 1898-1967. Each vol. has a
       bibl. of books and arts., mainly in Spanish, paralleling text, and
       indexes of names (subjects and scholars) and of titles.
YWMLS 62:212

6/68   Martínez Cachero, J. M. <u>Historia</u> <u>de</u> <u>la</u> <u>novela</u> <u>española</u> <u>entre</u> <u>1936</u>
       <u>y</u> <u>1975</u>. Madrid: Castalia, 1979. 505 pp.
Annotated bibl. of books and arts., pp. 373-469, 235 entries, with a
       subject index in 10 broad categories (pp. 375-76).
YWMLS 79:352-53--praises bibl.; BHS 58 (1981):162

• DRAMA •

6/69   Molera Manglano, L. <u>Teatro</u> <u>español</u> <u>contemporáneo</u>. Madrid:
       Nacional, 1974. 420 pp.
Covers from the 1930s. No bibls. or index.
YWMLS 75:315

• AUTHORS •

6/70   [Bibls. on special subjects.] In <u>García</u> <u>Lorca</u> <u>Review</u>, 1 (1973)--.
In each issue (annual). 8 (1980):36-46: a bibl. of books, arts. and a
       U. S. and a French diss. on "Poeta en Nueva York."

6/71   Colecchia, Francesca. <u>García</u> <u>Lorca</u>: <u>A</u> <u>Selectively</u> <u>Annotated</u> <u>Bib-</u>
       <u>liography</u> <u>of</u> <u>Criticism</u>. N. Y. & London: Garland, 1979. 313 pp.
Lorca's theatre, pp. 123-201, more than 500 entries in 12 sections,
       incl. the individual plays. Cites books, book revs. and arts. in
       Spanish, English, etc. Most items annotated in a phrase or 1-2
       sentences.
Hispania 64 (1981):315--prefers this to the next entry

6/72   Laurenti, Joseph L.   Federico García Lorca y su mundo: Ensayo de
       una bibliografía general.   Metuchen, N. J.: Scarecrow, 1974.
       282 pp.
2247 entries, in classified order.   Teatro: 530 entries, incl. sections
       on each play.   Relaciones literarias: nearly 100 entries.   Index
       of names (subjects and scholars).   This bibl. lists diss., as
       found in DAI, studies in the E. European langs., and some studies
       in Spanish not to be found in Colecchia (6/71); Colecchia lists a
       number of studies in Spanish and English not in this.
YWMLS 74:314

6/73   Pollin, Alice M.   A Concordance to the Plays and Poems of Federico
       García Lorca.   Ithaca, N. Y. & London: Cornell U. Pr., 1975.   1180
       pp.
Separate concordances for the plays and for the poems.
MLR 72 (1977):723-24; BHS 54 (1977):89

6/74   Carrión Gútiez, Manuel, ed.   Bibliografía machadiana (bibliografía
       para un centenario).   Madrid: Biblioteca Nacional, 1976.   295 pp.
Publs. by and about Manuel and Antonio Machado y Ruiz, incl. critical
       studies in books and journals, mostly in Spanish.
YWMLS 76:299

6/75   López Landeira, Richard.   An Annotated Bibliography of Gabriel
       Miró (1900-1978).   N. p.: Soc. of Spanish and Spanish American
       Studies, 1978.   200 pp.
Lists eds., transls. and studies of Miró and his works, in classified
       order.   Cites U. S., Spanish and other European diss.
YWMLS 78:320

6/76   Ruiz-Fornells, Enrique.   A Concordance to the Poetry of Leopoldo
       Panero.   University: U. of Alabama Pr., 1978.   725 pp.

6/77   King, Charles L.   Ramón J. Sender: An Annotated Bibliography, 1928-

<u>1974</u>.   Metuchen, N. J.: Scarecrow, 1976.   287 pp.

Pp. 221-63: studies on Sender, incl. U. S. and Spanish diss.

6/78   Fernández, Pelayo Hipólito.   <u>Bibliografía</u> <u>crítica</u> <u>de</u> <u>Miguel</u> <u>de</u>
       <u>Unamuno</u> (<u>1888</u>-<u>1975</u>).   Madrid: Porrúa Turanzas, 1976.   336 pp.

By year of publ.   Index of scholars.

BHS 55 (1978):166-67--v fav

6/79   Lima, Robert.   <u>An</u> <u>Annotated</u> <u>Bibliography</u> <u>of</u> <u>Ramón</u> <u>del</u> <u>Valle-Inclán</u>.
       University Park: Pennsylvania St. U. Libraries, 1972.   401 pp.

Lists eds., transls., and studies (books, arts. and U. S. diss.) in
       classified order.   A few annotations.

BHS 53 (1976):77--"exhaustive and up-to-date"; HR 43 (1975):440-42

● ● PORTUGUESE LITERATURE ● ●

[Some of the works cited in the Spanish section above also cover Portu-
       guese literature, as noted.]

● BIBLIOGRAPHIES ●

6/80   Zubatsky, David S.   "An Annotated Bibliography of Portuguese Au-
       thor Bibliographies."   In <u>Luso-Brazilian</u> <u>Review</u>, 15 (1978):44-62.

6/81   Moisés, Massaud, et al., eds.   <u>Bibliografia</u> <u>da</u> <u>literatura</u> <u>portu-</u>
       <u>guêsa</u>.   São Paulo: Saraiva, Ed. da Universidade, 1968.   383 pp.

Selective.   Eds. and studies (books and arts., almost all in Portuguese)
       arranged by period and author.   Camões: 10 pp.   Index of scholars.

● HANDBOOKS ●

6/82   Coelho, Jacinto do Prado.   <u>Dicionário</u> <u>de</u> <u>literatura</u>.   Pôrto:
       Figueirinhas, 1979.

3rd ed.   1st ed. 1960.   3 vols.   1526 pp.   Incl. Brazilian and Galician
       literatures.   Illus.   Decadentismo: 3 cols., incl. brief bibl.,

largely on the term as applied to Portuguese literature, 1880-
1920. Decadentismo como tema literário: 2+ cols., with ref. to
Portuguese literature, 16th-19th c. Don Juan: 5+ cols., in Portuguese and Brazilian literature. Camões: 4 3/4 cols, plus 3/4 col.
bibl.; Lusíadas: 7 cols., plus 1/2 col. bibl.

6/83 Cochofel, João José, ed. Grande dicionário da literatura portu-
      guêsa e de teoria literária. Lisboa: Iniciativas editorialis,
      1970--.
Publ. in fascicles. Vol. 1, 1977, 772 pp., A-Bobo. Afonso o Sábio: 2
      cols., with bibl. "In his pref. the ed. states that special atten-
      tion will be paid to literary theory and that arts. on Portuguese
      literary periodicals and associations, and on the influence of
      foreign literatures on Portuguese will appear besides the usual en-
      tries on authors and their works." YWMLS 70:335
YWMLS 70:335; 72:281--"contains some important arts."; 72:296

6/84 Moisés, Massaud, ed. Literatura portuguêsa moderna: Guia biográ-
      fico, crítico e bibliográfico. São Paulo: Cultrix, 1973. 202 pp.
Brief entries, few more than 1 p., giving brief biographies, list of
      publs. and a signed paragraph of critical commentary. A few en-
      tries conclude with a list of critical studies, mostly books. 9
      entries on schools, etc., as listed on pp.201-02, with names of
      associated writers.

● HISTORY ●

6/85 Moisés, Massaud. A literatura portuguêsa. São Paulo: Cultrix,
      1972. 338 pp.
10th ed. 1st ed. 1960.

● AUTHORS ●

6/86 Nogueira, Julio. Dicionário e gramática de "Os Lusíadas." Rio de

Janeiro: Freitas Bastos, 1960. 438 pp.

Alphabetical list, mixing words and allusions from the text with gram-
matical and rhetorical concepts, all with brief quotations and
exact refs. to text.

YWMLS 61:217

6/87 Iannone, Carlos Alberto. Bibliografia de Fernando Pessoa. São
Paulo: Eds. Quíron, 1975. 84 pp.

2nd ed. 681 entries for books and arts., chiefly in Portuguese, by author. Index of names.

● ● LATIN AMERICAN LITERATURES ● ●

● BIBLIOGRAPHIES ●

6/88 Bryant, Shasta M. A Selective Bibliography of Bibliographies of
Hispanic American Literature. Austin: Inst. of Latin American
Studies, U. of Texas, 1976. (Guides and Bibliographies Series, 8)
100 pp.

Incl Brazil. Appr. 650 bibls., from books and journals. Subject index.

YWMLS 77:404

6/89 Zubatsky, David S. "An Annotated Bibliography of Latin American
Author Bibliographies." In Chasqui: Revista de literatura latino-
americana, 6:1 (1976)-8:2 (1979).

In 6 installments. 1: Mexico. 6:1 (1976):43-70. 2: Central America &
the Caribbean. 6:2 (1977):41-72. 3: Colombia, Ecuador & Venezuela. 6:3 (1977):45-68. 4: Brazil. 7:1 (1977): 35-54; 5: Bolivia, Chile, Paraguay & Peru. 7:3 (1978):34-79. 6: Argentina &
Uruguay. 8:2 (1979):47-94. Annotated. Incl. books, arts. and
parts of books.

6/90 Gropp, Arthur Eric. A Bibliography of Latin American Bibliographies. Metuchen, N. J.: Scarecrow, 1968. 515 pp.

Incl. Brazil. Books only. Broad subject arrangement, with detailed
    subject index. Suppl., 1971. 277 pp.

6/91 Gropp, Arthur Eric. A Bibliography of Latin American Bibliogra-
    phies Published in Periodicals. Metuchen, N. J.: Scarecrow, 1976.
2 vols. 1031 pp. Incl. Brazil. Literature: pp. 712-27, appr. 185 en-
    tries.

6/92 Cordeiro, Daniel Raposo, ed. A Bibliography of Latin American
    Bibliographies: Social Sciences and Humanities. Metuchen, N. J.:
    Scarecrow, 1979--.
BHS 57 (1980):271

6/93 Handbook of Latin American Studies. 1936--.
Annual. Covers 1935--. Incl. Brazil and the West Indies. Briefly an-
    notated bibls. on various fields of research, each preceded by a
    brief (1-2 pp.) essay noting the major publs. of the year. 40
    (1978), publ. 1979. Literature: pp. 361-534 , 1500 entries. Incl.
    books of fiction, poetry and plays, with a separate section of
    transls. into English, and books, arts. and chapters in books of
    criticism. Indexes of subjects, incl. names, and of authors, incl.
    scholars, poets, novelists and playwrights.
Since 27 (1965) the even-numbered vols. and years survey the humanities:
    literature, linguistics, art, film [since 38 (1976)], folklore
    [since 34 (1972)], history, music and philosophy, for a two-year
    period. The odd-numbered vols. survey work in the social sciences.

6/94 HAPI: Hispanic American Periodicals Index. 1979--.
Annual. Covers 1975--. Incl. Brazil. Lists arts. on all aspects of
    Latin American culture and society from "200 major journals" by
    subject and author.

6/95 Index to Latin American Periodical Literature, 1929-1960. Boston:
    Hall, 1962.

9 vols. Suppl., 1961-65, 2 vols., 1968; suppl., 1966-1970, 2 vols.,
     1980. Arts. from journals and yearbooks publ. in the U. S., Eu-
     rope, and Latin America. Miguel Asturias, in the 1966-70 suppl.,
     has 36 entries, incl. a few essays by him and a number of studies
     of his works. (See also next entry)

6/96 Index to Latin American Periodicals: Humanities and Social Sci-
     ences. 1963-75.
9 annual vols. publ., covering 1961-69. Lists arts. from periodicals
     publ. in Latin America, incl. Brazil and Haiti. 4 (1964)-9 (1969)
     are 4 uncumulated quarterly installments bound together.
This and 6/95 are based on card-files kept at the Pan American Union's
     Columbus Memorial Library, Washington, D. C. The basic set of
     6/95 covers a large number of journals publ. in Latin America; for
     the 1960s 6/95 is an index to arts. on Latin-American topics from
     journals publ. outside of Latin America. However, it still incl.
     some Latin American serials, possibly yearbooks, which were not
     covered by 6/96.

6/97 Sánchez, Luis Alberto. Repertorio bibliográfico de la literatura
     latino-americana. Lima: Univ. Nacional Mayor de San Marcos, 1955--.
5 vols. publ. 1: [General.] 1955. 124 pp. 2: Brasil. Bolivia. 1957.
     100 pp. 3: Chile. Colombia. 1962. 282 pp. 4: Cuba. Ecuador.
     1962. 242 pp. 5: Contribución a la bibliografía de la literatura
     peruana. 1969. 279 pp.

6/98 "Bibliografía hispánica." In Revista hispánica moderna, 1 (1934/
     35)-35 (1969/70).
Books, arts. and book revs. on Spanish and Spanish-American literature.

· TRANSLATIONS ·

6/99 Shaw, Bradley A. Latin American Literature in English Translation:
     An Annotated Bibliography. N. Y.: NYU Pr., 1976. 144 pp.

Incl. Brazil and the non-Hispanic literatures of the region. 624 en-
    tries. Annotated. Suppl., 1975-1978, N. Y.: Center for Inter-
    American Relations, 1979, 23 pp.
LALR no. 13 (Fall-Winter, 1978): 82-84-v fav

6/100 Freudenthal, Juan R. and Patricia M. Freudenthal. Index to An-
    thologies of Latin American Literature in English Translation.
    Boston: Hall, 1977. 199 pp.
BHS 56 (1979):86

6/101 Hulet, Claude Lyle. Latin American Poetry in English Translation:
    A Bibliography. Washington, D. C.: Pan American Union, 1965. 192
    pp.
Incl. transls. publ. in books and journals. See 6/133 for a suppl. to
    the Brazilian section.

6/102 Hulet, Claude Lyle. Latin American Prose in English Translation:
    A Bibliography. Washington, D. C.: Pan American Union, 1964. 191
    pp.
Sections incl. Drama, Essay, Novel and Short Story, subdivided by nation.

● HANDBOOKS ●

6/103 Bradbury, Malcolm, Eric Mottram and Jean Franco. Penguin Compan-
    ion to American Literature. N. Y.: McGraw-Hill, 1971. 384 pp.
Latin American writers, pp. 283-384. Brief entries, incl. a few on
    movements, etc., most by Jean Franco.
YWMLS 71:365--"mistakes, omissions and often dubious contents," ref. to
    Brazilian entries; 74:398--"useful"

6/104 Reichardt, Dieter. Lateinamerikanische Autoren: Literaturlexikon
    und Bibliographie der deutschen Übersetzungen. Tübingen & Basel:
    Erdmann, 1972. 718 pp.
Arranged by country. Bibls. of works and German transls. only.

HLAS 34:4372

6/105 Foster, David W. and Virginia R. Foster. Modern Latin American
        Literature. N. Y.: Ungar, 1975. (Library of Literary Criticism)
2 vols. Passages (up to 2 pp.) from books and arts., incl. some transl.
        from Spanish, Portuguese and German, with full citations to the
        originals.
HLAS 38:6492; BHS 54 (1977):93--unfav

● HISTORY ●

6/106 Sánchez, Luis Alberto. Historia comparada de las literaturas
        americanas. Buenos Aires: Losada, 1973-76.
1:     Desde los orígenes hasta el barroco. 1973. 401 pp.
2:     Del naturalismo neoclásico al naturalismo romántico. 1973. 464
        pp.
3:     Del naturalismo al posmodernismo. 1974. 371 pp.
4:     Del vanguardismo a nuestros días. 1976. 446 pp.
Also covers U. S., Haitian and Brazilian literatures. Vol. 4 contains a
        bibliography by Susana Zanetti, pp. 323-81, of appr. 1350 entries,
        and an index to names as subjects covering the whole set.

● THEATER ●

6/106a Lyday, Leon F. and George W. Woodyard. A Bibliography of Latin
        American Theater Criticism, 1940-1974. Austin: Inst. of Latin
        American Studies, U. of Texas, 1976. (Guides and Bibliographies
        Series, 10) 243 pp.
2360 entries for books, book revs., arts. and U. S. diss., by scholar.
        Occasional brief notes. Index of names and 40 general topics.
YWMLS 77:405-418

● ● SPANISH-AMERICAN LITERATURES ● ●

● BIBLIOGRAPHIES ●

6/107 Flores, Ángel. Bibliografía de escritores hispanoamericanos: A
Bibliography of Spanish American Writers, 1609-1974. N. Y.: Gordian, 1975. 318 pp.

Sections on nearly 200 writers, in 3 A-Z sections, separated by brief
    addenda. Section I, pp. 1-56: writers born before 1850; II, pp.
    71-180: writers born after 1850; III, pp. 185-314: "Otros escri-
    tores notables, 1888-1974." No section of general studies. Lists
    books and arts. in Spanish and English, occasionally in other
    langs., and U. S. diss. Donoso: pp. 219-20, 49 studies, incl.
    book revs. García Márquez: pp. 112-15, appr. 120 studies. Incl.
    studies not listed in Foster (6/117) or Becco and Foster (6/118),
    while each of them lists studies not here.

6/108 Lozano, Stella. Selected Bibliography of Contemporary Spanish-
American Writers. Los Angeles: Latin American Studies Center,
California St. U., 1979. 149 pp.

Lists books and arts. in Spanish and English, occasionally in other
    langs., on 47 writers, publ. primarily 1974-78. Cites U. S. diss.
    Studies from before 1974 are cited for 23 women writers, several
    of whom are covered more extensively in Flores (6/107).

6/109 Rela, Walter. Guía bibliográfica de la literatura hispanoamericana desde el siglo XIX hasta 1970. Buenos Aires: Pardo, 1971.
613 pp.

Cites books only: bibls., histories, handbooks and anthologies. Index
    of names (scholars and subjects), pp. 573-613. Table of contents
    posing as an index of general topics, pp. 569-71.

YWMLS 71:353

6/110 Leavitt, Sturgis Elleno, ed. Revistas hispanoamericanas: Índice

bibliográfico, <u>1843</u>-<u>1935</u>. Santiago de Chile: Toribio Medina,
   1960. 589 pp.
Covers 56 periodicals from 13 countries. Lists arts. by author under
   broad subject headings. Literary criticism: pp. 159-269, appr.
   4200 entries, many briefly annotated. Also sections of literary
   works, by form. Index of names, incl. authors of literary works
   and critical studies cited, and authors named in titles or annotations. Errata, 6 pp., Lexington: U. of Kentucky Library, 1961.
   (Occasional Contribution, 123)
Hispania 61 (1978):645; YWMLS 61:179; HR 30 (1962):168-71

● HANDBOOK ●

6/111   Foster, David W., ed. <u>A</u> <u>Dictionary</u> <u>of</u> <u>Contemporary</u> <u>Latin</u> <u>Ameri</u>-
   <u>can</u> <u>Authors</u>. Tempe: Center for Latin American Studies, Arizona
   St. U., 1975. 110 pp.
Brief signed arts., few more than 1 col., on living writers, with bibl.
   of works only. Borges: 1+ col.
YWMLS 76:389; BHS 54 (1977):92--useful but uneven

● HISTORIES ●

6/112 <u>Historia</u> <u>literaria</u> <u>de</u> <u>hispanoamérica</u>. México: Andrea, 1966-73.
Arrangement, **indexing and scope of bibls. differ.** There seem to be no
   vols. on poetry.
1:   Alegría, Fernando. <u>Historia</u> <u>de</u> <u>la</u> <u>novela</u> <u>hispanoamericana</u>. 1966.
   301 pp. 3rd ed. 1st ed. 1959 (as <u>Breve</u> <u>historia</u>. . . .)
YWMLS 66:278; HLAS 30:2809
2:   Leal, Luis. <u>Historia</u> <u>del</u> <u>cuento</u> <u>hispanoamericano</u>. 1971. 187 pp.
   2nd ed. 1st ed. 1966.
3:   Arrom, José Juan. <u>Historia</u> <u>del</u> <u>teatro</u> <u>hispanoamericano</u>: Época
   <u>colonial</u>. 1967. 151 pp. 2nd ed. 1st ed. 1956.
YWMLS 68:322; HLAS 30:2796
4:   Dauster, Frank N. <u>Historia</u> <u>del</u> <u>teatro</u> <u>hispanoamericano</u>: <u>Siglos</u>

XIX y XX. 1973. 167 pp. 2nd ed. 1st ed. 1966.

HLAS 36:6824

5:    Carter, Boyd G. Historia de la literatura hispanoamericana a
      través de sus revistas. 1968. 271 pp.

YWMLS 68:330; HLAS 32:3600

6:    Earle, Peter G. and Robert G. Mead. Historia del ensayo hispano-
      americano. 1973. 172 pp. 2nd ed. 1st ed. 1956 (Breve historia
      . . . , by Mead).

BHS 53 (1976):269-70--mixed; Hispania 44 (1976):209-10; YWMLS 74:399

6/113 Valbuena Briones, Ángel. Literatura hispanoamericana. Barcelona:
       Gili, 1965. 556 pp.

2nd ed. 1st ed. 1962. Notes, but no bibls. Indexes of titles and
       authors. A companion to 6/20.

HLAS 25:4277

6/114 Anderson Imbert, Enrique. Spanish-American Literature: A History.
       Detroit: Wayne St. U. Pr., 1969.

2 vols. Brief bibl., index of names and detailed table of contents in
       each vol. Transl. of the 3rd Spanish ed. by John V. Falconieri,
       "revised and updated" by Elaine Malley.

● MODERNISM ●

6/115 Anderson, Robert Roland. Spanish American Modernism: A Selected
       Bibliography. Tucson: U. of Arizona Pr., 1970. 167 pp.

Books and arts. on 18 authors born 1848-82, and a section of general
       studies. José Marti: 629 entries. Subject indexes.

HLAS 34:3855; MLR 66 (1971):912-13

6/116 Henríquez Ureña, Max. Breve historia del modernismo. México:
       Fondo de Cultura Económica, 1962. 559 pp.

2nd ed. 1st ed. 1954. Index of names. Brief bibl.

● NOVEL ●

6/117 Foster, David W. The 20th Century Spanish-American Novel: A
       Bibliographic Guide. Metuchen, N. J.: Scarecrow, 1975. 227 pp.
Covers 56 writers, listing bibls., critical books and critical essays.
       Index of scholars.
YWMLS 76:390; BHS 54 (1977):93--"indispensible"

6/118 Becco, Horacio Jorge and David W. Foster. La Nueva narrativa
       hispanoamericana: Bibliografía. Buenos Aires: Pardo, 1976. 226
       pp.
Incl. sections on the literatures of 8 countries and on 15 writers, of
       which 13 are also in Foster (6/117). Lists works, transls. and
       criticism. Donoso: 70 entries, incl. 49 critical studies (Foster
       lists 35). García Márquez: 100 critical studies (Foster lists
       154). Both Foster and Becco and Foster list studies not in the
       other. See also 6/107.
YWMLS 76:390; BHS 54 (1977):360--perhaps insufficiently selective

6/119 Coll, Edna. Índice informativo de la novela hispanoamericana.
       N. p.: Ed. Universitaria, U. de Puerto Rico, 1974--.
1:     Las Antillas. 1974. 418 pp. (Puerto Rico, the Dominican Repub-
       lic and Cuba.)
2:     Centroamérica. 1977. 343 pp. (Costa Rica, El Salvador, Guata-
       mala, Honduras, Nicaragua and Panama.)
3:     Venezuela. 1978. 331 pp.
Biographies, up to 2 pp.; lists of works, often with plot summaries;
       bibls. of criticism in books and journals

6/120 Ocampo de Gómez, Aurora Maura. Novelistas iberoamericanos con-
       temporáneos: Obras y bibliografía crítica. México: U. Nacional
       Autónoma de México, Centro de Estudios Literarios, 1971--.
Publ. as parts of the Cuadernos del Centro de Estudios Literarios. 2
       (1971), "A", 48 pp.; 4 (1973), "B-Ch", 60 pp.; 6 (1974), "D-G", 74

pp.: 9 (1975), "H-M", 81 pp.

6/121 Alegría, Fernando. La Novela hispanoamericana, siglo XX. Buenos
       Aires: Centro Editor de América Latina, 1967. 62 pp.
Chapters on modernist novels, regionalism and neorealism.
HLAS 30:2809a; YWMLS 67:277

● PERIODICALS ●

6/122 Carter, Boyd G. Las Revistas literarias de Hispanoamérica: Breve
       historia y contenido. México: de Andrea, 1959. 282 pp.
Suppl. by J. E. Englekirk, "La Literatura y la revista literaria en
       Hispanoamérica," Revista iberoamericana, 26 (1961):9-79, 27 (1961):
       219-79, and 28 (1962):9-73. See also 6/112/5.
HR 38 (1970):445-46--v fav

● AUTHORS ●

6/123 Becco, Horacio Jorge. Jorge Luis Borges: Bibliografía total,
       1923-1973. Buenos Aires: Pardo, 1973. 244 pp.
Chapter 7: Crítica y biografía, pp. 111-205, appr. 1000 entries, by
       scholar, listing books, arts. and chapters in books, mostly in
       Spanish. No subject indexes.
YWMLS 73:366; HLAS 36:6625

6/124 Woodbridge, Hensley C. Rubén Darío: A Selective Classified and
       Annotated Bibliography. Metuchen, N. J.: Scarecrow, 1975. 231 pp.
Books, arts. and diss., incl. Spanish diss. Many direct quotations from
       works cited. Index of scholars.
YWMLS 76:385--critical of annotations; BHS 54 (1977):83x; HLAS 38:7147

6/125 Del Greco, Arnold Armand. Repertorio bibliográfico del mundo de
       Rubén Darío. N. Y.: Las Américas, 1969. 666 pp.
Studies, pp. 345-628, entries 1135-3179, by scholar. Index of names,

incl. some subjects; index of other subjects, but no index to Darío's works as subjects.

6/126 Pollin, Alice M. Concordancias de la obra poética de Eugenio
       Florit. N. Y.: NYU Pr./London: U. of London Pr., 1967. 574 pp.
Incl. the text of the poems in an unpaginated suppl.
YWMLS 68:338; HLAS 32:4370

6/127 Fau, Margaret Eustella. Gabriel García Márquez: An Annotated
       Bibliography, 1947-1979. Westport, Conn.: Greenwood Pr., 1980.
       198 pp.
Lists books and arts. by and books and arts. in various langs. about him.
       Cites diss. as found in DAI. The critical studies are pointlessly
       arranged by their form of publ. No subject index.

6/128 Scroggins, Daniel C. A Concordance of José Hernández "Martín
       Fierro." Columbia: U. of Missouri Pr., 1971. (U. of Missouri
       Studies, 53) 251 pp.
YWMLS 71:349; HLAS 34:3973

6/129 Becco, Horacio Jorge. Pablo Neruda: Bibliografía. Buenos Aires:
       Pardo, 1975. 260 pp.
III: Crítica, pp. 141-231, appr. 740 entries, by author, for books and
       arts., mostly in Spanish.
YWMLS 76:394; BHS 55 (1978):358; HLAS 38:7050

● ● BRAZILIAN LITERATURE ● ●
[Some of the works cited in the Portuguese section above also cover
       Brazilian literature, as noted. See the index.]

● BIBLIOGRAPHIES ●

6/130 Zubatsky, David S. "Annotated bibliography of Latin American
       Author Bibliographies." In Chasqui. (See 6/89)

4: Brazil.   7:1 (1977):35-54.

6/131 Basseches, Bruno. A Bibliography of Brazilian Bibliographies.
       Detroit: Blaine Ethridge, 1978.   185 pp.
Literature: 79 entries.   Index of names and subjects.
BHS 57 (1980):276

6/132 Carpeaux, Otto Maria. Pequena bibliografia crítica da literatura
       brasileira. Rio de Janeiro: Letras e Artes, 1964.   335 pp.
3rd ed. 1st ed. 1951. Bibl. of studies in books and journals.

• TRANSLATIONS •

6/133 Woodbridge, Hensley C. " A Bibliography of Brazilian Poetry in
       English Translation, 1965-1975." In Luso-Brazilian Review   15
       suppl. (1978):161-88.
Suppl. to 6/101.

• HANDBOOKS •

6/134 Pequeno dicionário de literatura brasileira. São Paulo: Cultrix,
       1980.   462 pp.
2nd ed. 1st ed. 1967. José Paulo Paes and Massaud Moisés, eds.   Brief
       signed arts., chiefly on authors, but also on movements, schools,
       places and a few critical terms. Modernismo: 2 pp. and 1/3 p.
       bibl. Sátira: 1+ p., on the history of satirical writing in Bra-
       zil. [Machado de] Assis: 1 1/3 p., bibls. of books by and books
       only in Portuguese about him.
YWMLS 68:344--"extremely useful"; HLAS 32:4674

6/135 Menezes, Raimundo de. Dicionário literário brasileiro. Rio de
       Janeiro & São Paulo: LTC, 1978.   803 pp.
2nd ed. 1st ed. 1969, in 5 vols. (Dicionário literário brasileiro ilu-
       strado--the 2nd ed. mercifully omits the illustrations.) Mostly

biographies, few longer than 1 col. [Machado de] Assis: 2 cols.,
plus 2 cols. bibl. Pp. 717-84: "Ismos literários, escolas e aca-
demias," entries up to several cols. Incl.critical terms.
YWMLS 71:365

● HISTORIES ●

6/136 Amora, Antônio Soares. História da literatura brasileira. São
      Paulo: Saraiva, 1974. 209 pp.
8th ed. 1st ed. 1955. Emphasis on the Romantic period (1833-68) to
      the present. IX: Simbolismo (1893-1922), pp. 156-89, incl. sec-
      tions on poetry and fiction, each with a bibl. as long or longer
      than the text, with bio-bibls. of the major authors. Bibls. cite
      books, arts. and chapters in books, in Portuguese only.

6/137 Bosi, Alfredo. História concisa da literatura brasileira. São
      Paulo: Cultrix, 1970. 571 pp.
Lengthy bio-bibl. notes. Index of names. 2nd ed., 1980, 571 pp.
YWMLS 71:366--"important and challenging"

6/138 A literatura brasileira. São Paulo: Cultrix, 1962-73.
1:    Castello, José Aderaldo. Manifestações literárias da era colonial
      (1500-1808/1836). 1962. 245 pp.
HLAS 28:2402
2:    Amora, Antônio Soares. O romantismo (1833/1838-1878/1881). 1967.
      356 pp.
3:    Pacheco, João. O realismo (1870-1900). 1963. 206 pp.
HLAS 28:2424
4:    Moisés, Massaud. O simbolismo (1893-1902). 1966. 293 pp.
HLAS 30:4657
5:    Bosi, Alfredo. O pré-modernismo. 1967. 158 pp.
6:    Martins, Wilson. O modernismo (1916-1945). 1973. 313 pp. 4th
      ed.
HLAS 28:2420

● FICTION ●

6/139 Gomes, Celuta Mereira. O conto brasileiro e sua crítica: Biblio-
     grafia (1841-1974). Rio de Janeiro: Biblioteca Nacional, 1977.
     (Coleção Rodolfo Garcia: Série B: Catálogos e bibliografias)
2 vols. 654 pp. 2nd ed. 1st ed in Anais da Biblioteca Nacional 87
     (1967). [Machado de] Assis: 116 entries for eds. and 73 for crit-
     ical studies.
HLAS 4):7715

● AUTHORS ●

6/140 Coelho Netto, Paulo. Bibliografia de Coelho Netto. Brasília:
     Inst. Nacional do Livro, 1972. (Coleção documentos, 4) 326 pp.
Works by and 900+ books and arts. about him, nearly all in Portuguese,
     by scholar.

6/141 Reis, Irene Monteiro. Bibliografia de Euclides da Cunha. Rio de
     Janeiro: Inst. Nacional do Livro, 1971. (Coleção documentos, 2)
     417 pp.
Works by and appr. 2050 books and arts. about, nearly all in Portuguese,
     by scholar.

VII

GERMAN LITERATURE

OUTLINE

● GERMAN LITERATURE ●

● BIBLIOGRAPHIES **of** BIBLIOGRAPHIES ●

7/1 Hansel, Johannes. Bücherkunde für Germanisten: Studienausgabe.
     Berlin: Schmidt, 1978. 202 pp.
7th ed., rev. by Lydia Tschakert. 1st ed. 1961. 1192 annotated entries,
     in classified order, with paragraphs of introduction and other
     commentary interspersed. Also covers lang. Lists bibls., hand-
     books, histories, etc. Does not cover individual authors (but see
     7/2). Originally this was a students' version of his Bücherkunde
     für Germanisten: Wie sammelt man das Schrifttum nach dem neuesten
     Forschungsstand, Berlin: Schmidt, 1959, 233 pp.
YWMLS 78:622; GL&L ns 24 (1970/71):216-17; MLR 63 (1968):515-16

7/2 Hansel, Johannes. Personalbibliographie zur deutschen Literatur-
     geschichte: Studienausgabe. Berlin: Schmidt, 1974. 258 pp.
2nd ed., rev. by Carl Paschek. 1st ed. 1967. Lists bibls. publ. as
     books or in books and journals. In 5 period sections. Eichen-
     dorff: gives refs. to the standard general bibls., then lists 3
     retrospective bibls., 1 current bibl., and 4 reviews of research;
     also notes journals, past and present, devoted to him, and librar-
     ies with collections of his manuscripts. Annotated.
YWMLS 75:538; GL&L ns 24 (1970/71):217-18--**unfav; MLR 64 (1969)**:686-88

7/3 Faulhaber, Uwe K. and Penrith Goff. German Literature: An Anno-
     tated Reference Guide. N. Y. & London: Garland, 1979. 398 pp.
A guide to sources of information on German literature and culture, and
     on general and European literature. Does not cover individual
     writers. Most entries have descriptive and evaluative comments.
     Classified arrangement, with many cross-refs. Index to names,
     titles and subjects. The tables of contents before each of the
     13 chapters are detailed and useful.
GQ 54 (1981):396-98

7/4 German Language and Literature: Select Bibliography of Reference
     Books. London: Inst. of Germanic Studies, U. of London, 1980.
     175 pp.
Ed. by L. M. Newman. 2nd ed. 1st ed. 1966. Annotated classified list
     of bibls., handbooks, histories, etc., but only appr. 156 entries
     deal specifically with literary studies.

7/5 Raabe, Paul. Einführung in die Bücherkunde zur deutschen Literatur-
     wissenschaft. Stuttgart: Metzler, 1980. 104 pp.
9th ed., with Werner Arnold and Ingrid Hannich-Bode. 1st ed. 1961. A
     bibliographic essay on research tools in German literature.

7/6 "Bibliographie germanistischer Bibliographien." In Jahrbuch für
     internationale Germanistik, 9 (1977)--.
In each issue (2/yr.). Classified, annotated list of bibls. in books
     and journals.

● BIBLIOGRAPHIES of RESEARCH ●

7/7 Bibliographie der deutschen Sprach- und Literaturwissenschaft.
     1957--.
Annual. Vols. 1-9, covering research of 1945-69, have been cumulated
     and supplemented by vol. 1 of 7/8; vol. 2 of 7/8, covering German
     literature since 1830, cumulates vols. 1-12 of this, listing publs.
     of 1945-72. Vol. 19 (1979), publ. 1981: 679 pp., 9143 entries in
     17 sections, each further subdivided. Sections 5 and 6 list stud-
     ies in German on general literary theory and history. Sections 7-
     17 list books, arts. and chapters in books in German, English and
     the other W. European langs. on German literature in general and
     by period, incl. 5 period divisions from Romanticism to the pre-
     sent. (The MLA Bibl. [1/9] divides all of German literature into
     only 5 periods.) Cites book revs. Lists U. S. diss., as found in
     DAI, and German diss. Indexes of names (subjects and scholars) and
     of other subjects, incl. themes, forms, movements, etc.

Recent vols. have been publ. about 6 months after the corresponding vol.
of the MLA. This lists a number of books and arts. not to be
found in the MLA, in addition to its refs. to book revs. and the
occasional German diss., but sometimes the MLA will list studies
not cited here. The subject indexes are unparalleled in the MLA
and very useful; the subject arrangement is much more detailed
and precise than that of the MLA. In 19 (1979) the section of
studies of themes in German literature, with about 90 entries, is
in nearly 70 subdivisions, incl. Einhorn, Tell (Wilhelm) and West-
wind. The Wolfram section has 40 entries, incl. 27 listed under
Parzival, as well as subsections on Titurel and Willehalm.

7/8 Köttelwesch, Clemens. Bibliographisches Handbuch der deutschen
Literaturwissenschaft, 1945-1969. Frankfurt am Main: Klostermann,
1971-79.
3 vols. I: Von den Anfängen bis zur Romantik. 2398 cols. II: 1830 bis
zur Gegenwart. 1996 cols. III: Register. 1008 cols. Vol. I
cumulates vols. 1-9 of the entry above (7/7); vol. II cumulates
vols. 1-12, and lists research publ. between 1945 and 1972.
Goethe: 330 cols., in classified order, incl. "Goethe und die
Antike," 3 cols., subdivided, and Faust, appr. 37 cols., subdivided, with sections of eds. and transls., and studies of various
aspects of the whole work, of the Ur-Faust, and of Faust I and II.
Cites book revs. Lists arts. in about 800 journals and 1000 collective volumes, as well as books and diss. Indexes of scholars,
of writers (incl. foreign writers), and of other subjects.

7/9 Germanistik: Internationales Referatenorgan mit bibliographischen
Hinweisen. 1960--.
4/yr. 22:1 (1981): 256 pp., 1810 entries, incl. many publ. in 1981, and
others to the late 1970s. Classified arrangement. Each issue is
in 34 sections, of which 17-31 cover general, comparative and
Germanic literature. The books cited are usually reviewed briefly.
Index of names (subjects and scholars) only, in issue 4.

7/10 Albrecht, Günter and Günther Dahlke. Internationale Bibliographie
      zur Geschichte der deutschen Literatur von den Anfängen bis zur
      Gegenwart. München-Pullach & Berlin: Dokumentation, 1969-77.

3 vols. in 4 parts. I: Von den Anfängen bis 1789. 1045 pp. II: Von
      1789 bis zur Gegenwart. 1030 & 1126 pp. III: Sachregister. 377 pp.
      Covers studies publ. largely to 1964 in E. Germany, Russia and E.
      Europe, as well as in W. Europe, the U. S., China, Japan and Korea.
      Many entries in the Cyrillic alphabet. Incl. diss., but not book
      revs. Goethe: 120 pp., divided and subdivided. The arrangement
      of this section is not obvious, nor is it shown in the table of
      contents. One must check the index vol., where Goethe has 8 pp.
      This work has a number of entries not in Köttelwesch (7/8), both
      in its coverage of publs. before 1945 and in its coverage of E.
      European and Slavic sources, but Köttelwesch has fuller coverage
      of recent western publs.
YWMLS 69:486

7/11 Jahresbericht für deutsche Sprache und Literatur. Berlin: Akade-
      mie, 1960--.

2 vols., covering publs. of 1940-45 and 1946-50. A 3rd vol. was plan-
      ned, to cover 1951-54, but has not been publ. Vol. 2 has about
      17,000 entries, in classified order, covering lang., theater and
      folklore, as well as literature. Indexes of scholars and of names
      and other subjects. This is meant to be a continuation of the 3
      following entries.

7/12 Jahresbericht über die Erscheinungen auf dem Gebiete der germa-
      nischen Philologie.

1 (1879)-42 (1920) and NF 1 (1921)-16/19 (1936/39). Covers through the
      end of the Middle Ages.

7/13 Jahresberichte für neuere deutsche Literaturgeschichte.
1 (1890)-26 (1915).

7/14 Jahresbericht über die wissenschaftlichen Erscheinungen auf dem
      Gebiete der neueren deutschen Literatur.
NF 1 (1921)-16/19 (1936/39).

7/15 Goedeke, Karl. Grundriss zur Geschichte der deutschen Dichtung
      aus den Quellen. Dresden: Ehlermann, 1884--. (Now publ. by
      Berlin: Akademie)
2nd ed. Intended to cover German literature through 1830. 15 vols.
      publ. 1884-1966. Several more vols. projected. Arranged and
      publ. chronologically, so that the vol. on the Middle Ages
      appeared nearly 100 years ago.
3rd ed., 1910--. Now publ. by Berlin: Akademie. Replaced vol. 4 of the
      2nd ed., Vom Siebenjährigen bis zum Weltkriege, covering appr.
      1750-1800. 5 parts publ., incl a bibl. on Goethe in 3 vols., 1910-
      13, with a suppl. covering 1912-1950, publ. in 1960.
Neue Folge. Berlin: Akademie, 1962--. Covers the literature of 1830-
      1880. Fascicles mainly covering the letter "A" have been publ.
See Hartmut Rambaldo, Grundriss zur Geschichte der deutschen Dichtung
      von Karl Goedeke: Index, Nendeln: KTO, 1975, 393 pp., for an index
      of the names and pseudonyms of the authors covered by these sets.

● REVIEW of RESEARCH ●

7/16 "Sonderheft Forschungsreferate." In Deutsche Vierteljahrsschrift
      für Literaturwissenschaft und Geistesgeschichte.
Irregular. Lengthy reviews of research on various topics, incl. aspects
      of German literature, were publ. in a suppl. issue, through 47
      (1973). Wolfgang Frühwald, "Stationen der Brentano-Forschung,
      1924-1972," 47 (1973):182-269 (Sonderheft). See 7/105.

● DISSERTATIONS ●

7/17 Norman, Frederick. Theses in German Studies: A Catalogue of
      Theses and Dissertations in the Field of Germanic Studies (exclu-

ding English) Approved **for Higher** Degrees **in the Universities of**
Great Britain **and** Ireland between 1903 **and** 1961. London: Inst. of
Germanic Langs., U. of London, 1962. 46 pp.

Suppls. covering 1962-67 and 1967-72, each 18 pp., were publ. in 1968 &
1973. Suppl., 1972-77, publ. 1980, 57 pp., incl. additions for
1903-71, not seen. Author listing with subject index. Incl. Dutch
and Scandinavian literatures.

7/18 Germanistische Dissertationen in Kurzfassung. 1975--. (Jahrbuch
für internationale Germanistik, Reihe B.)

Annual. 4 (1979): 291 pp., entries 120-62. 6 to 10 pp. abstracts from
German, U. S., French, Czech, etc. diss., in German, English or
French, covering diss. submitted between 1973 and 1976, but
chiefly 1975-76. Index of names and other subjects.

7/19 "Verzeichnis der germanistischen Dissertationsvorhaben." In
Jahrbuch für internationale Germanistik, 2 (1970)--.

Irregular. Liste XIII, for 1975-78: 10 (1978):144-90. 512 entries,
incl. completed diss. mentioned in both previous publ. lists: XI,
in 2 (1970):5-257 and XII, in 6 (1974):167-99.

• FESTSCHRIFTEN •

7/20 Hannich-Bode, Ingrid, ed. Germanistik in Festschriften von den
Anfängen (1877) bis 1973. Stuttgart: Metzler, 1976. (Repertorien
zur deut. Literaturgeschichte, 7) 441 pp.

List of Festschriften with contents, and a subject index. German literature, pp. 222-370, divided and subdivided; world and comparative
literature, pp. 370-90.

YWMLS 76:642; Monatshefte 71 (1979):187-88

• TRANSLATIONS •

7/21 Morgan, Bayard Quincy. A Critical Bibliography of German Litera-

ture in English Translation, 1481-1927. Stanford, Calif.: Stanford U. Pr., 1938. 690 pp.
2nd ed. Suppl., 1928-55, N. Y. & London: Scarecrow, 1965. A selected
    suppl. bibl., 1956-60, by Murray F. Smith was publ. 1972. All
    vols. cover many non-literary works. The vols. by Morgan cover
    transls. publ. as books and in certain anthologies; Smith's suppl.
    covers books only. The orig. vol. had some brief annotations.
MLR 61 (1966):722-24--unfav

7/22 O'Neill, Patrick. German Literature in English Translation: A
    Select Bibliography. Toronto, etc.: U. of Toronto Pr., 1981. 242
    pp.
Transls. publ. as books or in books, arranged by period. Unannotated.

● HANDBOOKS ●

7/23 Reallexikon der deutschen Literaturgeschichte. Berlin: de Gruyter,
    1958--.
Werner Kohlschmidt and Wolfgang Mohr, eds. Orig. ed. by Paul Merker
    and Wolfgang Stammler, 1927-31, in 4 vols. Publ. in fascicles.
    3 vols. to date, and fasc. 1/2-5/6 of vol. 4, through Trivial-
    literatur. Lengthy arts. on genres, movements, etc., but no bio-
    graphical arts. "Orient und orientalische Literaturen (Einflüsse
    auf Europa und Deutschland)," 62 pp., incl. a number of bibls.
    Teufelliteratur: nearly 37 pp. Symbolismus: 17+ cols., and nearly
    4 cols. bibl.
YWMLS 57:305--praises art. on Heldendichtung for "its combination of
    authoritative statement of fact with clarity and interest of pre-
    sentation"

7/24 Kosch, Wilhelm, ed. Deutsches Literatur-Lexikon: Biographisch-
    bibliographisches Handbuch. Bern & München: Francke, 1966--.
3rd ed., rev. by Bruno Berger and Heinz Rupp, et al. 1st ed. 1927-30;
    2nd ed. 1949-58. 7 vols. publ. to 1979, through Hogrebe. Brief

entries on writers, almost entirely bibliographical. Gottfried: 1
col. text, 7 cols. bibl., listing eds. and studies (books and
arts., chiefly in German or English, in classified order). Hei-
degger: 3 cols. The 2nd ed. contains entries for critical terms,
literary works, etc., omitted from the 3rd ed. A 1 vol. ed. based
on the 2nd ed. was publ. in 1963.

JEGP 78 (1979):290-92--notes changes in editorial policy between the 1st
and 6th vols.; 70 (1971):138-39; 71 (1972):406-07; 80 (1981):78-
80; Monatshefte 63 (1971):184; GQ 43 (1970):94-98; 46 (1973):129-32

7/25 Die deutsche Literatur: Biographisches und bibliographisches Lexikon. Bern, etc.: P. Lang, 1979--.

Of this project so far 3 issues have been publ. of IIB: Die deutsche
Literatur zwischen 1450-1620: Forschungsliteratur, Hans-Gert
Roloff, ed., 240 pp., 4352 entries, listing general works and
studies on Humanism and the Reformation in Europe and in Germany.
Section A will be a biographical handbook.

AUMLA no. 55 (May 1981):121-22--"a mammoth work of some 70 vols. [pro-
jected], each of 1000-1200 pp."

7/26 Wilpert, Gero von, ed. Deutsches Dichterlexikon: Biographisch-
bibliographisches Handwörterbuch zur deutschen Literaturgeschichte.
Stuttgart: Kröner, 1976. 791 pp.

2nd ed. 1st ed. 1963.

YWMLS 63:332 & 394--"reliable, comprehensive and up-to-date"

7/27 Albrecht, Günter, et al. Lexikon deutschsprachiger Schriftsteller
von den Anfängen bis zur Gegenwart. Kronberg: Scriptor, 1974.

3rd ed. 2 vols. 1st ed. 1961 (Deutsches Schriftstellerlexikon. . . .)
Slightly longer arts. than 7/26, but bibls. of eds. only.

7/28 Garland, Henry and Mary Garland. The Oxford Companion to German
Literature. Oxford: Clarendon, 1976. 977 pp.

Brief entries on writers; political and other figures and events, incl.

artists, etc.; literary works and characters, periods and movements. G. Grass: 1+ col.; U. Johnson: 1/2 col.; Don Juan: 2/3
col., mentioning 10 Don Juan versions, 3 of which are treated in
separate arts.

MLR 72 (1977):479-82; JEGP 76 (1977):392-96--unfav as regards accuracy
and emphases; YWMLS 76:568; 667--"succinctly informative and
dependable on leading 20th c. authors, but is far too often fac-
tually inaccurate about . . . minor or experimental writers"

7/29 Stammler, Wolfgang, ed. Deutsche Philologie im Aufriss. Berlin:
Schmidt, 1966.

2nd ed., orig. publ. 1957-62. 1st ed. 1952-57. 3 vols. 3050 cols.
I: Methodenlehre; Sprachgeschichte und Mundarten. II: Literaturgeschichte in Längsschnitten. III: Ausländische Einflüsse;
Kulturkunde und Religiongeschichte; Volkskunde. Lengthy arts.,
with bibls., covering all periods. Fritz Martini: "Poetik," I:
223-80; Kurt H. Halbach, "Epik des Mittelalters," II:397-684;
Harold Jantz, "Amerika im deutschen Dichten und Denken," III:309-
72. Register, publ. 1969, of names and some titles: Wolfram von
Eschenbach, 3/4 col.; Thomas Mann, 1/2 col., both variously subdivided.

YWMLS 57:305--2nd ed. takes account of latest research "chiefly in the
bibliographical and other notes"

● HISTORIES ●

7/30 Geschichte der deutschen Literatur von den Anfängen bis zur Gegenwart. Stuttgart: Reclam, 1965-80.

1:   Wehrli, Max. Vom frühen Mittelalter bis zum Ende des 16. Jahrhunderts. 1980. 1238 pp.
EG 38 (1981):238--v fav; for students and beginners
2:   Kohlschmidt, W. Vom Barock bis zur Klassik. 1965. 956 pp.
3:   Kohlschmidt, W. Von der Romantik bis zum späten Goethe. 2nd ed.
1979. 1st ed. 1974. 764 pp.

GL&L ns 31 (1977/78):289-90--v fav

4:　　Kohlschmidt, W. Vom Jungen Deutschland bis zum Naturalismus.
　　　　1975. 919 pp.

YWMLS 75:636

5:　　Lehnert, H. Vom Jugendstil zum Expressionismus. 1978. 1100 pp.

YWMLS 78:764--both an introduction and a detailed commentary

Bibls. of eds. and studies, chiefly books, in German. Indexes of names.

7/31　Boor, Helmut de and Richard Newald, eds. Geschichte der deutschen
　　　　Literatur von den Anfängen bis zur Gegenwart. München: Beck,
　　　　1964--.

8 vols. projected. 6 vols. to date. Each vol. has bibls., a chronology
　　　　and an index of names, or sometimes an index of names, titles and
　　　　other subjects.

1:　　Boor, Helmut de. Die deutsche Literatur von Karl dem Grossen bis
　　　　zum Beginn der höfischen Dichtung, 770-1170. 8th ed. 1971. 295
　　　　pp. 9th ed., 1979, 342 pp., not seen.

2:　　Boor, Helmut de. Die höfische Literatur: Vorbereitung, Blüte,
　　　　Ausklang, 1170-1250. 8th ed. 1969. 464 pp. 10th ed., 1979, 511
　　　　pp., not seen.

3:　　Boor, Helmut de. Die deutschen Literatur im späten Mittelalter:
　　　　Zerfall und Neubeginn, 1250-1450. Vol. 1: 1250-1350. 3rd ed.
　　　　1967. 590 pp. 4th ed. 1973, 610 pp., not seen. Vol. 2 not yet
　　　　publ.

4:　　Rupprich, Hans. Deutsche Literatur vom späten Mittelalter bis zum
　　　　Barock. Vol. 1: 1370-1520. 1970. 835 pp. Vol 2: 1520-1570.
　　　　1973. 554 pp.

GL&L ns 29 (1975/76):348-49; MLR 66 (1971):935-36; GL&L ns 29 (1975/76):
　　　　421-23; YWMLS 73:554-55; GQ 49 (1976):371-72--v fav

5:　　Newald, Richard. Deutsche Literatur vom Späthumanismus zur
　　　　Empfindsamkeit, 1570-1750. 6th ed. 1967. 592 pp.

6:　　Newald, Richard. Von Klopstock zu Goethes Tod, 1750-1832. Vol.
　　　　1: Ende der Aufklärung und Vorbereitung der Klassik. 5th ed.
　　　　1967. 438 pp. 6th ed., 1973, 438 pp., not seen. Vol. 2 not yet

publ.

7/32 Handbuch der deutschen Literaturgeschichte.   Abt. 1: Darstellungen.
       Bern & München: Francke, 1971--.

2:     Gaede, Friedrich. Humanismus, Barock, Aufklärung: Geschichte der
       deutschen Literatur vom 16. bis zum 18. Jahrhundert. 1971. 347
       pp.

GL&L ns 26 (1972/73):354-56; Monatshefte 65 (1973):84-85

4:     Just, Klaus Günther. Von der Gründerzeit bis zur Gegenwart:
       Geschichte der deutschen Literatur seit 1871. 1973. 702 pp.

JEGP 74 (1975):304-06--v fav; GL&L ns 31 (1977/78):310-12; YWMLS 73:612

Abt. 2 of the Handbuch is a set of 12 bibls., of which 11 only were
       publ. between 1969 and 1974.

7/33 Geschichte der deutschen Literatur von den Anfängen bis zur Gegen-
       wart. Berlin: Volk & Wissen, 1951--.

Nine 1 or 2 vol. sets to date. Klaus Gysi, et al., eds.

1:     Erb, Ewald, et al. Geschichte der deutschen Literatur von den
       Anfängen bis 1160. 3rd ed. 2 vols. 1976. 1147 pp.

MLR 61 (1966):147-51--praises bibl.

4:     Boeckh, Joachim, et al. Geschichte der deutschen Literatur von
       1480 bis 1600. 1960. 541 pp.

MLR 57 (1962):470-71

5:     Boeckh, Joachim, et al. Geschichte der deutschen Literatur von
       1600 bis 1700. 1962. 592 pp.

6:     Rieck, Werner, et al. Vom Ausgang des 17. Jahrhunderts bis 1789.
       1979. 955 pp.

7:     Dahnke, Hans-Dietrich, et al. Geschichte der deutschen Literatur
       1789 bis 1830. 1978. 967 pp.

8:     Böttscher, Kurt, et al. Geschichte der deutschen Literatur von
       1830 bis zum Ausgang des 19. Jahrhunderts. 1975. 2 vols. 1274 pp.

YWMLS 76:653

9:     Kaufmann, Hans, et al. Geschichte der deutschen Literatur vom
       Ausgang des 19. Jahrhunderts bis 1917. 1974. 600 pp.

GQ 49 (1976):544-45

10:   Kaufmann, Hans, et al. Geschichte der deutschen Literatur: 1917
      bis 1945. 1973. 754 pp.

GQ 49 (1976):544-45

11:   Haase, Horst, et al. Geschichte der deutschen Literatur: Liter-
      ature der Deutschen Demokratischen Republik. 1976. 907 pp.

7/34 Martini, Fritz. Deutsche Literaturgeschichte von den Anfängen bis
     zur Gegenwart. Stuttgart: Kröner, 1978. 727 pp.

17th ed. 1st ed 1949. Covers through the 1960s.

YWMLS 61:373--notes of the 11th ed. that it differs from the 9th ed.
     "mainly in the modern period, but also has many small changes
     in the 19th c. sections . . . ."

7/35 Robertson, John George. A History of German Literature. Edin-
     burgh: Blackwood, 1970. 817 pp.

6th ed., rev. by Dorothy Reich, et al. 1st ed. 1902. Chronological
     table, pp. 677-708, covering ca. 750-1970. Bibls., pp. 711-97,
     books only, arranged to parallel text. Literary passages cited
     in German only.

MLR 67 (1972):935-36x

7/36 Pasley, Malcolm, ed. Germany: A Companion to German Studies.
     N. Y.: Harper & Row, 1972. 678 pp.

New ed. 1st ed. 1932, by Jethro Bithell. 3 chapters on literature;
     others on philosophy, music and history. Index of names and other
     subjects.

MLR 68 (1973):436-38x; Monatshefte 67 (1975):283-84; GL&L ns 29
     (1975/76):232-34; GQ 48 (1975):179-81m

7/37 Daemmrich, Horst S. and Diether H. Haenicke, eds. The Challenge
     of German Literature. Detroit: Wayne St. U. Pr., 1971. 432 pp.

10 chapters by various scholars covering from the High Middle Ages to

the 1960s. Index of names as subjects. All quotations in English.
GQ 46 (1973):465-67; YWMLS 74:613

• CHRONOLOGIES •

7/38 Frenzel, Herbert Alfred and Elisabeth Frenzel. Daten deutscher
      Dichtung: Chronologischer Abriss der deutschen Literaturgeschichte.
      Köln: Kiepenheuer & Witsch, 1971. 766 pp.
4th ed. 1st ed. 1953. Annotated. Covers through 1968.

7/39 Schmitt, Fritz and Gerhard Fricke. Deutsche Literaturgeschichte
      in Tabellen. Bonn: Athenäum, 1949-52.
3 vols. I: 750-1450, 182 pp.; II: 1450-1770, 2nd ed., 1960, 243 pp.;
      III: 1770 bis zur Gegenwart, 306 pp. Arranged by period and genre.
      Much biographical and bibliographical information. Many folding
      charts. Index of names and titles in each vol.

7/40 Schmitt, Fritz and Jörn Göres. Abriss der deutschen Literatur-
      geschichte in Tabellen. Frankfurt am Main: Athenäum, 1969. 265
      pp.
5th ed. 1st ed. 1955.

7/41 Burger, Heinz Otto, ed. Annalen der deutschen Literatur: Eine
      Gemeinschaftsarbeit zahlreicher Fachgelehrter. Stuttgart:
      Metzler, 1971. 838 pp.
2nd ed., orig. publ. in fascicles, 1961-62. 1st ed. 1952. A narrative
      history, but arranged strictly chronologically. Chronological
      table, pp. 761-810, covering 2000 BC-1900 AD.
GQ 46 (1973):160-63m; MLR 67 (1972):934-35x

• POETRY •

7/42 Haller, Rudolf. Geschichte der deutschen Lyrik. Bern & München:
      Francke, 1967--.

I: Vom Ausgang des Mittelalters bis zu Goethes Tod. 487 pp. No more
    publ. Notes, but no bibl. Index of names only.

7/43 Klein, Johannes. Geschichte der deutschen Lyrik von Luther bis
    zum Ausgang des Zweiten Weltkrieges. Wiesbaden: Steiner, 1960.
    906 pp.
2nd ed., rev. & enl. 1st ed. 1957. Index of first lines and titles, pp.
    879-906.
YWMLS 60:365

● FICTION ●

7/44 Emmel, Hildegard. Geschichte des deutschen Romans. Bern & Mün-
    chen, 1972-78.
3 vols. Vol. 1 covers through Goethe and Hoffmann; vol. 2 through Kafka,
    Musil, Mann and Broch; Vol 3 (Der Weg in die Gegenwart) through
    Grass and Johnson.
YWMLS 72:541; 78:784; GQ 48 (1975):422-24; 50 (1977):205; 53 (1980):257-
    58; GL&L ns 28 (1974/75):76-77--unfav as regards critical method-
    ology, fav as a source of information

7/45 Klein, Johannes. Geschichte der deutschen Novelle von Goethe bis
    zur Gegenwart. Wiesbaden: Steiner, 1960. 674 pp.
4th ed., rev. & enl. 1st ed. 1954.
YWMLS 60:365

● DRAMA ●

7/46 Kosch, Wilhelm. Deutsches Theater-Lexikon: Biographisches und
    bibliographisches Handbuch. Klagenfurt & Wien: Kleinmayr, 1953--.
Now publ. by Bern & München: Francke. 21 fascicles, 2016 pp., to date,
    in 2+ vols., through Schletter, but nothing publ. since 1971.
    German-language theater: playwrights, actors, etc.; cities as cen-
    ters of theatrical activity; people and events as subjects of

plays; some entries on plays.

● THEMES ●

7/47 Schmitt, Franz Anselm and Kurt Bauerhorst. Stoff- und Motivge-
      schichte der deutschen Literatur: Eine Bibliographie. Berlin &
      N. Y.: de Gruyter, 1976. 437 pp.
3rd ed. 1st ed. 1959. A bibl. of studies (books and arts.) of themes in
      German literature, excluding studies of a theme in the work of a
      single author, but including studies of a theme in European or
      world literature, if they touch upon German literature. Cites
      U. S. and German diss.; cites book revs. Alphabetical arrange-
      ment, with cross-refs. and a classified list of headings, pp. 387-
      401. Geld: 4 entries; Sappho: 5 entries; Berlin: 20 entries;
      Vater und Sohn: 12 entries. Teufelsbund (in the classified list):
      refs. to 6 headings, incl. Blocksberg, Faust and Theophilus.
JEGP 76 (1977):441; YWMLS 77:609-10--v fav; MLR 62 (1967):739-40

● MEDIEVAL ●

• BIBLIOGRAPHIES •

7/48 Bibliographien zur deutschen Literatur des Mittelalters. Berlin:
      Schmidt, 1966--.
Ulrich Pretzel and Wolfgang Bachofer, eds. Lists books, book revs., arts.
      and chapters in books; also diss. in German. Classified arrange
      ment. Occasional brief notes.
1:    Krogmann, Willy and Ulrich Pretzel. Bibliographie zum "Nibe-
      lungenlied" und zur "Klage." 1966. 75 pp.
MLR 63 (1968):1000-01
2:    Pretzel, Ulrich and Wolfgang Bachofer. Bibliographie zu Wolfram
      von Eschenbach. 2nd ed. 1968. 114 pp.
GL&L ns 24 (1970/71):274; GQ 43 (1970):264-65
3:    Tervooren, Helmut. Bibliographie zum Minnesang und zu den

Dichtern aus "Des Minnesangs Frühling." 1969. 91 pp.

GL&L ns 25 (1971/72):313-14; JEGP 70 (1971):108-09; MLR 66 (1971):439

4:    Scholz, Manfred Günter. Bibliographie zu Walther von der Vogel-
      weide. 1969. 144 pp.

Monatshefte 63 (1971):162-63; GL&L ns 25 (1971/72):312-13; JEGP 70
      (1971):109; GQ 45 (1972):372-73; MLR 67 (1972):205

5:    Steinhoff, Hans-Hugo. Bibliographie zu Gottfried von Strassburg.
      1971. 110 pp.

JEGP 72 (1973):262-65; GQ 46 (1973):277-80--fav, but critical of org.;
      YWMLS 71:545--v fav; praises org.; MLR 69 (1974):219-20

6:    Neubuhr, Elfriede. Bibliographie zu Hartmann von Aue. 1977. 168
      pp.

YWMLS 77:641

7:    Belkin, Johanna and Jürgen Meier. Bibliographie zu Otfrid von
      Weissenburg. 1975. 137 pp.

YWMLS 75:559

• HANDBOOK •

7/49 Ruh, Kurt. Die deutsche Literatur des Mittelalters: Verfasser-
      lexikon. Berlin: de Gruyter, 1977--.

3 vols., 1280 cols., to date, through Hildegard. Incl. arts. on anony-
      mous works. Gottfried von Strassburg: 14 cols. of text in 9 sec-
      tions, and 1 1/2 cols. bibl. Hildebrandslied: 14 cols. text, 2
      1/2 cols. bibl. The orig. ed., by Wolfgang Stammler, was publ. in
      4 vols. and a suppl. by de Gruyter, 1933-55.

MLR 76 (1981):495

• AUTHORS •

7/50 Picozzi, Rosemary. A History of Tristan Scholarship. Bern: Lang,
      1971. (Kanadische Studien zur deutschen Sprache und Literatur, 5)
      164 pp.

Deals mainly with Gottfried.

YWMLS 71:545-46

7/51 Bäuml, Franz. A Concordance to the Nibelungenlied. Leeds: Maney,
      1976. (Compendia, 7) 901 pp.
YWMLS 76:586-87; MLR 73 (1978):226-27; Monatshefte 49 (1977):226

7/52 Bumke, Joachim. Die Wolfram von Eschenbach-Forschung seit 1945:
      Bericht und Bibliographie. München: Fink, 1970. 436 pp.
Indexes incl. scholars and subjects. Bibl. of more than 700 entries,
      incl. U. S. and German diss.
JEGP 70 (1971):709-11--v fav; MLR 67 (1972):203-05

● 16th and 17th CENTURIES ●

● BIBLIOGRAPHIES ●

7/53 Pyritz, Hans and Ilse Pyritz, eds. Bibliographie zur deutschen
      Literaturgeschichte des Barockzeitalters. Bern & München: Francke,
      1980--.
9 fascicles projected; 2 publ. to date, 306 pp., chiefly on general
      topics and anonymous works. Lists books and arts. in German,
      English, etc.

7/54 Gabel, Gernot Uwe. Drama und Theater des deutschen Barock: Eine
      Handbibliographie der Sekundärliteratur. Hamburg: n. p., 1974.
      182 pp.
Classified arrangement, covering 42 writers.
YWMLS 75:605

● 18th and EARLY 19th CENTURIES ●

● BIBLIOGRAPHIES ●

7/55 [Bibliographies and reviews of research on 18th century culture.]

In Das Achtzehnte Jahrhundert, 1 (1977)--.

In each issue.

7/56 Internationale Bibliographie zur deutschen Klassik, 1750-1850.
      11/12 (1964/65)--.

Irregular. 1 or 2/yr. Folge 23 (1976), publ. 1980: 384 pp., 3234 en-
      tries, in 3 sections. I: general studies, in classified order;
      II: authors (Heine: 130 entries, incl. eds., transls. and 100+
      studies, by scholar); III: book revs. A few brief annotations.
      Lists books and arts. in various langs., incl. Japanese, and Ger-
      man diss. Index of names (subjects and scholars) and a few other
      subjects. Folge 7-10 publ. in Weimarer Beiträge 9 (1963)-10
      (1964); Folge 1-6 in Zeitschrift für deutsche Literaturgeschichte
      6 (1960)-8 (1962), continuing a bibl. in Weimarer Beiträge 1
      (1955)-4 (1958). (A comparison with Goethe-Jahrbuch is at 7/67.)
GL&L ns 26 (1972/73):273

• HISTORIES •

7/57 Wiese, Benno von, ed. Deutsche Dichter des 18. Jahrhunderts: Ihr
      Leben und Werke. Berlin: Schmidt, 1977. 1086 pp.

Essays by various scholars on 42 writers. Lessing: 40 pp., incl. 8 pp.
      bibl. Chronological tables (1720-1810), pp. 1031-63. Index of
      names.

YWMLS 78:692; JEGP 78 (1979):292-94--"up-to-date bibls., readable criti-
      cal biographies"; GQ 53 (1980):107-09

7/58 Wiese, Benno von. Deutsche Dichter der Romantik: Ihr Leben und
      Werke. Berlin: Schmidt, 1971. 530 pp.

Essays on 18 writers, each with brief bibl. and notes. No chronology.
GQ 48 (1975):168-71M

7/59 Hughes, Glyn Tegai. Romantic German Literature. London: Arnold,
      1980. 183 pp.

Bibl., classified and with evaluative comments, pp. 133-76.   Index of
    names and other subjects.
MLR 76 (1981):508-09; MLN 95 (1980):713-15; YWMLS 79:798--praises text
    and esp. bibl.; JEGP 79 (1980):605-06

• FICTION •

7/60 Kunz, Josef. Deutsche Novelle zwischen Klassik und Romantik.
    Berlin: Schmidt, 1971. (Grundlagen der Germanistik, 2) 175 pp.
2nd ed. 1st ed. 1966. Goethe through Kleist. Bibls. of books, arts.
    and diss. in German with each chapter.

• PERIODICALS •

7/61 Wilke, Jürgen. Literarische Zeitschriften des 18. Jahrhunderts
    (1688-1789). Stuttgart: Metzler, 1978.
2 vols. Vol. II: a survey of the journals in 7 chapters, incl. one on
    the journals associated with Lessing and his circle.
YWMLS 78:716; Monatshefte 73 (1981):109-10

7/62 Index zu deutschen Zeitschriften der Jahre 1773-1830. Nendeln:
    KTO, 1979--.
Paul Hocks and Peter Schmidt, eds. Abt. 1: Zeitschriften der Berliner
    Spätaufklärung. 3 vols. 1013 pp. I: contents of 16 periodicals,
    issue by issue; II: index of names, incl. subjects and a "Gattungs-
    register," a selective index to titles of arts.; III: complete
    key-word index to title of arts., incl. words cited in "Gattungs-
    register," but excl. names cited in index of names.

7/63 Estermann, Alfred. Die deutschen Literatur-Zeitschriften, 1815-
    1850: Bibliographien, Programme, Autoren. Nendeln: KTO, 1978.
8 vols. Incl. journals from before 1815. Gives publ. and editorial
    history, quotations from statements of editorial policy, lists of
    authors (without specific titles of citations) and locations in

German libraries.

• AUTHORS •

7/64 Schlick, Werner. Das Georg-Büchner-Schrifttum bis 1965: Eine
      internationale Bibliographie. Hildesheim: Olms, 1968. 227 pp.
Eds., transls. into various langs., and studies by scholar. Indexes,
      incl. subjects.

7/65 "Eichendorff-Bibliographie." In Aurora, 13 (1953)--.
38 (1978):159-61, 55 entries, publs. of 1976-77. Some very brief notes.

7/66 Krabiel, Klaus-Dieter. Joseph von Eichendorff: Kommentierte Stu-
      dienbibliographie. Frankfurt am Main: Athenäum, 1971, 90 pp.
400 entries for books, arts., chapters in books and diss., in German and
      English. Classified arrangement. Some brief annotations. Index
      of scholars.

7/67 "Goethe-Bibliographie." In Goethe-Jahrbuch, 89 (1972)--.
There are now 4 annual bibls. with extensive sections on Goethe studies.
      This, 97 (1980):291-324, for 1978, but incl. publs. of 1977 also,
      lists 68 eds. and transls. of his works and nearly 350 studies in
      6 sections; section 5: 128 studies of individual works, by work
      studied, although this is not made obvious. It covers books and
      arts. in German, English and other W. and E. European langs., as
      well as Japanese, and German diss. Occasional brief notes. Index
      of scholars. This may note passages in books and diss. and arts.
      in journals not directly devoted to Goethe or even to literature,
      e. g., on Cervantes or Schubert. Internationale Bibliographie zur
      deutschen Klassik (7/56), 23 (1976):107-57, 500+ entries, lists
      55 eds. and transls. and studies in 5 sections, incl. 22 studies
      of individual works, with the title of each work clearly printed
      as a sub-heading. There are a number of refs. to theater pro-
      ductions and films. Book revs. are listed in a suppl. (pp.

298-344, 520+ entries, by book) with an extremely inconvenient
system of cross-refs. by entry number only. Bibliographie der
deutschen Sprach und Literatur (7/7), 19 (1979):313-24, publ. 1981,
lists eds. but not transls. and 157 studies in 6 sections, incl.
studies of genres, of individual works, by work with clear subheads, and of his influence, etc. Lists book revs. Cites fewer
German diss. less promptly than Goethe-Jahrbuch. The MLA International Bibliography (1/9), 1980 II:231-34, 160 entries, by
scholar, has to recommend it (besides its familiarity) the facts
that it is the most prompt to appear, lists more English-lang.
studies (incl. diss. from DAI) and concentrates otherwise on published research in the W. European langs., but its organization is
no organization at all. For most purposes BDSL will probably be
preferable because of its arrangement, although it is less thorough
than the first 2.

7/68 "Goethe-Bibliographie." In Goethe: Neue Folge der Jahrbuch der
Goethe-Gesellschaft, 14/15 (1952/53)-33 (1971).
The predecessor of 7/67. Covers 1951-69 and therefore continues 7/70.

7/69 Pyritz, Hans Werner. Goethe-Bibliographie. Heidelberg: Winter,
1968.
Rev. ed. by Klaus Schröter and Helmut Riege. 1st ed. 1955-65. 2 vols.
Covers through 1964. Studies of Goethe's literary works, in
classified order, incl. sections on individual works: I:551-790,
entries 6933-10191; suppl. for 1955-64 in II:163-248, entries
1396-2333.
JEGP 58 (1959):334-37; 66 (1967):418-20; 70 (1971):359-60

7/70 **Goedeke, Karl.** Grundriss zur Geschichte der deutschen Dichtung.
(See 7/15)
Vol. 4, pt. 2-5 of the 3rd ed. is a Goethe bibl. through 1950.

7/71 Zastrau, Alfred. Goethe-Handbuch: Goethe, seine Welt und Zeit in

Werk _und_ _Wirkung_. Stuttgart: Metzler, 1961--.
2nd ed. 1st ed. by Julius Zeitler, in 3 vols., 1916-18. Publ. in fas-
      cicles. Vol. 1: Aachen-Farbenlehre, 2280 cols. Vol. 4: a collec-
      tion of maps illus. his travels. No more publ?
JEGP 58 (1959):337-42

7/72 _Goethe-Wörterbuch_. Stuttgart, etc.: Kohlhammer, 1966--.
Publ. in fascicles. Vol. 1: A-azurn, 1307 pp. Fasc. 1-3 of vol. 2
      publ. through 1981.
MLR 63 (1968):695-97; 64 (1969):935-36

7/73 Fischer, Paul. _Goethe-Wortschatz: Ein sprachgeschichtliches Wör-_
      terbuch zu Goethes sämtlichen Werken. Leipzig: Rohmkopf, 1929.
      905 pp.
Cites passages and gives definitions.

7/74 "Heine-Literatur." In _Heine-Jahrbuch_, 1962--.
19 (1980):281-91, for 1978/79. Books and arts.

7/75 Wilhelm, Gottfried and E. Galley. _Heine-Bibliographie_. Weimar:
      Arion, 1960.
2 vols. Vol. 2: 294 pp., listing books and arts. in German, English,
      French and other W. and E. European langs., and U. S. and German
      diss. Classified arrangement. More than 400 entries on Heine's
      influence in German (by period) and abroad (by country). Indexes
      of scholars and of subjects. Continued by S. Seifert, _Heine-Bib-_
      liographie, _1954-1964_, Berlin & Weimar: Aufbau, 1968, 395 pp.
MLR 57 (1962):287-88

7/76 Hermand, Jost. _Streitobjekt_ Heine: Ein _Forschungsbericht_ _1945-_
      _1975_. Frankfurt am Main: Athenäum Fischer, 1975. 199 pp.
A review of research, emphasizing German-lang. publs. (and dividing some
      chapters into separate sections for W. and E. Germany). Also
      notes research in English, French, Spanish, etc. Incl. German,

French and U. S., etc., diss.
YWMLS 75:643

7/77 "Hölderlin-Bibliographie." In Hölderlin-Jahrbuch, 9 (1955/56)--.
Covers from 1951-55. Vol 19/20, for 1971-73: more than 50 pp., appr.
   480 entries (to entry 4196). Not in 21 (1978-79).

7/78 Kohler, Maria and Alfred Kelletat. Hölderlin-Bibliographie, 1938-
   1950. Stuttgart: Landesbibliothek, 1953. 103 pp.

7/79 Böschenstein, Bernhard. Konkordanz zu Hölderlins Gedichten nach
   1800. Göttingen: Vanderhoeck & Ruprecht, 1964. 94 pp.
No context.

7/80 Voerster, Jürgen. 160 Jahre E. T. A. Hoffmann-Forschung, 1805-
   1965: Eine Bibliographie mit Inhaltserfassung und Erläuterungen.
   Stuttgart: Eggert, 1967. 227 pp.
List of studies in classified order. Section C/VI: studies of themes,
   etc.; 6 pp. in 21 subdivisions, incl. 10 refs. on dreams, cited by
   scholar and title, with page refs., full publ. data being found in
   a bibl. of 1264 entries. Occasional brief notes. C/VIII: studies
   of his influence.

7/81 Seifert, Siegfried. Lessing-Bibliographie. Berlin & Weimar: Aufbau, 1973. 857 pp.
6313 entries in classified order. Books and arts. in German, English
   and other langs., and U. S. and European diss.
Monatshefte 67 (1975):198-99; GQ 49 (1976):265

7/82 "Schiller-Bibliographie." In Jahrbuch der deutschen Schiller-
   gesellschaft, 6 (1957)--.
Irregular. Every 3-5 years. Covers from 1958-61. 23 (1979):549-612,
   covering 1974-78. Classified arrangement. Lists eds., transls.
   and studies, citing books and book revs. and arts. in books and

journals. A few brief annotations.

7/83 Vulpius, Wolfgang. Schiller-Bibliographie, 1893-1958. Weimar:
       Arion, 1959. 569 pp.
Continued by his Schiller-Bibliographie, 1959-1963, Berlin & Weimar:
       Aufbau, 1967, 204 pp., and by Peter Wersig, Schiller-Bibliographie,
       1964-1974, Berlin: Aufbau, 1977, 254 pp.
YWMLS 78:711

● MID 19th CENTURY and AFTER ●

• BIBLIOGRAPHY •

7/84 Wiesner, Herbert, Irena Živsa and Christoph Stoll. Bibliographie
       der Personalbibliographien. München: Nymphenburger, 1970. 160
       pp.
Vol. 3 of Kunisch's Handbuch der deutschen Gegenwartsliteratur (7/85).
       Lists bibls. of eds. and criticism, publ. as books or in journals,
       incl. bibls. attached to studies.
MLR 69 (1974):471x

• HANDBOOKS •

7/85 Kunisch, Hermann. Handbuch der deutschen Gegenwartsliteratur.
       München: Nymphenburger, 1969-70.
2nd ed., rev. by Herbert Wiesner. 3 vols. Vols. 1 & 2: mostly biogra-
       phical arts. on writers active this century, with brief bibls.
       II: 333-452: a collection of arts. by various scholars on 6 move-
       ments in recent German literature, from Expressionism. Index of
       names. See 7/84 for vol. 3. The Austrian entries have been
       transl. in 7/92.

7/86 Arnold, Heinz Ludwig. Kritisches Lexikon zur deutschsprachigen
       Gegenswartliteratur. München: Text + Kritik, 1978--.

Loose-leaf format, supplemented and up-dated regularly. Covers living
   writers only. Each entry: biography; signed essay (5-15 pp.) on
   work; list of works, incl. contributions to journals; list of
   studies, books and arts., in German and English. Grass: 16 pp.
   essay; bibl. of 159 studies through 1980, incl. some U. S. diss.

7/87 Lennartz, Franz. Deutsche Schriftsteller der Gegenwart: Einzel-
      darstellung. Stuttgart: Kröner, 1978. 825 pp.
11th ed. 1st ed. 1938. Brief entries, with bibls. on living writers.
   Previous eds. had several different titles.
YWMLS 79:831--"a most useful handbook"

7/88 Endres, Elisabeth. Autorenlexikon der deutschen Gegenwartslite-
      ratur, 1945-1975. Frankfurt: Fischer, 1975. 202 pp.
More than 350 entries. Brief biographies, a general critical comment
   and brief notes on the principal works. Bibl. of works and of
   critical studies in German, incl. German diss.

7/89 Albrecht, Günter, et al. Schriftsteller der DDR. Leipzig: Biblio-
      graphisches Institut, 1975. 656 pp.
2nd ed., unrev. 1st ed. 1974. Incl. entries on scholars, critics, etc.
   Brief entries, few as long as 2 pp. Brecht: 7+ pp. text, 1+ p.
   bibl., listing books by Brecht only.

7/90 Kürschners deutscher Literatur-Kalender. Berlin: de Gruyter,
      1879--.
Irregular, appr. every 5 years. 1978, 1374 pp. A biographical handbook
   of living German-lang. writers. Minimal biographical facts and
   list of publs. Similar information on writers who have died this
   century is given in Nekrolog zu Kürschners Literatur-Kalender,
   1901-1935 and 1936-1970, Berlin: de Gruyter, 1936 & 1973, 976 cols.
   and 871 pp.

7/91 Domandi, Agnes Körner. Modern German Literature: A Library of

Literary Criticism. N. Y.: Ungar, 1972.

2 vols. Excerpts from books and arts. in English or transl. from German, on "more than 200 authors" active since 1900.

Monatshefte 66 (1974):178-79--neg; GQ 47 (1974):471-73--v unfav

7/92 Ungar, Frederick, ed. Handbook of Austrian Literature. N. Y.: Ungar, 1973. 296 pp.

Signed arts., usually 2-7 pp., with bibls. of works and criticism. A transl. and adaptation of the Austrian entries in 7/85.

• HISTORIES •

7/93 Wiese, Benno von. Deutsche Dichter des 19. Jahrhunderts: Ihr Leben und Werk. Berlin: Schmidt, 1979. 687 pp.

2nd ed. 1st ed. 1969. 23 essays by various scholars. Büchner: 24 pp., incl. 2 pp. bibl.

GL&L ns 25 (1971-72):286-87; JEGP 70 (1971):123-25; MLR 66 (1971):464-65

7/94 Wiese, Benno von. Deutsche Dichter der Moderne: Ihr Leben und Werk. Berlin: Schmidt, 1975. 624 pp.

3rd ed. 1st ed. 1965. Essays by various scholars on writers from Nietzsche to Benn and Brecht.

MLR 66 (1971):464-65

7/95 Wiese, Benno von. Deutsche Dichter der Gegenwart: Ihr Leben und Werk. Berlin: Schmidt, 1973. 686 pp.

40 essays by various scholars. G. Grass: 23 pp.; U. Johnson: 15 pp.

7/96 Kindlers Literaturgeschichte der Gegenwart in Einzelbänden: Autoren, Werke, Themen, Tendenzen seit 1945. München & Zürich: Kindler, 1971-77.

1: Lattmann, Dieter, ed. Die Literatur der Bundesrepublik Deutschland. 1973. 800 pp. A general chapter and sections on poetry, prose and drama. Biographies, pp. 712-77. Index of names and titles.

2:    Franke, Konrad, ed. Literatur der Deutschen Demokratischen Repub-
      lik. 1974. 678 pp. 2nd ed. 1st ed. 1971.
GL&L ns 27 (1973/74):336-37x

3:    Spiel, Hilde, ed. Die Zeitgenössischen Literatur Österreichs.
      1976. 758 pp.
GQ 51 (1978):251-52; YWMLS 76:671-72

4:    Gsteiger, Manfred, ed. Die Zeitgenössisch Literatur Österreichs.
      Schweiz. 1974. 752 pp. Chapters on the 4 langs.
GQ 49 (1976):540

5:    Radler, Rudolf, ed. Die deutschsprachige Sachliteratur. 1977.
      992 pp. Incl. chapters on biography and autobiography and on
      literary scholarship and criticism.

• POETRY •

7/97 Paulus, Rolf and Ursula Steuler. Bibliographie zur deutschen Lyrik
      nach 1945: Forschung, Autoren, Anthologien. Wiesbaden: Athenaion,
      1977. 263 pp.
2nd ed. 1st ed. 1974. Covers 14 poets as well as general studies, incl.
      studies of themes, schools, etc. Paul Celan: appr. 170 studies,
      most in German, incl. appr. 95 by poem studied, and many cross-
      refs. Index of scholars.
MLR 72 (1977):252-53

• FICTION •

7/98 Kunz, Josef. Deutsche Novelle im 19. Jahrhundert. Berlin:
      Schmidt, 1978. (Grundlagen der Germanistik, 10) 182 pp.
2nd ed. 1st ed. 1970. Covers from the 1820s to Raabe and Fontane.
      Bibls. of books, arts. and diss. and notes with each chapter.
YWMLS 70:590--unfav

7/99 Kunz, Josef. Deutsche Novelle im 20. Jahrhundert. Berlin:

Schmidt, 1977. (Grundlagen der Germanistik, 23) 240 pp.
From Hauptmann to the mid-century.
YWMLS 77:736

• PERIODICALS •

7/100 Laakmann, Dagmar and Reinhard Tgahrt. Literarische Zeitschriften
    und Jahrbücher, 1880-1970: Verzeichnis der im Deutschen Literatur-
    archiv erschlossenen Periodica. Marbach: Deutsche Schillergesell-
    schaft, 1973. 227 pp.
Gives publ. and editorial history, but no notes on contents.
Monatshefte 66 (1974):435-36

7/101 Schlawe, Fritz. Literarische Zeitschriften. Stuttgart: Metzler,
    1965-71.
2nd ed. 1st ed. 1961-62. 2 vols. I: 1885-1910. 110 pp. II: 1910-
    1933. 113 pp. Gives publ. and editorial history, notes on con-
    tributors, etc.
MLR 57 (1962):460-61

7/102 King, Janet K. Literarische Zeitschriften, 1945-1970. Stuttgart:
    Metzler, 1974. 105 pp.
GQ 50 (1977):224-25M

7/103 Analytische Bibliographien deutschsprachiger literarischer Zeit-
    schriften. Berlin & Weimar: Aufbau, 1972--.
A series of vols. by various scholars on the journals publ. by German
    exiles. Bd. 3: Mass und Wirt, Zürich, 1937-40, by Volker Riedel,
    1973. 77 pp. Introductory essay, the contents of each issue, in-
    dexes of contributors and of subjects.

• EXPRESSIONISM •
[See also 1/196]

7/104 Raabe, Paul. Index Expressionismus: Bibliographie der Beiträge
    in den Zeitschriften und Jahrbüchern des literarischen Expression-
    ismus, 1910-1925. Nendeln: KTO, 1972.
18 vols. in 5 "series," incl. indexes by author, genre and subject. See
    also his Zeitschriften und Sammlungen des literarischen Expres-
    sionismus: Repertorium der Zeitschriften, Jahrbücher, Anthologien,
    Sammelwerke, Schriftenreihen und Almanache, 1910-1921, Stuttgart:
    Metzler, 1964, 263 pp., an annotated list ·of 182 publs.
TLS 23 March, 1973, p. 332--v unfav; critical of accuracy; GQ 47 (1974):
    167M

7/105 Brinkmann, Richard. Expressionismus: Internationale Forschung zu
    einem internationalen Phänomen. Stuttgart: Metzler, 1980. 360 pp.
Covers Expressionism in literature and the other arts. Chapters on
    themes; on Dada and Surrealism; on journals, poetry, drama, etc.
    Bibl. of 673 entries. Suppl. list of diss. in German and English.
    Offered as a suppl.to Deutschen Vierteljahrsschrift (7/16).

7/106 Stark, Michael. Literaturlexikon des deutschen Expressionismus.
    Stuttgart: Kröner, 198-.
Not yet publ.

• AUTHORS •

7/107 Lyon, James K. and Craig Inglis. Konkordanz zur Lyrik Gottfried
    Benns. Hildesheim & N. Y.: Olms, 1971. 524 pp.
Line or more of context.
Monatshefte 65 (1973):201-04

7/108 Neumann, Peter Horst. Wort-Konkordanz zur Lyrik Paul Celans bis
    1967. München: Fink, 1969. 134 pp.

No context.
MLR 65 (1970):714x

7/109 O'Neill, Patrick. Günter Grass: A Bibliography, 1955-1975. To-
      ronto & Buffalo: U. of Toronto Pr., 1976. 108 pp.
Lists eds. and transls as well as studies (books, arts. and passages in
      books) in English and German. Lists diss. as found in DAI.
GQ 51 (1978):414-15

7/110 "Hofmannsthal-Bibliographie." In Hofmannsthal-Blätter, 1(1968)--.
Covers from 1964. In each issue (2/yr.) 21/22 (1979):166-73. Classi-
      fied arrangement, incl. section of studies on individual works,
      and of comparative studies.

7/111 Koch, Hans-Albrecht and Uta Koch, eds. Hugo von Hofmannsthal:
      Bibliographie, 1964-1976. Freiburg im Breslau: n. p., 1976.
      (Hofmannsthal-Forschungen, 4) 175 pp.
Nearly 1400 entries for studies, listing books, arts. and chapters in
      books in various langs. and U. S. and European diss. Classified
      arrangement, with cross-refs. and indexes of names (subjects and
      scholars), of his works, and of other topics. Occasional brief
      annotations. Continues a bibl. by Horst Weber, Hugo von Hofmanns-
      thal: Bibliographie des Schrifttums, 1892-1963, Berlin: de Gruyter,
      1966, 254 pp., which is arranged by year of publ., with indexes.
GQ 51 (1978):420-21

7/112 Sondrup, Stephen P. and Craig Inglis. Konkordanz zu den
      Gedichten Hugo von Hofmannsthals. Salt Lake City, Utah: Brigham
      Young U. Pr., 1978. 474 pp.
Context of several lines of verse.

7/113 Flores, Angel. A Kafka Bibliography, 1908-1976. N. Y.: Gordian
      Pr., 1976. 193 pp.
Pp. 147-86: Kafka's works, by title (in English), with citations to arts.

and passages in books.
GQ 51 (1978):119-20--"helpful, but often imprecise"

7/114 Järv, Harry. Die Kafka-Literatur: Eine Bibliographie. Malmö:
       Cavefors, 1961. 381 pp.
MLR 58 (1963):300-01

7/115 Speidel, Walter. A Complete Contextual Concordance to Franz
       Kafka, Der Prozess. Leeds: Maney, 1978. (Compendia, 9) 1004 pp.
YWMLS 78:810; JEGP 80 (1981):305-06; CHum 14 (1980):63-64

7/116 Jonas, Klaus W. Die Thomas-Mann-Literatur. Berlin: Schmidt,
       1972-79.
2 vols., covering 1896-1955 and 1956-1975. Various indexes, incl. Mann's
       works, and themes.
Library, 6 ser., 2 (1980):377-78; JEGP 73 (1974):92-93; 79 (1980):422-23;
       Monatshefte 66 (1974):312-13; GQ 48 (1975):131M; MLR 65 (1970):
       951-52

7/117 Matter, Harry. Die Literatur über Thomas Mann: Eine Biblio-
       graphie, 1898-1969. Berlin & Weimar: Aufbau, 1972.
2 vols. Classified arrangement. Indexes incl. Mann's works and other
       subjects.
JEGP 73 (1974):92-93; Monatshefte 66 (1974):83-87--v fav, reviewed by
       Jonas, ed. of 7/116

7/118 Goldsmith, Ulrich K., et al., eds. Rainer Maria Rilke: A Verse
       Concordance to his Complete Lyrical Poetry. Leeds: Maney, 1980.
       (Compendia, 10) 1593 pp.
See also James Ronald Bartlett, A Word Index to Rainer Maria Rilke's
       German Lyric Poetry, Ann Arbor, Mich.: UMI, 1976, 2 vols. in 3
       parts, which, however, does not give a context.

7/119 Wetzel, Heinz. Konkordanz zu den Dichtungen Georg Trakls.

Salzburg: Müller, 1971.   (Trakl-Studien, 7)   818 pp.
Line or more of context.

VIII

LITERATURE IN ENGLISH

OUTLINE

ENGLISH and AMERICAN LITERATURE
      Bibliography of Bibliographies 8/1
      Bibliography 8/2
      Reviews of Research 8/3-8/4
      Dissertations 8/5-8/6
      Handbook 8/7
      Poetry 8/8
ENGLISH LITERATURE
      Bibliographies 8/9-8/10
      Handbooks 8/11-8/12
      Histories 8/13-8/15
            Chronology 8/16
      Poetry 8/17-8/18
      Fiction 8/19-8/21
      Drama 8/22
      Periods
            Old English
                  Bibliographies 8/23-8/25
                  Review of Research 8/26
                  Poetry 8/27
                  Beowulf 8/28
            Middle English
                  Reviews of Research 8/29-8/30
                  Authors and Works
                        Chaucer 8/31-8/36

● ● LITERATURE in ENGLISH ● ●

● ● ENGLISH and AMERICAN LITERATURE ● ●

● BIBLIOGRAPHIES ●

8/1 Schweik, Robert C. and Dieter Riesner. Reference Sources in English
     and American Literature. N. Y.: Norton, 1977. 258 pp.
1217 entries in classified order. Indexes of subjects and of scholars.
     Annotations, sometimes to 4-5 sentences. Does not list reference
     materials on individual writers.
AmLS 77:514; Review 2 (1980):373-83--v unfav

8/2 Annual Bibliography of English Language and Literature. 1921--.
Covers from 1920. Annual. Slow to appear. 52 (1977), publ. 1980: 757
     pp., 12734 entries. Covers the English lang., folklore, and liter-
     ature in English, worldwide. Literary studies are arranged by
     period or century, without geographic subdivisions. Has always
     incl. studies written in the European langs., now incl. the E.
     European langs. Lists U. S. and British diss. Cites book revs.
     The organization is similar to that of the MLA Bibl. (1/9), in
     that it is organized by period and author primarily; general stud-
     ies are collected under broad subject headings. The lack of geo-
     graphic subdivisions will sometimes be a disadvantage. Consider-
     able coverage of minor, popular or non-literary writers. Even for
     recent years this will often cite studies not to be found in the
     MLA (in addition to the book revs. and British diss.), while the
     MLA will list materials not in this, and for the years before 1956
     the coverage of research by British, Commonwealth and European
     scholars will be very useful. Index of scholars which incl. a
     list of the subject sections. Cross-refs. give author and title
     of study, as opposed to the cross-refs. by entry number only in
     the MLA.

● REVIEWS of RESEARCH ●

8/3 The Year's Work in English Studies. 1921--.
Covers from 1919. Annual. 59 (1978), publ. 1980, 556 pp. Bibl. essays
    surveying books and arts. from appr. 400 journals, mostly in En-
    glish, but some in German, a few in French. Has had sections on
    U. S. literature since 35 (1954). Since 56 (1975) the index of
    authors and subjects has made some attempt to indicate studies of
    themes, genres, etc. Index of scholars.

8/4 Bateson, Frederick W. and Harrison T. Meserole. A Guide to English
    and American Literature. London & N. Y.: Longman, 1976. 334 pp.
3rd ed. 1st ed. 1965. Lists and evaluates histories and studies of
    periods, genres, themes, etc., from Middle English to the mid-20th
    c., and eds. and studies of the principal authors. Covers books
    mostly, some arts.
SCN 36 (1978):23-24; AmLS 76:193-94

● DISSERTATIONS ●

8/5 McNamee, Lawrence F. Dissertations in English and American Liter-
    ature: Theses Accepted by American, British and German Univer-
    sities, 1865-1964. N. Y. & London: Bowker, 1968. 1124 pp.
Suppls., 1964-1968, 1969, 450 pp. and 1969-1973, 1974, 690 pp. Classi-
    fied arrangement. Chapter 16: Comparative Literature, in about 75
    sections, on influences, transls., and comparative studies of
    British literature. (Similar studies of American literature are
    in chapter 34: American Literary Relations.) Also covers Irish,
    Canadian and Australian literatures and dissertations.

8/6 Gabel, Gernot U. and Gisela R. Gabel. Dissertations in English and
    American Literature: Theses Accepted by Austrian, French and Swiss
    Universities, 1875-1970. Hamburg: n. p., 1977. 198 pp.

● HANDBOOK ●

8/7 Great Writers of the English Language.   N. Y.: St. Martin's Pr.,
     1979.
James Vinson, ed., D.L. Kirkpatrick, assoc. ed. 3 vols. Poets, 1141 pp.
     Novelists and Prose Writers, 1367 pp. Dramatists, 648 pp. Outline
     biography, list of works and of studies, and a signed critical
     comment. Incl. living writers and writers from the Commonwealth
     countries.

● POETRY ●

8/8 Kuntz, Joseph M. and Nancy Martinez. Poetry Explication: A Check-
     list of Interpretation since 1925 of British and American Poems,
     Past and Present. Boston: Hall, 1980. 570 pp.
3rd ed. 1st ed. 1950. Arts. from more than 100 journals and chapters
     and passages from books, arranged by poet and poem, from Chaucer
     to Dickey. Whitman: 11 pp., more than 60 poems. Yeats: 23 pp.;
     "Sailing to Byzantium": 56 entries.

● ● ENGLISH LITERATURE ● ●

● BIBLIOGRAPHIES ●

8/9 The New Cambridge Bibliography of English Literature. Cambridge:
     The University Pr., 1969-77.
George Watson, ed. 4 vols. and index vol. I: 600-1660. 1974. 2476+
     cols. II: 1660-1800. 1971. 2082+ cols. III: 1800-1900. 1969.
     1948+ cols. IV: 1900-1950. 1972. 1408+ cols.
Each vol. is arranged by type of literature: poetry, drama, fiction,
     prose, etc., and each section is further divided and subdivided,
     esp. into author sections, listing original and modern eds. and
     biographical and critical studies, by year of publ. An author who
     wrote in more than 1 form will be covered in 1 section only.

Eliot: 50 cols. in vol. 4, under Poetry; Beckett: 20 cols. in vol. 4, under Drama. The index vol. incl. the headings of all sections and subsections (names, anonymous works and other topics, e. g., "Italian Literature, Relations with," citing sections in all 4 vols.), but does not list individual studies, either by subject or by scholar.

The original Cambridge Bibliography of English Literature was publ. in 4 vols. in 1940, F. W. Bateson, ed. It covered a number of topics not in the New Cambridge, such as the literatures of the Commonwealth countries.

Scriblerian 4 (1971/72):25

8/10 The Shorter New Cambridge Bibliography of English Literature. Cambridge & N. Y.: Cambridge U. Pr., 1981. 1612+ cols.

An adaptation of the New Cambridge (8/9), omitting nearly all refs. to journal arts. and many refs. to even recent books, though adding some refs. to books publ. through the mid-1970s. Wyatt: 8 studies, incl. 2 publ.1542; Sterne: 13 20th c. refs., incl. 4 not in 8/9.

● HANDBOOKS ●

8/11 Harvey, Sir Paul. The Oxford Companion to English Literature. Oxford: Clarendon Pr., 1967. 961 pp.

4th ed. 1st ed. 1932. Brief entries on authors, characters, works (at least 16 entries on Dickens' works, under title), and much miscellaneous data. Incl. brief entries on classical and European writers and anonymous works.

8/12 Harvey, Sir Paul. Concise Oxford Dictionary of English Literature. Oxford: Clarendon Pr., 1970. 628 pp.

2nd ed., rev. by Dorothy Eagle. 1st ed. 1939. Brief entries on writers (up to several cols.), works, characters from literature, mythology, the Bible, etc. Swift: 2 cols., condensed from OCEL (8/11). At least 16 entries for Dickens' works.

● HISTORIES ●

8/13 Baugh, Albert C., ed. A Literary History of England. N. Y.: Ap-
      pleton-Century-Crofts, 1967. 1605 pp.
2nd ed. 1st ed. 1948. Revision of text largely limited to details.
      Lengthy unpaginated section of suppl. notes. Separately paged
      index of names, titles and other subjects.

8/14 Sampson, George. The Concise Cambridge History of English Litera-
      ture. Cambridge: The University Pr., 1970. 976 pp.
3rd ed., rev. and with additional chapters by R. C. Churchill. 1st ed.
      1941. Incl. the literatures of all the English-speaking countries.
      The original Cambridge History of English Literature, Cambridge:
      The University Pr., 1907-27, was ed. in 15 vols. by A. W. Ward and
      A. R. Waller, with chapters by various scholars on all aspects of
      literature, incl. travel writers, etc. Full bibls. and an index
      which noted themes, influences, etc.
YWES 70:15; RES ns 22 (1971):174-78

8/15 The Oxford History of English Literature. Oxford: The Clarendon
      Pr., 1945--.
13 vols. in 17 parts now projected. Orig. ed. by F. P. Wilson and
      Bonamy Dobrée. All vols. have a very lengthy annotated bibl.
      Most have a detailed chronology. The indexes are brief and simple.
      9 vols. and pt. 1 of another publ. to date, covering from the late
      Middle Ages to the early 19th c. and an unsatisfactory vol. on the
      modern period.

● CHRONOLOGY ●

8/16 Annals of English Literature, 1475-1950. The Principal Publica-
      tions of Each Year Together with an Alphabetical Index of Authors
      with Their Works. Oxford: Clarendon Pr., 1961. 380 pp.
2nd ed. 1st ed. 1935. Also notes births and deaths of authors, etc.

MLR 57 (1962):625

● POETRY ●

8/17 Dyson, A. E., ed. English Poetry: Select Bibliographical Guides.
        London: Oxford U. Pr., 1971. 375 pp.
Essays surveying research on 20 poets, from Chaucer to Eliot.
YWES 71:288

8/18 Routledge History of English Poetry. London & Boston: Routledge,
        Kegan, Paul, 1977--.
R. A. Fowkes, ed.
1:     Pearsall, Derek. Old English and Middle English Poetry. 1977.
        352 pp.
YWES 77:53, 79, 111; MLR 76 (1981):651-54
3:     Rothstein, Eric. Restoration and Eighteenth Century Poetry, 1660-
        1780. 1981. 242 pp.
TLS 1 Jan., 1982, p. 4
4:     Jackson, J. R. de J. Poetry of the Romantic Period. 1980. 334
        pp.
English 29 (1980):239-45; N&Q ns 28 (1981):438-39x

● FICTION ●

8/19 Bell, Inglis F. and Donald Baird. The English Novel, 1578-1956: A
        Checklist of Twentieth-Century Criticisms. Denver: Swallow, 1958.
        168 pp.
Criticism from certain books and journals, by author and novel. Incl.
        Commonwealth writers.

8/20 Palmer, Helen H. and Anne Jane Dyson. English Novel Explication:
        Criticisms to 1972. Hamden, Conn.: Shoe String Pr., 1973. 329 pp.
Lists criticism publ. 1958-72 in certain books and journals. Meant to
        suppl. 8/19; see also suppl., 1976, 305 pp., by Peter L. Abernethy.

8/21 Dyson, A. E., ed. The English Novel: Select Bibliographical
      Guides. London: Oxford U. Pr., 1974. 372 pp.
Surveys of research on 20 novelists, Bunyan to Joyce.
YWES 74:27; YES 6 (1976):265-66

● DRAMA ●

8/22 Wells, Stanley, ed. English Drama Excluding Shakespeare: Select
      Bibliographical Guides. London: Oxford U. Pr., 1975. 303 pp.
17 chapters surveying research on periods or on groups of playwrights.
      See 8/63 for a companion vol. on Shakespeare.
YWES 75:17

● OLD ENGLISH ●

• BIBLIOGRAPHIES •

8/23 "Old English Bibliography." In Old English Newsletter,   3
      (1969/70)--.
In issue no. 2 (Spring). 14:2 (Spring, 1981):55-86. 10 sections, incl.
      Anglo-Latin, book revs., and research in progress. 3: Literature:
      pp. 60-67; 3b: Individual Poems, pp. 62-66. Lists books and arts.
      in English, German, French, etc. and diss. as found in DAI. Publs.
      of 1979-80, chiefly. This is more prompt to appear than the bibl.
      in ASE (8/24); the differences in arrangement and esp. contents
      are slight, but tend to favor this one.

8/24 "Bibliography." In Anglo-Saxon England, 1 (1972)--.
Annual. Covers 1971--. Classified, covering history, archaeology, art,
      etc., as well as literature. 9 (publ. 1981):281-318, for 1979. 9
      sections. Section 3: Old English Literature, pp. 288-94; 3b:
      Poetry, in 3 subsections (General; Beowulf; Other), pp. 289-93.

8/25 Greenfield, Stanley B. and Fred C. Robinson. A Bibliography of

Publications on Old English Literature, to the End of 1972.
Toronto & Buffalo: U. of Toronto Pr., 1980. 437 pp.
3 sections: General; Poetry (Seafarer: appr. 50 entries); Prose. Cites
    books and book revs., arts., and U. S. and other diss. A few very
    brief annotations. Beowulf: pp. 126-97, entries 1632-3196A, in 10
    sections, incl. some items within the scope of Short (8/28) but
    not found there, while Short lists a few items not to be found
    here. Indexes of scholars and of subject sections, but no subject
    access to individual studies. Cross-refs.

• REVIEW of RESEARCH •

8/26 "The Year's Work in Old English Studies." In Old English News-
    letter, 1 (1967)--.
In issue no. 1 (Fall). 14:1 (Fall, 1980):15-79, for 1979. Incl. studies
    of lang., history, culture and archaeology. Beowulf: pp. 48-52.

• POETRY •

8/27 Bessinger, Jess B. and Philip H. Smith. Concordance to the Anglo-
    Saxon Poetic Records. Ithaca, N. Y. & London: Cornell U. Pr.,
    1978. 1510 pp.
Incl. Beowulf. See also their A Concordance to Beowulf, Ithaca, N. Y.:
    Cornell U. Pr., 1969, 373 pp.
N&Q ns 26 (1979):347-48; YWES 78:63; JEGP 69 (1970):161-62; MLR 65
    (1970):863-65

• BEOWULF •

8/28 Short, Douglas D. Beowulf Scholarship: An Annotated Bibliography.
    N. Y. & London: Garland, 1980. 353 pp.
More than 1100 entries for books, arts., and chapters in books in vari-
    ous langs., incl. Russian, arranged by year of publ. Selective
    listing of studies publ. before 1950. Indexes of scholars and of

subjects.

● MIDDLE ENGLISH ●

● REVIEWS of RESEARCH ●

8/29 A Manual of the Writings in Middle English, 1050-1500. New Haven:
    Conn. Academy of Arts and Sciences, 1967--.
J. Burke Severs [then Albert E. Hartung], gen. ed. 6 vols., 2194 pp.,
    to date. Surveys by various scholars of the manuscripts and eds.
    of, and research on Middle English works and writers, incl. Sir
    Gawain (vol. 2), Malory (vol. 3) and the ballads (vol. 6). Orig.
    ed. by John Edwin Wells, A Manual of the Writings in Middle En-
    glish, 1050-1400, New Haven, Conn.: Yale U. Pr., 1916, 1155 pp.,
    with 9 suppls., 1919-51.

8/30 Recent Middle English Scholarship and Criticism: Survey and Desid-
    erata. Pittsburgh: Duquesne U. Pr., 1971. 107 pp.
J. Burke Severs, ed. Covers Piers Plowman, Sir Gawain, the romances and
    the Canterbury Tales.
YWES 71:80

● AUTHORS and WORKS ●

8/31 "Chaucer Research, [year]: Report." In Chaucer Review, 1
    (1966/67)--.
Annual. Lists books and arts., research in progress, incl. diss., and
    completed but unpubl. research. All sections arranged by scholar.
    15 (1980):356-79, report no. 41, for 1980.

8/32 Baugh, Albert C. Chaucer. Arlington Heights, Ill.: AHM, 1977.
    (Goldentree Bibls.) 161 pp.
2nd ed. 1st ed. 1968. Classified arrangement. Most of book is devoted
    to individual works.

8/33 Griffith, Dudley D. Bibliography of Chaucer, 1908-1953. Seattle:
      U. of Washington Pr., 1955. 398 pp.
Books and book revs., arts. and U. S. and foreign diss., in classified
      order. Canterbury Tales: pp. 151-247; by tale, pp. 163-247.
      Index of scholars and subjects. A few very brief annotations.

8/34 Crawford, William R. Bibliography of Chaucer, 1954-1963. Seattle
      & London: U. of Washington Pr., 1967. 144 pp.
Books, book revs., arts. and U. S. diss. Classified arrangement.

8/35 Baird, Lorrayne Y. A Bibliography of Chaucer, 1964-1973. Boston:
      Hall, 1977. 287 pp.
Books, book revs., arts. and U. S. diss. Classified arrangement. Some
      brief annotations.
ES 62 (1981):383-85

8/36 Tatlock, John S. P. and Arthur G. Kennedy. A Concordance to the
      Complete Works of Geoffrey Chaucer and to the Romaunt of the Rose.
      Washington, D. C.: Carnegie Inst. of Washington, 1927. 1110 pp.

8/37 Andrew, Malcolm. The Gawain-Poet: An Annotated Bibliography,
      1839-1977. N. Y. & London: Garland, 1979. 256 pp.
Critical writings on Sir Gawain and the Grene Knight, pp. 120-206, by
      scholar. Index of scholars and of lines specifically commented
      on. No other subject access. See also Roger A. Hambridge, "Sir
      Gawain and the Green Knight: An Annotated Bibliography, 1950-
      1972," in Comitatus 4 (1973):49-84.
YWES 74:101

8/38 Kottler, Barnet and Alan M. Markman. A Concordance to Five Middle
      English Poems. N. p.: U. of Pittsburgh Pr., 1966. 761 pp.
Covers Sir Gawain and the other poems of its manuscript.

8/39 Life, Page West. Sir Thomas Malory and the Morte Darthur: A

Survey of Scholarship and Annotated Bibliography. Charlottesville:
    U. Pr. of Virginia, 1980. 297 pp.
Classified arrangement. Indexes of scholars (called "Index of Names")
    and of subjects (incl. names and titles).
Speculum 56 (1981):456--"exemplary annotations," "the survey tends to
    simplify opinions"; Library 6th ser, 3 (1981):248-49x

8/40 Kato, Tomomi. A Concordance to the Works of Sir Thomas Malory.
    Tokyo: U. of Tokyo Pr., 1974. 1659 pp.
Brief context.
YWES 75:105-06

● 16th and EARLY 17th CENTURIES ●

● BIBLIOGRAPHIES ●

8/41 [Bibliographies on various writers.] In English Literary Renais-
    sance, 1 (1971)--.
A. J. Colaianne and W. L. Godshalk, "Recent Studies in Sidney (1970-
    1977)," 8 (1978):212-33, continuing a survey by Godshalk covering
    1945-69 in 2 (1972).

8/42 "Literature of the Renaissance." In Studies in Philology 20
    (1923)-66 (1969).
Through 35 (1938) covered English literature only. See 1/157.

● HANDBOOK ●

8/43 Ruoff, James E. Crowell's Handbook of Elizabethan and Stuart
    Literature. N. Y.: Crowell, 1975. 468 pp.
Arts. on writers, some literary works, and literary and cultural topics
    (Satire; Criticism, literary; etc.).
YWES 76:154; SCN 35 (1977):26-27; LRN 2 (1977):187-89

● POETRY ●

8/44   Donow, Herbert S. A Concordance to the Sonnet Sequences of Daniel,
       Drayton, Shakespeare, Sidney and Spenser. Carbondale: S. Illinois
       U. Pr., 1969. 772 pp.

● DRAMA ●

8/45   Ribner, Irving and Clifford Huffman. Tudor and Stuart Drama. Ar-
          lington Heights, Ill.: AHM, 1978. (Goldentree Bibls.) 121 pp.
2nd ed. 1st ed. 1966. Excl. Shakespeare (see 8/59).
LRN 4 (1979):101-04

8/46   Logan, Terence P. and Denzell S. Smith. A Survey and Bibliography
          of Recent Studies in English Renaissance Drama. Lincoln: U. of
          Nebraska Pr., 1973-78.
Reviews of research, by various scholars. Excl. Shakespeare.
1:   The Predecessors of Shakespeare. 1973. 348 pp. Marlowe and
        others.
YWES 73:189
2:   The Popular School. 1975. 299 pp. Covers Webster, Middleton,
        Dekker and others.
YWES 76:148
3:   The New Intellectuals. 1977. 370 pp. Jonson, Chapman, Marston
        and others.
SCN 36 (1978):49; SQ 31 (1980):443-44
4:   The Later Jacobean and Caroline Dramatists. 1978. 279 pp. Beau-
        mont and Fletcher, Massinger, Ford and others.
SCN 38 (1980):35-36

8/47   Stagg, Louis C. Index to the Figurative Language of the Tragedies
          of Shakespeare's Chief 17th-Century Contemporaries. Memphis, Tenn.:
          Memphis St. U. Pr., 1977. (Distr. by Ann Arbor: UMI) 520 pp.
Rev. and enlarged. Orig. publ. in parts, 1967-70. Covers Webster,

Jonson, Chapman and 4 others, in separate lists. Several lines of context.

8/48 Holzknecht, Karl J. Outlines of Tudor and Stuart Plays, 1497-1642.
      N. Y.: Barnes & Noble, 1947. 442 pp.
Excl. Shakespeare (see 8/69).

• AUTHORS •

8/49 Roberts, John R. John Donne: An Annotated Bibliography of Modern
      Criticism, 1912-1967. Columbia: U. of Missouri Pr., 1973. 323 pp.
Books, arts. and passages in books, chiefly in English, by year of publ.
      Index of scholars, of names as subjects, and of Donne's works.
SCN 37 (1979):73

8/50 Combs, Homer Carroll and Zay Rusk Sullens. A Concordance to the
      English Poems of John Donne. Chicago: Packard, 1940. 418 pp.

8/51 Roberts, John R. George Herbert: An Annotated Bibliography of
      Modern Criticism, 1905-1974. Columbia & London: U. of Missouri
      Pr., 1978. 280 pp.
800 entries, by year of publ. Books and arts. in English and other langs.
      Indexes incl. names and other subjects, and Herbert's works.
RES ns 31 (1980):346-48; Ren&R ns 4 (1980):119x; MQ 13 (1979):59; SCN
      37 (1979):73

8/52 DiCesare, Mario A. and Rigo Mignani. A Concordance to the Com-
      plete Writings of George Herbert. Ithaca, N. Y. & London: Cornell
      U. Pr., 1977. 1319 pp.
Ren&R ns 4 (1980):119x; YWES 78:194

8/53 Brock, Dewey H. and James M. Welsh. Ben Jonson: A Quadricentennial
      Bibliography, 1947-1972. Metuchen, N. J.: Scarecrow, 1974. 166
      pp.

Separate sections for books (noting reviews), arts., and English lang.
    diss. Index of scholars, of titles of Jonson's works, and of
    names as subjects. Occasional brief annotations.

8/54 Friedenreich, Kenneth. Christopher Marlowe: An Annotated Bibliog-
    raphy of Criticism since 1950. Metuchen, N. J.: Scarecrow, 1979.
    150 pp.
Sections on each play. Books, arts., chapters in books and diss. as
    found in DAI.

8/55 Chan, Lois Mai and Sarah A. Pedersen. Marlowe Criticism: A Bibli-
    ography. Boston: Hall, 1976. 226 pp.
Classified arrangement, incl. sections on his works. Lists books, arts.
    and chapters in books, and diss. from the U. S. and Europe.

8/56 Crawford, Charles. The Marlowe Concordance. Louvain: Uystpruyst,
    1911-32. 1453 pp.
Louis Ule, A Concordance to the Works of Christopher Marlowe, Hildesheim
    & N. Y.: Olms, 1979 (Elizabethan Concordance Series, 1), 596 pp.,
    gives no context, though it concords each play separately, an ad-
    vantage in the case of Marlowe.

8/57 "Shakespeare: Annotated World Bibliography." In Shakespeare
    Quarterly, 1 (1950)--.
In issue no. 4 (Autumn). Lists books, arts., diss. and reviews of books
    and productions. Indexes of scholars and of subjects, incl. names
    and other topics. 31 (1980):468-659, 2859 entries. Individual
    works: pp. 540-621; the sonnets: pp. 605-608, appr. 72 entries.

8/58 "Shakespeare-Bibliographie für [year] mit Nachträgen aus früheren
    Jahren." In Shakespeare-Jahrbuch.
There are 2 concurrent bibls. of this title, both in yearbooks publ. by
    a Shakespeare-Gesellschaft, this one in Weimar, DDR, the other
    (called simply Jahrbuch) by the Deutsche Shakespeare-Gesellschaft

(West) of Heidelberg. The Weimar Shakespeare Jahrbuch claims
descent from the Shakespeare-Jahrbuch of the Deutschen Shakespeare-
Gesellschaft, 1 (1865)-71 (1935), which itself contained a bibliography. The bibl. in the Weimar Shakespeare Jahrbuch lists studies on literary and theatrical topics in various langs., incl.
English and the E. European langs. The Heidelberg Jahrbuch lists
mainly German-lang. studies, incl. Swiss and Austrian.

Weimar: 115 (1979):207-312, for 1977. 1929 entries, listing books,
    book revs., arts. and diss. Index of names (subjects and scho-
    lars). Some brief annotations.

Heidelberg: 1980, **pp.** 275-333, covering 1978. 665 entries. Books, book
    revs. and arts.

The bibl. in Shakespeare Quarterly usually has been available nearly a
    year or more before that in the Weimar Shakespeare Jahrbuch.   In
    addition, a number of the entries in Weimar 115 (1979) had been
    reported in Shakespeare Quarterly's bibl. for 1976 [28 (1977)].
    The classified arrangement of the Quarterly is more detailed than
    that of Weimar and the indexes incl. topics as well as names.
    Weimar does offer more extensive coverage of European research.

8/59 Bevington, David M. Shakespeare. Arlington Heights, Ill.: AHM,
      1978. (Goldentree Bibls.) 259 pp.

4689 entries for books and arts., mainly in English. Classified ar-
      rangement, incl. 115 pp. on the plays. Studies in Genre: pp. 85-
      108, nearly 450 entries, divided and subdivided. Cross-refs.
      Index of scholars.

SQ 32 (1981):120-21--praises arrangement; YWES 78:129

8/60 Ebisch, W. and Levin L. Schücking. A Shakespeare Bibliography.
      Oxford: Clarendon Pr., 1931. 294 pp.

Suppl., 1930-35, 1937, 104 pp. Selective listing of books and arts.,
      incl. many 19th c. publs.

8/61 Smith, Gordon R. A Classified Shakespeare Bibliography, 1936-

<u>1958</u>. University Park: Pennsylvania St. U. Pr., 1963. 784 pp.
Books, book revs., chapters in books, and arts., in various langs. Incl.
U. S. and European diss. Section XIII: Shakepeare's Influence
Outside of England, divided by nation and subdivided by period,
then specific author. Occasional notes. No indexes.

8/62 "The Year's Contributions to Shakespearian Studies." In <u>Shake</u>-
<u>speare</u> <u>Survey</u>: <u>An</u> <u>Annual</u> <u>Survey</u> <u>of</u> <u>Shakespearian</u> <u>Study</u> <u>and</u> <u>Produc</u>-
<u>tion</u>, 1 (1948)--.
32 (1979):211-47. Bibl. essays on 1): critical studies; 2): Shakepeare's life, times and stage; and 3): textual studies. 33 (1980),
publ. 1981.

8/63 Wells, Stanley, ed. <u>Shakespeare</u>: <u>Select</u> <u>Bibliographical</u> <u>Guides</u>.
N. Y.: Oxford U. Pr., 1973. 300 pp.
17 essays surveying research, incl. 13 on the plays, singly or in
groups.
MLR 69 (1974):843-44; RES ns 26 (1975):207-08

8/64 Bergeron, David M. <u>Shakespeare</u>: <u>A</u> <u>Study</u> <u>and</u> <u>Research</u> <u>Guide</u>. Lon-
don: Macmillan, 1976. 145 pp.
A review of research, chiefly noting books, entirely in English.
YWES 76:111--prefers Wells; SQ 28 (1977):116-19

8/65 Velz, John W. <u>Shakespeare</u> <u>and</u> <u>the</u> <u>Classical</u> <u>Tradition</u>: <u>A</u> <u>Critical</u>
<u>Guide</u> <u>to</u> <u>Commentary</u>, <u>1660-1960</u>. Minneapolis: U. of Minnesota Pr.,
1968. 459 pp.
2487 numbered entries, arranged by play. Sometimes lengthy (10-15 sentences) descriptive and evaluative notes. Cites books, arts., and
U. S. and European diss. Index of scholars and subjects, incl.
names, Latin and Greek words and phrases, etc. Cleopatra: 99 entries, cited by entry number only, as a character in <u>Antony</u> <u>and</u>
<u>Cleopatra</u>, plus 35 entries under other subheadings.
RES ns 21 (1970):202-04--v fav; SQ 24 (1973):94; ShakS 5 (1969):372-73

8/66   Champion, Larry S. King Lear: An Annotated Bibliography. N. Y.:
       Garland, 1980. (Garland Shakespeare Bibliographies, 1)
2 vols. 8 broad subject sections. Index, incl. subjects.

8/67   Hayashi, Tetsumaro. Shakespeare's Sonnets: A Record of 20th Cen-
       tury Criticism. Metuchen, N. J.: Scarecrow, 1972. 163 pp.
2503 entries for books, arts. and passages in books, in English only.
       Criticism of specific sonnets, pp. 93-110.

8/68   Campbell, Oscar J. and Edward G. Quinn. A Shakespeare Encyclo-
       pedia. London: Methuen, 1966. 1014 pp.
Brief unsigned arts. on his plays, characters and contemporaries; on peo-
       ple associated with Shakespearean production and scholarship, to
       the present; and on other topics. Comedy of Errors: 13 cols.,
       incl. 1 col. on sources, 2+ on plot, and 4 1/4 cols. of quotations
       from critics.
YWES 67:139; RES ns 19 (1968):70-73--v fav; MLR 65 (1970):140-41

8/69   Watt, Homer A., Karl J. Holzknecht and Raymond Ross. Outlines of
       Shakespeare's Plays. N. Y.: Barnes & Noble, 1934. 212 pp.

8/70   Spevack, Marvin. The Harvard Concordance to Shakespeare. Cam-
       bridge: Harvard U. Pr., 1973. 1600 pp.
His A Complete and Systematic Concordance to the Works of Shakespeare,
       Hildesheim: Olms, 1968-80, 9 vols., treats the same data more ex-
       pansively, incl. concordances arranged work by work and character
       by character, vols. 1-3.
JEGP 74 (1975):121-23x; RES ns 26 (1975):474-75

8/71   Washington, Mary A. Sir Philip Sidney: An Annotated Bibliography
       of Modern Criticism, 1941-1970. Columbia: U. of Missouri Pr.,
       1972. 199 pp.
831 entries. Defense of Poesie: 118 entries. Books, chapters in books

and arts., mostly in English. Diss., as found in <u>DAI</u>, and foreign
diss. Index of scholars and subjects, chiefly names and Sidney's
works.

8/72 [Bibliographies of Spenser studies.] In <u>Spenser Newsletter</u>, 1
      (1969)--.
Each issue consists entirely of "Books: Reviews and Notices," "Articles:
   Abstracts and Notices," "Notices of Reviews," "Dissertation Ab-
   stracts," and a list of work in progress.

8/73 McNeir, Waldo F. <u>Edmund Spenser: An Annotated Bibliography, 1937-
      1972</u>. Pittsburgh: Duquesne U. Pr., 1975. 490 pp.
2nd ed. 1st ed., 1962. Continues Frederic I. Carpenter, <u>A Reference
   Guide to Edmund Spenser</u>, Chicago: U. of Chicago Pr., 1923, 333 pp.
   and its suppl. by Dorothy F. A. Evans, Baltimore, Md.: Johns
   Hopkins Pr./London: Oxford U. Pr., 1937, 242 pp. See also B. J.
   Vondersmith, "A Bibliography of Criticism of <u>The Faerie Queen</u>,
   1900-1970," in Richard C. Frushell and B. J. Vondersmith, eds.,
   <u>Contemporary Thought on Edmund Spenser</u>, Carbondale, etc.: Southern
   Illinois U. Pr., 1975, pp. 150-213.
YWES 76:156; SCN 36 (1978):37-39--ref. to McNeir; YES 8 (1978):331;
   YWES 75:186; SpNews 6 (1975):41x--ref. to Vondersmith

8/74 Osgood, Charles G. <u>A Concordance to the Poems of Edmund Spenser</u>.
      Washington, D. C.: Carnegie Inst., 1915. 997 pp.
See also Einar Bjorvand, <u>A Concordance to Spenser's Fowre Hymnes</u>, Oslo:
   Universitetsforlaget, 1973, 112 pp.
YWES 73:212

8/75 Jentoft, Clyde W. <u>Sir Thomas Wyatt and Henry Howard, Earl of Sur-
      rey: A Reference Guide</u>. Boston: Hall, 1980. 192 pp.
Books, passages in books, and arts., in English and other langs. U. S.
   diss. Index, incl. scholars, Wyatt's and Surrey's works, names
   and other topics.

8/76   Hangen, Eva C. A Concordance to the Complete Poetical Works of
Sir Thomas Wyatt. Chicago: U. of Chicago Pr., 1941. 527 pp.

● MID 17th and 18th CENTURIES ●

● BIBLIOGRAPHIES ●

8/77   Lund, Roger D. Restoration and Early Eighteenth Century English
Literature, 1660-1740: A Selected Bibliography of Resource Mate-
rials. N. Y.: MLA, 1980. 42 pp.
Annotated.

8/78   The Eighteenth Century: A Current Bibliography. (See 1/160 &
1/161).
The installments from 5 (1926) through 49 (1970) chiefly covered English
literature, 1660-1800.

8/79   "Some Current Publications." In Restoration: Studies in English
Literary Culture, 1660-1700, 1 (1977)--.
2/yr. Books, arts. and diss. from DAI. Notes on most entries, of 1-4
sentences, occasionally evaluative. 4:2 (Fall, 1980):81-104;
studies of individual writers, pp. 81-94.
YWES 78:217-18--"admirably comprehensive and up-to-date"

8/80   "Recent Articles" and "Foreign Reviews." In The Scriblerian and
the Kit-Cats, 1 (1968/69)--.
2/yr. Covers Gay, Pope, Swift, and Addison and Steele (the latter from
4:2 [Spring, 1972]), as well as the minor figures of their circles.
YWES 78:237

8/81   Barker, Arthur E. Seventeenth Century: Bacon through Marvell.
Arlington Heights, Ill.: AHM, 1979. (Goldentree Bibls.) 132 pp.
Nearly 2400 unannotated entries, most concerned with writers. Lists
books and arts., in English.

MiltonQ 14 (1980):69

8/82   Bond, Donald F. <u>The</u> <u>Age</u> <u>of</u> <u>Dryden</u>.   N. Y.: Appleton-Century-
       Crofts, 1970.   (Goldentree Bibls.)   103 pp.

8/83   Bond, Donald F. <u>The</u> <u>Eighteenth</u> <u>Century</u>.   N. Y.: AHM, 1975.
       (Goldentree Bibls.)   180 pp.
Books and arts., in English.   2916 entries in classified order, incl.
       2000+ on authors.   Indexes of scholars and of subjects.

• REVIEW of RESEARCH •

8/84   [Review articles on various topics.]   In <u>Philological</u> <u>Quarterly</u>,
       55 (1976)--.
In issue no. 4 (Fall).   Usually 4 or 5 essays; topics have varied, but
       have covered forms (drama, fiction, criticism) and periods (Res-
       toration, Augustan, Age of Johnson).
YWES 77:210; 78:217

• AUTHORS •

8/85   Latt, David J. and Samuel Holt Monk.   <u>John</u> <u>Dryden</u>: <u>A</u> <u>Survey</u> <u>and</u>
       <u>Bibliography</u> <u>of</u> <u>Critical</u> <u>Studies</u>, <u>1895-1974</u>.   Minneapolis: U. of
       Minnesota Pr., 1976.   199 pp.
Revision by Latt of a bibl. by Monk, publ. 1950.   Books, arts. and diss.
       in classified order, with many cross-refs. and with indexes.
YWES 76:190-91; ES 60 (1979):796-97x

8/86   Zamonski, John A.   <u>An</u> <u>Annotated</u> <u>Bibliography</u> <u>of</u> <u>John</u> <u>Dryden</u>: <u>Texts</u>
       <u>and</u> <u>Studies</u>, <u>1949-1973</u>.   N. Y. & London: Garland, 1975.   147 pp.
Classified arrangement, incl. a lengthy section on his works.
ES 60 (1979):795-96x

8/87   Montgomery, Guy, Mary Jackman and Helen S. Agoa.   <u>Concordance</u> <u>to</u>

the Poetical Works of John Dryden. Berkeley: U. of California Pr.,
    1957. 722 pp.
No context.

8/88 "Abstracts." In Milton Quarterly, 1 (1967)--.
In most issues. Arts. in English only. 15:2 (May, 1981):70-71. 14
    abstracts. 1 (1967)-3 (1969) called Milton Newsletter.

8/89 Hanford, James Holley and William A. McQueen. Milton. Arlington
    Heights, Ill.: AHM, 1979. (Goldentree Bibls.) 111 pp.
Rev. ed. 1st ed. 1966. 1650 entries, in classified order. Books and
    arts., chiefly in English. Paradise Lost: nearly 250 entries, by
    scholar. Some very brief notes.
MiltonQ 14 (1980):68-69

8/90 Stevens, David Harrison. Reference Guide to Milton, from 1800 to
    the Present Day. Chicago: U. of Chicago Pr., 1930. 302 pp.
Suppl. by Harris F. Fletcher, Contributions to a Milton Bibliography,
    1800-1930. . . , Urbana: U. of Illinois, 1931, 166 pp.

8/91 Huckabay, Calvin. John Milton: An Annotated Bibliography, 1929-
    1968. Pittsburgh: Duquesne U. Pr., 1969. 392 pp.
2nd ed. 1st ed. 1960. 3932 entries, in classified order. Books, book
    revs., arts. and chiefly U. S. diss. Nearly all entries in
    English. Many very brief annotations.
YWES 69:231--v unfav; SN 42 (1970):471-73--inaccurate and inconsistent

8/92 A Milton Encyclopedia. Lewisburg, Pa.: Bucknell U. Pr./London:
    Associated U. Pr., 1978--.
William B. Hunter, gen. ed. 8 vols. to date, A through Z. 9th vol.
    planned, to contain bibls. Signed arts. on names (characters, con-
    temporaries, and earlier and later writers), etc. Angels: 6 cols.;
    Envy: 2 1/2 cols.; Shelley: 5 1/2 cols.
MiltonQ 12 (1978):110-11; 14 (1980):25-27; 15 (1981):62-64; YWES 78:

202-03

8/93 Ingram, William and Kathleen Swaim. A Concordance to Milton's
      English Poetry. Oxford: Clarendon Pr., 1972. 683 pp.
See also Gladys W. Hudson, Paradise Lost: A Concordance, Detroit: Gale,
      1970, 361 pp.
YWES 70:238

8/94 Tobin, James E. Alexander Pope: A List of Critical Studies Pub-
      lished from 1895 to 1944. N. Y.: Cosmopolitan Science and Art
      Service Co., 1945. 30 pp.
414 entries.

8/95 Lopez, Cecilia L. Alexander Pope: An Annotated Bibliography, 1945-
      1967. Gainesville: U. of Florida Pr., 1970. 154 pp.
682 annotated entries, in classified order. Index of names (subjects
      and scholars) and titles of Pope's works.
YWES 70:265--"appallingly casual" about details

8/96 Bedford, Emmett G. and Robert J. Dilligan. A Concordance to the
      Poems of Alexander Pope. Detroit: Gale, 1976.
2 vols.

8/97 Hannaford, Richard Gordon. Samuel Richardson: An Annotated Bibli-
      ography of Critical Studies. N.Y.& London: Garland, 1980. 292 pp.
1460 entries, briefly annotated. Suppl. list of U. S. and foreign diss.
      Indexes of scholars and of subjects.

8/98 Hartley, Lodwick. Laurence Sterne in the Twentieth Century: An
      Essay and a Bibliography of Sternean Studies, 1900-1965. Chapel
      Hill: U. of North Carolina Pr., 1966. 189 pp.
Books and arts. in English and other langs., by scholar. Brief annota-
      tions. Index of names (scholars and subjects).

8/99 Hartley, Lodwick. Laurence Sterne: An Annotated Bibliography,
      1965-1977, with an Introductory Essay-Review of the Scholarship.
      Boston: Hall, 1978. 103 pp.
409 entries, in 5 sections, incl. IV: Criticism, subdivided by work, and
      V: Literary Influence and Reputation.

8/100 Landa, Louis A. and James E. Tobin. Jonathan Swift: A List of
       Critical Studies Published from 1895 to 1945. N. Y.: Cosmopolitan
       Science and Art Service Co., 1945. 62 pp.
573 entries. 115 on Gulliver's Travels.

8/101 Stathis, James J. A Bibliography of Swift Studies, 1945-1965.
       Nashville, Tenn.: Vanderbilt U. Pr., 1967. 110 pp.
659 entries, in classified order. More than 170 entries on Gulliver's
       Travels.
MLR 64 (1969):401x

8/102 Campbell, Hilbert H. James Thomson, 1700-1748: An Annotated Bib-
       liography of Selected Editions and the Important Criticism. N. Y.
       & London: Garland, 1976. 157 pp.
605 entries. Books and arts. in English and other langs., and U. S.
       diss. and M. A. theses. Index of names (subjects and scholars).

● ROMANTIC MOVEMENT ●

8/103 The Romantic Movement: A Selective and Critical Bibliography.
       (See 1/167 and 1/168)

8/104 "Current Bibliography." In Keats-Shelley Journal: A Periodical
       Devoted to Keats, Shelley, Byron, Hunt and Their Circles, 1
       (1952)--.
30 (1981):221-65. 438 entries for eds. and transls. into various lang.,
       and for books, arts., and diss. as found in DAI. Brief annota-
       tions. Cites book revs. Sections on the authors, with index of

names (subjects and scholars) and titles as subjects.
The annotations in The Romantic Movement may be longer than the ones
    here, but occasionally this comments on a title not annotated in
    the other. This lists a number of items not in The Romantic Move-
    ment (1/167 - 1/168).
YWES 78:287

8/105 Keats, Shelley, Byron, Hunt and Their Circles: A Bibliography,
    July 1, 1950-June 30, 1962. Lincoln: U. of Nebraska Pr., 1964.
    323 pp.
David Bonnell Green and Edwin Graves Wilson, eds. Index of names (sub-
    jects and scholars) and titles or first lines. Reprints the first
    12 installments of 8/104.

8/106 Keats, Shelley, Byron, Hunt and Their Circles: A Bibliography,
    July 1, 1962-December 31, 1974. Lincoln: U. of Nebraska Pr., 1978.
    487 pp.
Robert A. Hartley, ed. Index of names (subjects and scholars) and
    titles and first lines.
YES 11 (1981):304-05--regrets lack of index to general subjects

8/107 Reiman, Donald H. English Romantic Poetry, 1800-1835: A Guide to
    Information Sources. Detroit: Gale, 1979. 294 pp.
8 sections, incl. 1 each on the 5 major poets, divided and subdivided.
    Annotated. Indexes incl. subject index.
N&Q ns 28 (1981):439-40x

• REVIEWS of RESEARCH •

8/108 Jordan, Frank, ed. The English Romantic Poets: A Review of Re-
    search and Criticism. N. Y.: MLA, 1972. 468 pp.
3rd ed. 1st ed. by Thomas M. Raysor, 1950. Covers Wordsworth, Cole-
    ridge, Byron, Shelley and Keats.
YWES 72:304

8/109 Houtchens, Carolyn W. and Lawrence H. Houtchens, eds. The En-
     glish Romantic Poets and Essayists: A Review of Research and Crit-
     icism. N. Y.: MLA, 1966. 395 pp.
Rev. ed. 1st ed. 1957. Covers Blake, Carlyle, Scott and others.

• AUTHORS •

8/110 "Blake and His Circle: A Checklist of Recent Scholarship." In
     Blake: An Illustrated Quarterly,
In issue no. 2 (Fall). 15 (1981/82):83-93. 233 entries for books, book
     revs. and arts., as well as exhibition catalogs and diss. as found
     in DAI. Some brief notes. Incl. more than 100 studies of Blake.

8/111 Bentley, Gerald E., Jr. A Blake Bibliography: Annotated Lists of
     Works, Studies and Blakeana. Minneapolis: U. of Minnesota Pr./Ox-
     ford: Oxford U. Pr., 1964. 393 pp.
Section VI: Biography and Criticism, pp. 215-360, entries 604-2197, by
     scholar. Index, incl. names and Blake's works as subjects.

8/112 Damon, Samuel Foster. A Blake Dictionary: The Ideas and Symbols
     of William Blake. Providence, R. I.: Brown U. Pr., 1965. 460 pp.
Usually brief arts. London: 3 cols., plus 1 1/3 cols. on related sub-
     jects. Reprinted, with a new 70 pp. index, by Boulder, Colo.:
     Shambala (distr. by N. Y.: Random House), 1979.
BlakeN 14 (1980/81):131-35; MLR 65 (1970):153-55

8/113 Erdman, David V. A Concordance to the Writings of William Blake.
     Ithaca, N. Y.: Cornell U. Pr., 1967.
2 vols. 2317 pp.
MLR 65 (1970) 155x

8/114 Santucho, Oscar José. George Gordon, Lord Byron: A Comprehensive
     Bibliography of Secondary Materials in English, 1807-1974. Metu-
     chen, N. J.: Scarecrow, 1977. 641 pp.

"A Critical Review of Research," by Clement Tyson Goode, Jr., pp. 1-166.
    The bibl. is arranged chronologically, occasionally briefly anno-
    tated, and indexed by scholar.
YWES 77:266; YES 10 (1980):300-01

8/115 Young, Ione Dodson. A Concordance to the Poetry of Byron. Aus-
    tin, Texas: Pendleton Pr., 1965.
4 vols. 1698 pp.

8/116 Hagelman, Charles W. and Robert J. Barnes. A Concordance to By-
    ron's Don Juan. Ithaca, N. Y.: Cornell U. Pr., 1967. 981 pp.

8/117 "Coleridge Scholarship: An Annual Register." In Wordsworth
    Circle, 4 (1973)--.
Review essay surveying books and arts. In issue no. 3 (Summer).

8/118 Caskey, Jefferson D. and Melinda M. Stapper. Samuel Taylor Cole-
    ridge: A Selective Bibliography of Criticism, 1935-1977. Westport,
    Conn.: Greenwood Pr., 1978. 174 pp.
2054 entries. 11 sections of criticism of major individual works, en-
    tries 1-655. Occasional brief notes.

8/119 Logan, (Sister) Eugenia. A Concordance to the Poetry of Samuel
    Taylor Coleridge. St Mary-of-the-Woods, Ind.: n. p., 1940. 901
    pp.

8/120 MacGillivray, James R. Keats: A Bibliography and Reference Guide,
    with an Essay on Keats' Reputation. Toronto: U. of Toronto Pr.,
    1949. 210 pp.
80 pp. separately paged survey of Keats criticism.

8/121 Becker, Michael G., et al. A Concordance to the Poems of John
    Keats. N. Y.: Garland, 1981. 719 pp.

8/122 Dunbar, Clement. A Bibliography of Shelley Studies, 1823-1950.
       N. Y.: Garland, 1976. 320 pp.
3271 numbered entries, by year of publ. No subject index.
YWES 76:236

8/123 Ellis, Frederick Startridge. A Lexical Concordance to the Poeti-
       cal Works of Percy Bysshe Shelley: An Attempt to Classify Every
       Word Found Therein According to Its Signification. London: Quar-
       itch, 1892. 818 pp.

8/124 "Wordsworth Scholarship: An Annual Register." In Wordsworth and
       His Circle, 4 (1973)--.
In issue no. 3 (Summer). A review essay surveying books and arts.

8/125 Logan, James V. Wordsworthian Criticism: A Guide and Bibliog-
       raphy. Columbus: Ohio St. U., 1947. 304 pp.
I: Trends in Criticism, pp. 3-153; II: Bibliography, incl. books and
       arts., 1850-1944, by year of publ., pp. 167-275. Indexes incl.
       names (subjects and scholars): Wordsworth: 4+ cols., subdivided by
       topic, incl. titles of his works. The 2nd ed., 1961, was unre-
       vised.

8/126 Henley, Elton F. and D. H. Stam. Wordsworthian Criticism, 1945-
       1964: An Annotated Bibliography. N. Y.: New York Public Library,
       1965. 107 pp.
Rev. ed. 1st ed. 1960. 643 entries, by year of publ. Index of names,
       incl. subjects, and titles of Wordsworth's works.

8/127 Stam, David H. Wordsworthian Criticism, 1964-1973: An Annotated
       Bibliography, Including Additions to Wordsworthian Criticism,
       1945-1964. N. Y.: New York Public Library and Readex Books, 1974.
       116 pp.
More than 550 entries.
YWES 74:361

8/128 Cooper, Lane. A Concordance to the Poems of William Wordsworth.
       London: Smith, Elder, 1911. 1136 pp.

● MID-19th CENTURY ●

● BIBLIOGRAPHIES ●

8/129 "Victorian Bibliography for [year]." In Victorian Studies, 1
       (1958/59)--.
In issue no. 4 (June). Covers British history and culture of the latter
       2/3 of the 19th c. 23 (1980):531-609, for 1979. Classified and
       annotated. Section V: literary history; VI: studies of authors.
       Lists books and book revs., and arts., largely in English, and
       diss. as found in DAI. Orig. appeared in Modern Philology 30
       (1932/33)-54 (1956/57), but collected in next 4 entries.

8/130 Templeman, William D., ed. Bibliographies of Studies in Victo-
       rian Literature for the Thirteen Years 1932-1944. Urbana: U. of
       Illinois Pr., 1945. 450 pp.

8/131 Wright, Austin, ed. Bibliographies of Studies in Victorian
       Literature for the Ten Years 1945-1954. Urbana: U. of Illinois
       Pr., 1956. 310 pp.

8/132 Slack, Robert C., ed. Bibliographies of Studies of Victorian
       Literature for the Ten Years 1955-1964. Urbana: U. of Illinois
       Pr., 1967. 461 pp.

8/133 Freeman, Ronald E., ed. Bibliographies of Studies in Victorian
       Literature for the Ten Years 1965-1974. N. Y.: AMS, 1981. 876
       pp.
These 4 books collect the bibls. from 8/129, with cumulated indexes.
       The index in 8/130 is of names as subjects; the other 3 have in-
       dexes of names, incl. scholars and subjects, and other subjects.

The index in 8/133 is particularly detailed.

8/134 Buckley, Jerome H. Victorian Poets and Prose Writers. Arlington
        Heights, Ill.: AHM, 1978. (Goldentree Bibls.) 96 pp.
2nd ed. 1st ed. 1966.

• POETRY •

8/135 "A Guide to the Year's Work in Victorian Poetry." In Victorian
        Poetry, 1 (1963)--.
In issue no. 3 (Autumn). 18 (1980):241-92. 10 essays covering books
        and arts., largely or entirely in English, on poets, incl. Brow-
        ning, Hopkins and Tennyson, on several groups or schools, and on
        general topics.

8/136 Faverty, Frederic E., ed. Victorian Poets: A Guide to Research.
        Cambridge, Mass.: Harvard U. Pr., 1968. 423 pp.
2nd ed. 1st ed. 1956. 11 chapters, covering Tennyson, Browning, Hop-
        kins and others.

• FICTION •

8/137 Watt, Ian. The British Novel: Scott through Hardy. Northbrook,
        Ill.: AHM, 1973. (Goldentree Bibls.) 134 pp.

8/138 Stevenson, Lionel, ed. Victorian Fiction: A Guide to Research.
        Cambridge, Mass.: Harvard U. Pr., 1964. 440 pp.
12 chapters on the Brontës, Eliot, Dickens, Thackeray and others.
YWES 64:310; MLR 62 (1967):120-21

8/139 Ford, George H., ed. Victorian Fiction: A Second Guide to Re-
        search. N. Y.: MLA, 1978. 401 pp.
A continuation of Stevenson. 70+ pp. on Dickens.
YWES 78:311

• PROSE •

8/140 DeLaura, David J., ed. Victorian Prose: A Guide to Research.
       N. Y.: MLA, 1973. 560 pp.
Reviews of research on the Carlyles, Newman, Ruskin and others.
YWES 73:355; RES ns 26 (1975):238-39

• AUTHORS •

8/141 "Robert and Elizabeth Barrett Browning: An Annotated Bibliog-
       raphy." In Browning Institute Studies, 1 (1973)--.
Annual. Covers from 1971. 8 (1980):177-86, for 1978. 106 entries, for
       books, book revs., arts. and diss. from DAI. Descriptive annota-
       tions. Index of names (subjects and scholars), titles of the
       Brownings' works, and a few other topics. See also "A Checklist
       of Publications" in Studies in Browning and His Circle, 1 (1973)--.

8/142 Broughton, Leslie Nathan, Clark S. Northrup and Robert Pearsall.
       Robert Browning: A Bibliography, 1830-1950. Ithaca, N. Y.: Cor-
       nell U. Pr./London: Oxford U. Pr., 1953. 446 pp.

8/143 Peterson, William S. Robert and Elizabeth Barrett Browning: An
       Annotated Bibliography, 1951-1970. N. Y.: The Browning Inst.,
       1974. 209 pp.
Section C: Biography, Criticism and Miscellaneous, pp. 39-180. Books,
       book revs. and arts., mostly in English. Cites diss., incl. MA
       theses. Arranged by year of publ., with indexes of the Brownings'
       works and other subjects, incl. names, and of scholars.

8/144 Broughton, Leslie Nathan and Benjamin F. Stelter. A Concordance
       to the Poems of Robert Browning. N.Y.: Stechert, 1924-25. 2 vols.

8/145 Hudson, Gladys W. An Elizabeth Barrett Browning Concordance.
       Detroit: Gale, 1973. 4 vols. 2074 pp.

8/146 Gold, Joseph. The Stature of Dickens: A Centenary Bibliography.
       Toronto: U. of Toronto Pr., for the U. of Manitoba Pr., 1971. 236
       pp.
General studies, pp. 3-114, by year of publ.; studies of his works, pp.
       115-202, by work and year of publ. Index of scholars. Cites
       books and arts. in various langs.

8/147 Fenstermaker, John J. Charles Dickens, 1940-1975: An Analytical
       Subject Index to Periodical Criticism of the Novels and Christmas
       Books. Boston: Hall, 1979. 302 pp.
English-lang. arts. only. Classified arrangement.

8/148 "Recent Studies on Dickens: [years]." In Dickens Studies Annual:
       Essays on Victorian Fiction, 8 (1980)--.
8(1980):299-324. Surveys of research on other novelists will be publ.
       at intervals: 8 (1980): surveys of Thackeray and Eliot studies.

8/149 Dunn, Richard J. David Copperfield: An Annotated Bibliography.
       N. Y.: Garland, 1981. (Garland Dickens Bibls., 8) 256 pp.
Not seen.

● LATE 19th CENTURY and AFTER ●

• FICTION •

8/150 Wiley, Paul L. The British Novel: Conrad to the Present. North-
       brook, Ill.: AHM, 1973. (Goldentree Bibls.) 137 pp.
44 novelists, Bennett to Woolf. Joyce: pp. 65-71, appr. 130 entries.

8/151 [Bibliographies on various topics.] In Modern Fiction Studies,
       1 (1955)--.
Issues no. 1 (Spring) and 3 (Autumn) are devoted to a special subject,
       usually an author, usually British or American, and incl. a bibl.
       26:1 (Spring, 1980): "Criticism of Doris Lessing: A Selected

Checklist," pp. 167-75, in 11 sections, citing books and arts., in
English. 24:1 (Spring, 1978): "Studies of the Modern Novel and
the City: A Selected Checklist," pp. 147-53, with 3 pp. on American fiction, 1+ on European, 5 items on Latin American.

8/152 Adelman, Irving and Rita Dworkin. The Contemporary Novel: A
       Checklist of Critical Literature on the British and American Novel
       since 1945. Metuchen, N. J.: Scarecrow, 1972. 614 pp.
Covers novelists active since 1945 only, but incl. all the novels of the
       writers listed, whenever publ. Criticism from certain books and
       journals, by novelist and novel.

                            • AUTHORS •

8/153 Federman, Raymond and John Fletcher. Samuel Beckett: His Works
       and Critics: An Essay in Bibliography. See 4/84.

8/154 "Current JJ Checklist." In James Joyce Quarterly, 14:2 (Winter,
       1977)--.
In every issue. 19:1 (Fall, 1981):63-68. Chiefly a list of recent
       books and arts., by scholar. Also sections on eds., transls.,
       films., etc. Previously an annual bibl., "Supplemental JJ Bibli-
       ography," 1 (1963/64)-15 (1977/78).

8/155 Deming, Robert H. A Bibliography of James Joyce Studies. Boston:
       Hall, 1977. 264 pp.
5885 entries for books and arts. in English and various other langs.,
       diss., etc., in a classified arrangement. Section A3b: Joyce and
       other Writers--Comparisons and Contrasts: pp. 28-38, entries 609-
       817; Proust: 15 entries. Index of scholars. Cross-refs.
Review 2 (1980):185-87x

8/156 Hanley, Miles Lawrence. Word Index to James Joyce's Ulysses.
       Madison: U. of Wisconsin Pr., 1951. 392 pp.

No context. See also Leslie Hancock, Word Index to James Joyce's Por-
trait of the Artist, Carbondale: Southern Illinois U. Pr., 1967,
145 pp., and Wilhelm Füger, Concordance to James Joyce's Dub-
liners, with a Reverse Index, a Frequency List and a Conversion
Table, Hildesheim & N. Y.: Olms, 1980, 875 pp.

8/157 "Recent Criticism of Virginia Woolf." In Virginia Woolf Quarterly, 1 (1972/73)--.
In issue no. 1 (Fall). Gives abstracts.

8/158 Majumdar, Robin. Virginia Woolf: An Annotated Bibliography of
Criticism, 1915-1974. N. Y. & London: Garland, 1976. 118 pp.
638 entries, listing books and arts., mostly in English. Some brief annotations. Suppl. list of reviews of her books.

8/159 Jochum, K. P. S. W. B. Yeats: A Classified Bibliography of Criticism. Urbana: U. of Illinois Pr., 1978. 801 pp.
"The Irish Literary and Dramatic Revival," pp. 543-684. Brief annotations. Indexes incl. names, Yeats' works, and selected other subjects. Note also the brief (5 or 6 entries) annotated bibls. in
each issue of Yeats/Eliot Review (2/yr.).
N&Q ns 26 (1979):599--v fav; Review 1 (1979):233-36x; YWES 78:415-16

8/160 Parrish, Stephen M. A Concordance to the Poems of W. B. Yeats.
Ithaca, N. Y.: Cornell U. Pr., 1963. 968 pp.
MLR 59 (1964):285-86

8/161 Domville, Eric. A Concordance to the Plays of W. B. Yeats.
Ithaca, N. Y.: Cornell U. Pr, 1972.
2 vols. 1558 pp.

● ● ANGLO-IRISH LITERATURE ● ●

● BIBLIOGRAPHY ●

8/162 "Bibliographical Bulletin." In <u>Irish University Review</u>: <u>A Journal of Irish Studies</u>, 2 (1972)--.
In issue no. 2 (Autumn). 10 (1980):253-92, for 1979. Books, arts., and
chapters in books, in various langs., but chiefly English, in
classified order, chiefly by author studied. Incl. literary works
and eds. Compiled by the International Assn. for the Study of
Anglo-Irish Literature.

● REVIEW of RESEARCH ●

8/163 <u>Anglo-Irish Literature</u>: <u>A Review of Research</u>. N. Y.: MLA, 1976.
596 pp.
Richard J. Finneran, ed. Chapters on seven 20th c. writers, incl. Yeats
and Joyce, and 3 general chapters, incl. 1 on 19th c. writers.
YWES 76:370-71; IUR 10 (1980):300-02--v fav; LRN 2 (1977):187-89

● HANDBOOK ●

8/164 <u>Dictionary of Irish Literature</u>. Westport, Conn.: Greenwood Pr.,
1979. 815 pp.
Robert Hogan, ed. in chief. Arts. on writers and other topics. O'Casey:
10 1/2 pp.; Abbey Theatre: 10 pp. No entries on writers in Irish,
but a history of Gaelic literature, by Seamus O'Neill, pp. 17-64.
Chronology, 432 AD-1977, pp. 728-41. Index, mainly of names and
titles.

● ● SCOTTISH LITERATURE ● ●

● BIBLIOGRAPHY ●

8/165 Annual Bibliography of Scottish Literature. 1970--.
Annual. Covers from 1969.

● ● COMMONWEALTH LITERATURE ● ●

● BIBLIOGRAPHIES ●

8/166 "Annual Bibliography of Commonwealth Literature." In Journal of
      Commonwealth Literature, 1 (1965)--.
In issue no. 2 (December). 15:2 (Dec., 1980):5-175, in regional sec-
      tions. Covers Africa, in 3 parts, Australia, Canada, India, the
      West Indies, etc. Each section opens with an introductory essay
      noting the important publs. of the year. Lists literary works as
      well as criticism in books and journals.

8/167 Index to Commonwealth Little Magazines. 1966--.
Covers from 1964-65. Every other year, but irregular. 1974-1975, publ.
      1976, 491 pp. Covers literary journals from the British Isles,
      incl. the Republic of Ireland, and Africa and Australia. Indexes
      by author and subject.
LRN 3 (1978):186-88--the 1974-1975 vol.

8/168 New, William H. Critical Writings on Commonwealth Literatures.
      University Park: Pennsylvania State U. Pr., 1975. 333 pp.
Arranged by region and author. Books, arts. and passages in books, and
      U. S., European and Commonwealth diss. Index of scholars.

● HANDBOOK ●

8/169 Ferres, John H. and Martin Tucker. Modern Commonwealth Litera-

ture: A Library of Literary Criticism. N. Y.: Ungar, 1977. 561
pp.
Passages from books and arts., with exact citations to the originals.

● ● AFRICAN LITERATURE ● ●

● BIBLIOGRAPHIES ●

8/170 Lindfors, Bernth. Black African Literature in English: A Guide
    to Information Sources. Detroit: Gale, 1979. 477 pp.
Part 1: Genre and Topical Studies, pp. 3-240. 26 subsections. Part 2:
    Individual Authors, pp. 243-417, with many cross-refs. Lists
    books, arts. and U. S. and foreign diss. Occasional annotations.
    Indexes incl. subject and geographical indexes.
The standard current general bibliography of African studies is Inter-
    national African Bibliography: Current Books, Articles and Papers
    in African Studies, 1971--. The quarterly issues are arranged
    mostly by region or nation; they do not contain much on literature,
    and what there is is not easy to find. Annual index of scholars.
    This continues a bibl. publ. in Africa from 1929 to 1970, cumu-
    lated in Cumulative Bibliography of African Studies: Author Cata-
    logue [2 vols.] and Classified Catalogue [3 vols.], Boston: Hall,
    1973, which contains very little on literature. Africa South of
    the Sahara: Index to Periodical Literature, 1900-1970, by the
    Africa Section of the Library of Congress may also be useful for
    certain purposes (4 vols. and suppl., Boston: Hall, 1971).

8/171 Jahn, Janheinz and Claus P. Dressler. Bibliography of Creative
    African Writing. Millwood, N. Y.: Kraus-Thomson, 1973. 446 pp.
Literature and criticism by African writers, publ. as books, chiefly.
    Criticism and book reviews of works of African literature. Geo-
    graphic arrangement, with indexes, incl. index to African langs.

8/172 Baldwin, Claudia. Nigerian Literature: A Bibliography of Criti-

cism, 1952-1976. Boston: Hall, 1980. 147 pp.
1510 entries, nearly all listed under an author studied. Lists books
     and arts. in English or French and revs. of literary works but not
     of critical studies. Lists interviews. Indexes of scholars and
     of works.

• HANDBOOKS •

8/173 Jahn, Janheinz, Ulla Schild and Almut Nordmann. Who's Who in
       African Literature: Biographies, Works, Commentaries. Tübingen:
       Erdmann, 1972. 406 pp.
Brief entries, few longer than 1 p.

8/174 Herdeck, Donald E., et al. African Authors: A Companion to Black
       African Writing, 1300-1973. Rockville, Md.: Black Orpheus Pr.,
       1974. 605 pp.
"Vol. 1." No more publ. 2nd ed. 1st ed. 1973. Bio-bibliographies, pp.
     17-471, on 594 writers. Various appendixes and indexes.

• • AUSTRALIAN LITERATURE • •

• BIBLIOGRAPHIES •

8/175 Lock, Fred and Alan Lawson. Australian Literature: A Reference
       Guide. Melbourne: Oxford U. Pr., 1980. 120 pp.
New ed. 1st ed. 1977. List of reference sources, incl. bibls. on indi-
     vidual authors. Annotated.

8/176 "Annual Bibliography of Studies in Australian Literature." In
       Australian Literary Studies, 1 (1963/64)--.
In issue no. 3 (May). 9 (1980):346-62, for 1979. Lists books, book
     revs. and arts., incl. many from Australian newspapers and liter-
     ary magazines, by writer studied, with a general section.

• HISTORY •

8/177 Kramer, Leonie, ed. <u>Oxford</u> <u>History</u> <u>of</u> <u>Australian</u> <u>Literature</u>.
    Melbourne, etc.: Oxford U. Pr., 1981. 509 pp.
Bibl., pp. 429-90; bio-bibls. on authors, pp. 443-90. Text is in 3
    chapters: Fiction, Drama, Poetry.

● ● CANADIAN LITERATURE ● ●

• BIBLIOGRAPHIES •

8/178 <u>Canadian</u> <u>Essay</u> <u>and</u> <u>Literature</u> <u>Index</u>. 1975--.
Annual. Covers 1973--. Lists. arts. in periodicals and certain books.
    Incl. literary works as well as criticism. None publ. since 1977.

8/179 Gnarowski, Michael. <u>A</u> <u>Concise</u> <u>Bibliography</u> <u>of</u> <u>English</u>-<u>Canadian</u>
    <u>Literature</u>. Toronto: McClelland & Stewart, 1973. 127 pp.
Lists books by Canadian authors, with reviews, and "selected studies
    and articles."

8/180 Watters, Reginald Eyre. <u>On</u> <u>Canadian</u> <u>Literature</u>, <u>1806</u>-<u>1960</u>: <u>A</u>
    <u>Checklist</u> <u>of</u> <u>Articles</u>, <u>Books</u> <u>and</u> <u>Theses</u> <u>on</u> <u>English</u> <u>Canadian</u> <u>Liter</u>-
    <u>ature</u>, <u>Its</u> <u>Authors</u> <u>and</u> <u>Language</u>. Toronto: U. of Toronto Pr.,
    1966. 165 pp.
Part I: 14 sections of general studies. Part II, pp. 71-165: studies of
    authors.

8/181 Lecker, Robert and Jack David. <u>The</u> <u>Annotated</u> <u>Bibliography</u> <u>of</u>
    <u>Canada's</u> <u>Major</u> <u>Authors</u>. Boston: Hall, 1980--.
I: Atwood (Prose), Laurence, MacLennan, Richler, Roy. 1980. 262 pp.
    II: Atwood (Poetry), Cohen, Lampman, Pratt, Purdy. 1981. Lists
    works (incl. periodical publs.) and studies.
UTQ 50 (1980/81):155-56

• HANDBOOKS •

8/182 Story, Norah. The Oxford Companion to Canadian History and Liter-
       ture. Toronto, etc.: Oxford U. Pr., 1967. 935 pp.
Brief biographical arts., few more than 1 p. Lengthy survey arts., e. g.
       "Fiction in English," 15 pp. Index of titles. Incl. literature
       in French.

8/183 Toye, William, ed. Supplement to the Oxford Companion to Cana-
       dian History and Literature. Toronto, etc.: Oxford U. Pr., 1973.
       318 pp.
Mainly covers literature. "Fiction in English," 11 1/2 pp.
MLR 64 (1969):160-61

8/184 Sylvestre, Guy, Brandon Conron and Carl F. Klinck, eds. Écrivains
       canadiens/Canadian Writers: Un Dictionnaire biographique/A Bio-
       graphical Dictionary. Montréal: HMH, 1966. 186 pp.
New ed. 1st ed. 1964. Brief arts. in English or French. Chronological
       table, 1606-1965, pp. ix-xviii.

• HISTORIES •

8/185 Klinck, Carl F., ed. Literary History of Canada: Canadian Liter-
       ature in English. Toronto & Buffalo: U. of Toronto Pr., 1976.
2nd ed. 1st ed. 1965. 3 vols.
RES ns 28 (1977):508-09--v fav

8/186 Tougas, Gérard. La Littérature canadienne-française. Paris: PUF:
       1974. 270 pp.
5th ed. 1st ed. 1960. The 2nd ed. was transl. by Alto Lind Cook: His-
       tory of French-Canadian Literature, Toronto: Ryerson Pr., 1966,
       301 pp.

● ● CARIBBEAN LITERATURE ● ●

● BIBLIOGRAPHIES ●

8/187 Allis, Jeannette B. West Indian Literature: An Index to Criti-
       cism, 1930-1975. Boston: Hall, 1981. 353 pp.
Part I: studies in English of authors and their works, pp. 1-183. Part
       II: the studies from part I listed by their author, pp. 185-305.
WLWE 20 (1981):335-36

8/188 Bandara, Samuel B. "A Checklist of Theses and Dissertations in
       English on Caribbean Literature." In World Literature Written in
       English 20 (1981):319-34.
U. S., Canadian, British and West Indian diss., by scholar.

● HANDBOOK ●

8/189 Caribbean Writers: A Bio-bibliographical-critical Encyclopedia.
       Washington, D. C.: Three Continents, 1979. 943 pp.
Donald E. Herdeck, ed. English, French, Spanish and Dutch-lang. writers,
       by language., and much information on related topics. Most entries
       1-3 paragraphs. Derek Walcott: 9 cols., plus 3 cols. bibl.
RHL 81 (1981):852x

● ● AMERICAN LITERATURE ● ●

● BIBLIOGRAPHIES ●

8/190 Gohdes, Clarence L. F. Bibliographical Guide to the Study of the
       Literature of the U.S.A. Durham, N.C.: Duke U. Pr., 1976. 173 pp.
4th ed. 1st ed. 1959. Classified list of reference works and studies,
       usually books, with brief notes, sometimes evaluative. No entries
       on individual authors.
YES 10 (1980):229-31--v unfav

8/191 "Articles on American Literature Appearing in Current Period-
        icals." In American Literature, 1 (1929/30)--.
In every issue (4/yr.) Usually 12-17 pp., by subject, chiefly authors.

8/192 Leary, Lewis G. Articles on American Literature, 1900-1950.
        Durham, N. C: Duke U. Pr., 1954. 437 pp.

8/193 Leary, Lewis G. Articles on American Literature, 1950-1967.
        Durham, N. C.: Duke U. Pr., 1970. 751 pp.

8/194 Leary, Lewis G. and John Auchard. Articles on American Litera-
        ture, 1968-1975. Durham, N. C.: Duke U. Pr., 1979. 745 pp.
Classified arrangement. Appr. 3/4 of each vol. is devoted to studies of
        authors. General studies listed under 25 broad headings, incl.
        Foreign Influences and Estimates, Literary Trends and Attitudes,
        and Social and Political Aspects, all arranged by scholar, without
        subdivisions. Articles may be listed under two headings, if appro-
        priate, though this could be done more often. No indexes. Lists
        British and European studies, but coverage of foreign-lang. publs.
        was not systematic before the 1950s, and therefore this is only a
        partial suppl. to the MLA Bibl. before 1956 in this respect.
HJR 1 (1979/80):267-68--finds "too many" errors, incl. failure to make
        cross-refs.

● REVIEWS of RESEARCH ●

8/195 American Literary Scholarship: An Annual. 1965--.
Covers from 1963--. 1979, publ. 1981. 574 pp., in 22 chapters, incl.
        10 on a writer or a pair of writers, the others on periods, genres,
        or other topics. Poe: 12 pp. Whitman and Dickinson: 18 pp. Fic-
        tion, 1900 to the 1930s: 21 pp., but Faulkner and Fitzgerald and
        Hemingway are covered in 2 separate chapters totalling 44 pp.
        Number and contents of chapters has varied. Evaluates in some-
        times pungent terms books, arts. and chapters in books.

8/196 Leary, Lewis G. American Literature: A Study and Research Guide.
       N. Y.: St. Martin's Pr., 1976.   185 pp.
Bibl. essays surveying research. "Studies in Genre," pp. 28-39; "Major
       Writers," pp. 70-134.
AmLS 76:401

● DISSERTATIONS ●

8/197 Woodress, James, with Marian Koritz. Dissertations in American
       Literature, 1891-1966. Durham, N. C.: Duke U. Pr., 1968.   185 pp.
Rev. ed. 1st ed 1957. 4631 entries, in classified order, with more
       than half devoted to authors. Cross-refs. A more readable page
       than McNamee (8/5), and lists French and Scandinavian diss. among
       its coverage of European diss. Like McNamee, diss. are listed
       once only, with too few cross-refs.; for instance, the sections on
       themes in general do not give cross-refs. to studies of the theme
       in individual writers.

● HANDBOOKS ●

8/198 Hart, James D. The Oxford Companion to American Literature.
       N. Y.: Oxford U. Pr., 1965.   991 pp.
4th ed. 1st ed. 1941. Brief arts. of writers, books, literary journals
       and groups, etc. Chronology, pp. 961-91.

8/199 Dictionary of Literary Biography. Detroit: Gale, 1978--.
Lengthy signed entries, with bibls. of works and studies and notes on
       manuscript repositories. Illustrated.
1:     The American Renaissance in New England. 1978.   224 pp.
2:     American Novelists since World War II. 1978.   555 pp.
3:     Antebellum Writers in New York and the South. 1979.   383 pp.
Melville: 21 pp. of text, emphasizing biography, and 3 1/2 pp. bibl.
PoeS 14 (1981):18-19
4:     American Writers in Paris, 1920-1939. 1980.   426 pp.

5:     American Poets since World War II. 1980. 2 vols.
AL 53 (1981):161-62
6:     American Novelists since World War II: Second Series. 1980. 404 pp.
7:     Twentieth-Century American Dramatists. 1981. 2 vols.
9:     American Novelists, 1910-1945. 1981. 3 vols.

● HISTORIES ●

8/200 Literary History of the United States. N. Y.: Macmillan/London:
       Collier-Macmillan, 1974.
Robert E. Spiller, et al., eds. 4th ed. 1st ed. 1948. 2 vols. I:
       History. 1556 pp. II: Bibliography. 1466 pp. Changes in the
       history vol. for the 4th ed. are a new chapter on Dickinson and
       new or revised chapters on literature since 1945. The bibl. vol.
       consists of the orig. bibl. and 2 suppls.
RES ns 28 (1977):363-66

8/201 Spiller, Robert E. The Cycle of American Literature: An Essay In
       Historical Criticism. N. Y.: Macmillan, 1955. 318 pp.

8/202 Cunliffe, Marcus. The Literature of the United States. Balti-
       more: Penguin, 1967. 409 pp.
3rd ed. 1st ed. 1954. Bulk of book deals with 19th c. writers.

● BLACK WRITERS ●

8/203 Inge, M. Thomas, Jackson R. Bryer and Maurice Duke, eds. Black
       American Writers: Bibliographical Essays. N. Y.: St Martin's Pr.,
       1978.
2 vols. I: The Beginnings through the Harlem Renaissance and Langston
       Hughes. 217 pp. II: Wright, Ellison, Baldwin, Baraka. 187 pp.
AmLS 76:382-83--valuable, but vol. 1 uneven; YWES 78:428

● FICTION ●

8/204 Gerstenberger, Donna and George Hendrick. The American Novel,
       1789-1959: A Checklist of Twentieth-Century Criticism. Denver:
       Swallow, 1961. 333 pp.
Suppl., covering criticism of 1960-68, 1970, 459 pp. Lists criticism in
       journals and certain books, by novelist and novel.

● DRAMA ●

8/205 Eddleman, Floyd E. American Drama Criticism: Interpretations,
       1890-1977. Hamden, Conn., Shoe String Pr., 1979. 488 pp.
2nd ed. 1st ed. 1967, by Helen H. Palmer. Lists criticism from journals
       and certain books, by playwright and play.

● BEFORE 1900 ●

● REVIEWS of RESEARCH ●

8/206 Eight American Authors: A Review of Research and Criticism.
       N. Y.: Norton, 1971. 392 pp.
Rev. ed., by James Woodress, et al. 1st ed. 1956, by Floyd Stovall, ed.
       Covers Emerson, Hawthorne, James, Melville, Poe, Thoreau, Twain
       and Whitman. Whitman, by Roger Asselineau, 48 pp., in 8 sections;
       VI: Criticism, 19 pp. in 7 subdivisions, incl. one on the influ-
       ences on him. Also a section on research on his influence.

8/207 Rees, Robert A. and Earl N. Harbert, eds. Fifteen American Au-
       thors before 1900: Bibliographic Essays on Research and Criticism.
       Madison: U. of Wisconsin Pr., 1971. 442 pp.
Stephen Crane, Dickinson, and others. Incl. several 18th c. writers and
       2 surveys of southern literature.

• FICTION •

8/208 Holman, Clarence Hugh. The American Novel through Henry James.
    Arlington Heights, Ill.: AHM, 1979. 177 pp.
2nd ed. 1st ed. 1966. Cooper: pp. 31-37, 110+ entries.

• AUTHORS •

8/209 Buckingham, Willis J., ed. Emily Dickinson: An Annotated Bibli-
    ography: Writings, Scholarship, Criticism and Ana, 1850-1968.
    Bloomington & London: Indiana U. Pr., 1970. 322 pp.
English-lang. studies by form of publ. Foreign-lang. studies by lang.
    Incl. U. S. and European diss. Indexes incl. her poems, and
    scholars and subjects, incl. names and topics.
Note also the bibl. "Emily Dickinson: Annual Bibliography for [year],"
    in Dickinson Studies (orig. Emily Dickinson Newsletter). 40
    (June, 1981):71-85. Brief annotations.
AmLS 70:70-71--"impressively complete, accurate and usable"

8/210 Rosenbaum, Stanford Patrick. A Concordance to the Poems of Emily
    Dickinson. Ithaca, N. Y.: Cornell U. Pr., 1964. 899 pp.

8/211 "James Studies [years]: An Analytical Bibliographical Essay." In
    Henry James Review, 2 (1980/81)--.
2 (1980/81):132-52, covering 1978-79. A review of research.

8/212 McColgan, Kristin Pruitt. Henry James, 1917-1959: A Reference
    Guide. Boston: Hall, 1979. 389 pp.
By year of publ. Annotated. Suppl. list of diss., incl. British and
    European diss. Index, incl. scholars and titles of his works.
YES 11 (1981):339; AmLS 79:93-94--v fav

8/213 Scura, Dorothy McInnis. Henry James, 1960-1974: A Reference
    Guide. Boston: Hall, 1979. 490 pp.

YES 11 (1981):339; AmLS 79:93-94--v fav

8/214 Boswell, Jeanetta. Herman Melville and the Critics: A Checklist
    of Criticism, 1900-1978. Metuchen, N. J.: Scarecrow, 1981.
    pp.
By scholar, with index of Melville's works and other subjects.

8/215 Ricks, Beatrice and Joseph D. Adams. Herman Melville: A Refer-
    ence Bibliography, 1900-1972, with Selected Nineteenth-Century
    Materials. Boston: Hall, 1973. 532 pp.
AmLS 73:66--v unfav, esp. as regards the annotations and inaccuracy of
    citations

8/216 Cohen, Hennig and James Cahalan. A Concordance to Melville's
    Moby Dick. N. p.: Melville Soc., 1978. (Distr. by Ann Arbor: UMI)
3 vols.
AmLS 78:44-45--critical of choice of text

8/217 "Current Poe Bibliography." In Poe Studies, 2 (1969)--.
In issue no. 2 (December). 13 (1980):29-34. Early vols. called Poe
    Newsletter.

8/218 Dameron, J. Lasley. Edgar Allan Poe: A Bibliography of Criti-
    cism, 1827-1967. Charlottesville: U. Pr. of Virginia, for the
    Bibliographical Soc. of the U. of Virginia, 1974. 386 pp.
English-lang. criticism by scholar, pp. 1-276. Foreign-lang. criticism
    by scholar, pp. 279-353. Brief annotations. Index.
AmLS 74:33-34

8/219 Hyneman, Esther F. Edgar Allan Poe: An Annotated Bibliography of
    Books and Articles in English, 1827-1973. Boston: Hall, 1974.
    335 pp.
Pp. 170-251: criticism, 1900-1973, on individual works, by work studied.
AmLS 74:33-34

8/220 Booth, Bradford Allen and Claude E. Jones. A Concordance of the
       Poetical Works of Edgar Allan Poe. Baltimore: Johns Hopkins Pr.,
       1941. 211 pp.

8/221 Tenney, Thomas Asa. Mark Twain: A Reference Guide. Boston: Hall,
       1977. 443 pp.
By year of publ. Annotated. Index, pp. 409-43, chiefly of names (sub-
       jects and scholars): Clemens: 12 1/2 cols., incl. 8+ cols. on his
       works, by title. Annual suppls. in American Literary Realism,
       1870-1910, 10 (1977)--. 13 (1980):161-224, by year of publ.,
       annotated and with a 5 pp. introductory essay.
AmLS 77:87-88

8/222 "Whitman: A Current Bibliography." In Walt Whitman Review, 2
       (1956)--.
In each issue. Books and arts. from journals and newspapers, incl. some
       very odd stuff. Vols. 1-4 called Walt Whitman Newsletter.

8/223 Boswell, Jeanetta. Walt Whitman and the Critics: A Checklist of
       Criticism, 1900-1978. Metuchen, N. J. & London: Scarecrow, 1980.
       257 pp.
2752 entries, by scholar, listing books, arts., passages in books, and
       diss., as found in DAI, nearly all in English. Subject index, of
       names, his works, and other topics.

8/224 Eby, Edwin H. A Concordance of Walt Whitman's Leaves of Grass
       and Selected Prose Writings. Seattle: U. of Washington Pr., 1949-
       55. 964 pp.

● 1900 and AFTER ●

● REVIEW of RESEARCH ●

8/225 Bryer, Jackson R., ed. Sixteen Modern American Authors: A Survey
    of Research and Criticism. Durham, N. C.: Duke U. Pr., 1974. 673
    pp.
2nd ed. 1st ed. 1969 (Fifteen Modern American Authors. . . .) Covers
    Eliot, Faulkner, Hemingway, Pound and others.
AmLS 74:124

● HANDBOOKS ●

8/226 Hoffman, Daniel, ed. Harvard Guide to Contemporary American
    Writing. Cambridge, Mass. & London: Harvard U. Pr., 1979. 618 pp.
Covers from the end of World War II. 3 chapters on poetry, 3 on fiction,
    1 each on drama and criticism. Also chapters on Black, Jewish and
    women writers. No bibls. or notes. Index of names.
TLS Sept. 5, 1980, p. 969--v unfav; JEGP 79 (1980):271-75--v unfav

8/227 Popkin, Michael, ed. Modern Black Writers: A Library of Literary
    Criticism. N. Y.: Ungar, 1978. 519 pp.
Passages from critical studies, incl. some transl. from French, with
    exact citations to originals. Incl. U. S., Caribbean and African
    writers.

● POETRY ●

8/228 Malkoff, Karl. Crowell's Handbook of Contemporary American
    Poetry. N. Y.: Crowell, 1973. 338 pp.
Essays on poets, 1-20 pp., emphasizing criticism, with brief bibls. Also
    a few general arts. (Concrete poetry, New criticism) and a long
    introduction. Covers poets who first publ. after 1940.
AmLS 73:333-34--"very valuable"

• FICTION •

8/229 [Bibliographies on various topics.] In Modern Fiction Studies.
       See 8/151.

• AUTHORS •

8/230 Martin, Mildred. A Half-Century of Eliot Criticism: An Annotated
       Bibliography of Books and Articles in English, 1916-1965. Lewis-
       burg, Pa.: Bucknell U. Pr., 1972. 361 pp.

8/231 Frank, Mechthild, Armin P. Frank and K. P. S. Jochum. T. S. Eliot
       Criticism in English, 1916-1965: A Supplementary Bibliography.
       Edmonton, Alberta: Yeats/Eliot Review, 1978. 108 pp.
Suppl. to Martin's bibl.(8/230). Books, arts. and chapters in books, by
       year of publ. Lists doctoral diss. from the U.S., Canada, England,
       etc. Indexes incl. scholars and subjects, incl. Eliot's works.
       Note also the brief (5 or 6 entries) annotated bibls. in each
       issue of Yeats/Eliot Review (2/yr.), formerly T. S. Eliot Review.

8/232 Ricks, Beatrice. T. S. Eliot: A Bibliography of Secondary Works.
       Metuchen, N. J.: Scarecrow, 1980. 366 pp.
4319 numbered entries, in classified order. "The Waste Land:" 510 en-
       tries. Indexes of subjects and of scholars.

8/233 "Faulkner [year]: A Survey of Research and Criticism." In Missis-
       sippi Quarterly, 31 (1977/78)--.
In issue no. 3 (Summer). 34 (1980/81):343-66, for 1980. Classified
       arrangement. Annotations, sometimes evaluative. Based on material
       reported in the Faulkner section of the "Checklist of Scholarship
       on Southern Literature" in the preceding issue (no. 2 [Spring]),
       where full bibl. details are given. 34 (1980/81):153-277, by per-
       iod and author, briefly annotated; Faulkner: pp. 196-212.

8/234 McHaney, Thomas L. <u>William</u> <u>Faulkner</u>: <u>A</u> <u>Reference</u> <u>Guide</u>. Boston:
       Hall, 1976. 568 pp.
By year of publ. Annotated. Author/Title index, pp. 462-568, incl.
       scholars, titles of Faulkner's works, and appr. 90 general head-
       ings, e. g., Character Studies.
AmLS 76:120

8/235 Bassett, John. <u>William</u> <u>Faulkner</u>: <u>An</u> <u>Annotated</u> <u>Checklist</u> <u>of</u> <u>Crit</u>-
       icism. N. Y.: Lewis, 1972. 551 pp.
Studies of individual works, pp. 18-281.
AmLS 72:115

8/236 Capps, Jack L. <u>Go</u> <u>Down</u> <u>Moses</u>: <u>A</u> <u>Concordance</u>. N. p.: Faulkner
       Concordance Advisory Board, 1978. (Distr. by Ann Arbor: UMI)
2 vols. 867 pp. Concordances to <u>As</u> <u>I</u> <u>Lay</u> <u>Dying</u>, <u>Light</u> <u>in</u> <u>August</u>, <u>Re</u>-
       <u>quiem</u> <u>for</u> <u>a</u> <u>Nun</u>, and <u>The</u> <u>Sound</u> <u>and</u> <u>the</u> <u>Fury</u> have also been publ.
AmLS 78:159; 78:153-54

8/237 "Hemingway Checklist." In <u>Fitzgerald-Hemingway</u> <u>Annual</u>, 1970--
1979, pp. 463-83, by author, listing publs. of 1977 and 1978, chiefly.

8/238 Hanneman, Audre. <u>Ernest</u> <u>Hemingway</u>: <u>A</u> <u>Comprehensive</u> <u>Bibliography</u>.
       Princeton, N. J.: Princeton U. Pr., 1967. 568 pp.
Pp. 275-527: materials on Hemingway, incl. diss., in various langs. In-
       dex of names (subjects and scholars) and of titles of his works.
       <u>The</u> <u>Sun</u> <u>Also</u> <u>Rises</u>: 12 lines, by entry number, plus refs. to eds.
       and transls. Suppl., 1975, 393 pp.
AmLS 75:168-69

8/239 Wagner, Linda Welshimer. <u>Ernest</u> <u>Hemingway</u>: <u>A</u> <u>Reference</u> <u>Guide</u>.
       Boston: Hall, 1977. 363 pp.
Books and arts., most in English, by year of publ. Annotated. Index of
       scholars and titles of his works.
AmLS 77:165

IX

OTHER EUROPEAN LITERATURES

OUTLINE

DUTCH LITERATURE
     Bibliographies 9/1-9/2
     History 9/3
BELGIAN LITERATURE
     Bibliographies 9/4-9/5
SCANDINAVIAN LITERATURES
     Bibliographies 9/6-9/8
     Translations 9/9
     Histories 9/10-9/11
DANISH LITERATURE
     Bibliographies 9/12-9/13
     Translations 9/14
     Histories 9/15-9/16
     Author
         Kierkegaard 9/17
OLD NORSE-ICELANDIC
     Bibliography 9/18
     Translations 9/19
NORWEGIAN LITERATURE
     Bibliographies 9/20-9/22

● ● DUTCH LITERATURE ● ●

● BIBLIOGRAPHIES ●

9/1 Gobben, W. "Source Material for the Study of Dutch Literature: A
     Bibliographic Survey." In Dutch Studies 1 (1974):151-79.

9/2 Bibliografie van de nederlandse taal- en literatuurwetenschap.
     1970--.
Annual. Cumulated every 5 years (1975-79, 2 vols., 1171 & 455 pp.,
     publ. 1981). Classified arrangement, with indexes.

● HISTORY ●

9/3 Meijer, Reinder P. Literature of the Low Countries: A Short His-
     tory of Dutch Literature in the Netherlands and Belgium. The
     Hague & Boston: Nijhoff, 1978. 402 pp.
New ed. 1st ed. 1971. Very brief bibl. Index of names and titles.
     Covers through the mid-1950s; 100+ pp. on the 20th c.
YWMLS 78:833-34; 71:664--noting that it relates Dutch culture to that of
     Europe.

● ● BELGIAN LITERATURE ● ●

● BIBLIOGRAPHIES ●

9/4 Bibliographie nationale: Dictionnaire des écrivains belges et cata-
     logue de leurs publications, 1830-1880. Bruxelles: Weissenbruch,
     1886-1910.
4 vols. and suppl.

9/5 Culot, Jean Marie, et al. Bibliographie des écrivains française de
     Belgique, 1881-1950. Bruxelles: Palais de Academies, 1958--.
4 vols. to date. Vols. 2-4 cover through 1960. Vol. 4, M-N, 373 pp.,

publ. 1972. Maeterlinck: pp. 8-143; studies, by year of publ.,
pp. 65-143 (through 1965).

● ● SCANDINAVIAN LITERATURES ● ●

● BIBLIOGRAPHIES ●

9/6 "Contributions to Scandinavian Studies in Other Periodicals." In
     Scandinavica.
In issue no. 1 (May). Arranged by journal. 20 (1980/81):119-34.

9/7 Kvamme, Janet. Index Nordicus: A Cumulative Index to English-Lan-
     guage Periodicals on Scandinavian Studies. Boston: Hall, 1980.
     601 pp.
Covers 6 journals, incl. Scandinavian Review, Scandinavian Studies and
     Scandinavica. Scholars and subjects, alphabetically. Strindberg:
     6 2/3 cols. of arts. and revs. of studies, as well as 2 cols. of
     revs. of transls. and a few stories in transl.

9/8 Buchholz, Peter. "A Bibliographical Introduction to Medieval
     Scandinavia." In Bibliography of Old Norse-Icelandic Studies 9
     (1971):7-87.
Classified and annotated.

● TRANSLATIONS ●

9/9 Ng, Maria and Michael S. Batts. Scandinavian Literature in English
     Translation, 1928-1977. Vancouver: Canadian Assn. of Univ.
     Teachers of German, 1978. (CAUTG Publ., 3) 95 pp.
Incl. transls. publ. as books or in anthologies.
Scan 19 (1980):94-96

● HISTORIES ●

9/10 Rossel, Sven H. A History of Scandinavian Literature, 1870-1980.
       Minneapolis: U. of Minnesota Pr., 1981.   pp.
Transl. by Anne C. Ulmer. German ed. 1973. Not seen.
YWMLS 73:712--v fav

9/11 Brondsted, Mogens. Nordens litteratur. København: Glydendal, 1972.
I: For 1860. 427 pp. II: Efter 1860. 593 pp. Index of names. "Aims
       at (1) introducing the literature of one area to . . . readers
       from the other areas and (2) comparing and summarizing, period by
       period, literary tendencies and achievements within the entire
       Scandinavian area." YWMLS 72:646
YWMLS 72:646; 73:678; Scan 11 (1972):146-47

● DANISH LITERATURE ●

● BIBLIOGRAPHIES ●

9/12 Mitchell, Phillip M. A Bibliographical Guide to Danish Literature.
       Copenhagen: Munksgaard, 1951. 62 pp.
Books only, incl. general studies and eds., transls. and studies of in-
       dividual authors.

9/13 Dansk litteraturhistorisk bibliografi. 1968--.
Annual. Covers 1967--. Annotated. Cites book revs. By period and
       authors, with cross-refs., but index of scholars only. 1974, publ.
       1975. 630 entries in 10 sections; sections 3-6: literary history,
       by period. Aage Jørgensen, comp.

● TRANSLATIONS ●

9/14 Bredsdorff, Elias. Danish Literature in English Translation.
       Copenhagen: Munksgaard, 1950. 198 pp.

Incl. books and arts. in English on the major writers.

• HISTORIES •

9/15 Dansk litteratur historie. København: Politiken, 1976-77.
P. H. Traustedt, ed. 4th ed. 6 vols. Not seen. 1st ed., 1964. 4
      vols. Brief bibls. of eds. and studies, chiefly books, in each
      vol. Chronology in vol. 4, pp. 545-606, covering 200 AD to 1966,
      in 3 cols. Indexes of titles and of names.
YWMLS 78:850-51

9/16 Mitchell, Phillip M. A History of Danish Literature, with an
      Introductory Chapter by Mogens Haugsted. N. Y.: Kraus-Thomson,
      1971. 339 pp.
2nd ed. 1st ed. 1957. Covers through 1970. Very brief bibl. of books
      and arts. in English. Index of names and Danish and English ti-
      tles.
YWMLS 71:685-86

• AUTHOR •

9/17 Lapointe, Francois H. Sören Kierkegaard and His Critics. West-
      port, Conn. & London: Greenwood Pr., 1980. 430 pp.
Books and arts. in W. European langs., and U. S. and European diss.
      Classified arrangement.

• OLD NORSE and ICELANDIC •

• BIBLIOGRAPHY •

9/18 Bibliography of Old Norse-Icelandic Studies. 1964--.
Annual. Covers from 1963--. Books and arts., with some brief annota-
      tions, by scholar, with subject index. Each vol. also incl. an
      "introductory essay," e. g., 9/8.

• TRANSLATIONS •

9/19 Mitchell, Phillip M. and Kenneth H. Ober. Bibliography of Modern
      Icelandic Literature in Translation, Including Works Written by
      Icelanders in Other Languages. Ithaca, N. Y. & London: Cornell
      U. Pr., 1975. (Icelandica, 40) 317 pp.
JEGP 75 (1976):392-94; SS 49 (1977):490-91

• NORWEGIAN LITERATURE •

• BIBLIOGRAPHIES •

9/20 "Bibliografi til den norske litteratur for [year]." In Norsk
      litteraer årbok, 1966--.
Annual. Covers from 1965--. 1981, for 1980, pp. 216-35, in 2 cols.
      Authors, pp. 224-35. Lists books and arts. in Norwegian, English
      and other langs. 2 1/2 cols. on Ibsen, incl. sections on his
      plays.

9/21 Øksnevad, Reidar. Norsk litteratur-historisk bibliografi. Oslo:
      Glydendal, 1951-58.
2 vols., covering 1900-1945 and 1946-1955. Lists books, arts. and diss.,
      in Norwegian and other langs. Ibsen: 67+ pp. total. Index of
      scholars.

9/22 Naess, Harald. Norwegian Literary Bibliography, 1956-1970/Norsk
      litteratur-historisk bibliografi, 1956-1970. Oslo, etc.: Univer-
      sitetsforlaget, 1975. 128 pp.
Rev. ed. 1st ed. 1973. Ed. by Kaare Haukaas. 2990 entries, by period
      and author, mostly on the 19th and 20th cs. Ibsen: pp. 37-61, en-
      tries 747-1443, in classified order. Hedda Gabler: entries 1246-
      75. Lists books and arts. as well as eds. and transls., in various
      langs., chiefly Norwegian and English.
YWMLS 75:701; Scan 17 (1978):74-75

• HISTORIES •

9/23 Beyer, Edvard, ed. <u>Norges litteratur historie</u>. Oslo: Cappelens,
      1974-75.
6 vols. Lengthy bibl., chronological table (covering 400 AD to 1972),
      and index of names and anonymous titles in vol. 6. Ibsen: III:
      226-383.
YWMLS 75:697-98; Scan 15 (1976):172-74; 16 (1977):35-41--prefers the
      bibls. in the 1 vol. history by Beyer and Beyer (9/24).

9/24 Beyer, Harald and Edvard Beyer. <u>Norsk litteratur historie</u>. Oslo:
      Aschehoug, 1970. 479 pp.
3rd ed. 1st ed. 1939. Most of the book covers from Ibsen and his con-
      temporaries. Bibl., pp. 395-465, paralleling text. The 1st ed.
      was transl. into English by Einar Haugen: <u>A History of Norwegian</u>
      <u>Literature</u>, N. Y.: New York U. Pr., for the American Scandinavian
      Foundation, 1956, 370 pp. 4th ed., 1978, 597 pp., not seen.
SS 37 (1965):201-03; YWMLS 78:863--"copious up-to-date bibl.," pp. 479-
      581

• AUTHOR •

9/25 "Ibsen-bibliografi." In <u>Ibsenårbok</u>, 1955--.
Irregular. Covers from 1954--. 1978, pp. 178-201, listing books, arts.,
      and chapters and passages in books, in Norwegian, English and other
      langs.
YWMLS 75:708

9/26 Tedford, Ingrid. <u>Ibsen Bibliography, 1928-1957</u>. Oslo: Oslo U.
      Pr., 1961. 80 pp.
Books, arts. in books and journals and U. S. and European diss., by year
      of publ. Index of scholars.

9/27 Barranger, M. S. "Ibsen Bibliography, 1957-1967." In <u>Scandinavian</u>

<u>Studies</u> 41 (1969):243-58.
Books and arts., by author.

● SWEDISH LITERATURE ●

● BIBLIOGRAPHY ●

9/28 "Svensk litteraturhistorisk bibliografi." In <u>Samlaren</u>: <u>Tidskrift</u>
<u>för</u> <u>svensk</u> <u>litteraturhistorisk</u> <u>forskning</u>, 1881--.
Covers from 1880--. A separately paged supplement. 96 (1977), in 100
    (1981). 37 pp., in 7 sections. Authors, pp. 12-34; Strindberg:
    3+ cols., listing eds., transls., and studies by scholar, in Swed-
    ish, English and other langs. Some brief notes.

● HISTORY ●

9/29 Gustafson, Alrik. <u>A</u> <u>History</u> <u>of</u> <u>Swedish</u> <u>Literature</u>. Minneapolis:
    U. of Minnesota Pr., for the American Scandinavian Foundation,
    1961. 708 pp.
"Bibliographical Guide," pp. 567-644, citing books and arts. in Swedish,
    English and other langs., with evaluative commentary. List of
    transls. into English, pp. 645-60, by period and author, listing
    books only. Covers to the mid-1950s; 3/4 of the book covers 1800-
    1930s. Index of names and titles (in Swedish, sometimes also in
    English).
YWMLS 61:456; MLR 57 (1962):293-94

● AUTHOR ●

9/30 Lindström, Goran. "Strindberg Studies, 1915-1962." In <u>Scandi-</u>
    <u>navica</u> 2 (1963):27-50.
A review of trends in scholarship.

● ●   EAST EUROPEAN LITERATURES   ● ●

● BIBLIOGRAPHIES ●

9/31 Terry, Garth M. East European Languages and Literatures: A Sub-
      ject and Name Index to Articles in English-Language Journals,
      1900-1977. Oxford & Santa Barbara, Calif.: Clio, 1978. 275 pp.
Rev. ed. 1st ed. 1976. Lists arts. in English and French, alphabeti-
      cally by subject. Index of names (subjects and scholars).
YWMLS 79:1013-14

9/32 American Bibliography of Slavic and East European Studies.
      1957--.
Annual. Covers 1956--. 1977, publ. 1981: 272 pp., 6934 entries. 1976,
      publ. 1979: 229 pp., 5621 entries, in 17 sections, divided and
      subdivided. Section 11: Literature: 25 pp., 715 entries, covering
      general topics and 16 nations or languages, incl. Czech and Slovak,
      E. German (44 entries, incl. Brecht and Kafka), Greek, Hungarian,
      Polish (69 entries, incl. 30 on Conrad), Russian (445 entries,
      incl. sections on Pre-Soviet, Soviet and Emigré literatures, and
      on authors), Ukrainian and Yiddish. Lists U. S. and Canadian
      publs. only. Incl. book revs. Vols. for 1971-74 carried a suppl.
      on British publs. which has been continued in the entry below.
      Vols. for 1956-66 were called American Bibliography of Russian and
      East European Studies.

9/33 European Bibliography of Soviet, East European and Slavonic Stud-
      ies. 1977--.
Annual. Slow to appear. Lists books, arts., and book revs. from Brit-
      ish, French, Belgian, Swiss (French-lang. only), Austrian and W.
      German sources. 2 (1976), publ. 1979, by region and topic. Rus-
      sian literature: pp. 185-228, entries 2141-601, with sections on
      periods and on writers, A-Z. Replaces "Travaux et publications
      parus en français. . . ." in Cahiers du monde russe et soviétique

from 1963 to 1974, and the British suppl. in ABSEES (9/32), 1971-74.

● DISSERTATIONS ●

9/34 "Doctoral Dissertations on Russia, the Soviet Union and Eastern
     Europe Accepted by American, Canadian, British, Australian and New
     Zealand Universities [years]." In Slavic Review, 23 (1964)--.
38 (1980):728-41, by nation of origin, then nation or other subject.

● ● SLAVIC LITERATURES ● ●

● BIBLIOGRAPHIES ●

9/35 Wytrzens, Günther. Bibliographische Einführung in das Studium der
     slavischen Literaturen. Frankfurt am Main: Klostermann, 1972.
     (Zeitschrift für Bibliothekswesen und Bibliographie, 13) 348 pp.
Lists chiefly histories and bibls. of the various Slavic literatures.
YWMLS 72:779--"awkwardly arranged and unannotated, but convenient as a
     compendium which incl. Western publs."; SEEJ ns 17 (1973):322-23

9/36 Bamborschke, Ulrich. Bibliographie slavistischer Arbeiten aus
     deutschsprachigen Fachzeitschriften, 1964-1973, einschliessl.
     slavist. Arbeiten aus dt.-sprachigen nicht-slavist. Fest- und
     Sammelschriften, 1945-1973. Wiesbaden: in Kommission bei O. Har-
     rassowitz, 1976. (Bibliographische Mitteilungen des Osteuropa-
     Instituts an der Freien Universität, Berlin, 13)
2 vols. 736 pp. 6501 entries, by language and topic. Russian: pp. 249-
     511, in 3 sections (language, literature and art and culture), all
     divided and subdivided. Continues next entry.

9/37 Seemann, Klaus Dieter and Frank Siegmann. Bibliographie der
     slavistischen Arbeiten aus den deutsch-sprachigen Fachzeit-
     schriften, 1876-1963. Berlin: in Kommission bei O. Harrassowitz,

Wiesbaden, 1965. (Bibliographische Mitteilungen des Osteuropa-
Instituts an der Freien Universität, Berlin, 8) 422 pp.
4133 entries. Russian, pp. 170-253; Russian literature, pp. 187-239,
entries 1933-2599, incl. sections on periods.

● DISSERTATIONS ●

9/38 "Theses in Slavonic Studies Approved for Higher Degrees by British
      Universities. . . ." In Oxford Slavonic Papers.
13 (1967):135-59, for 1907-1966; ns 6 (1973):133-47, for 1967-1971; ns
      10 (1977):120-38, for 1972-1976. By topic, then region. Index of
      scholars and subjects.
YWMLS 73:770

9/39 Magner, Thomas F. Soviet Dissertations for Advanced Degrees in
      Russian Literature and Slavic Linguistics, 1934-1962. University
      Park: Dept. of Slavic Langs., Pennsylvania St. U., 1966. 100 pp.

● TRANSLATIONS ●

9/40 Lewanski, Richard C. The Slavic Literatures. N.Y.: New York Pub-
      lic Library and F. Ungar, 1967. (Literatures of the World in En-
      glish Translation) 630 pp.
Transls. publ. as books or in books and periodicals. By language, then
      author. Polish: pp. 72-145; Russian: pp. 145-405; Gogol: 7 cols.
      Does not cite title of work in original. Index of authors (but
      not translators) and English titles.

● HANDBOOK ●

9/41 Mihailovich, Vasa D., ed. Modern Slavic Literatures. N. Y.:
      Ungar, 1972-76.
2 vols. I: Russian Literature. 424 pp. II: Bulgarian, Czechoslovak,
      Polish, Ukranian and Yugoslav Literatures. 720 pp. Passages from

critical studies, incl. many transl. from the Slavic langs. Gives
full citations to originals.
CSP   19 (1977):392-93--"immensely useful," but critical of omissions;
SEEJ ns 17 (1973):451-52--unfav; 21 (1977):423-26--mixed

● HISTORY ●

9/42 Chyzhevs'kyi, Dmytro. Comparative History of Slavic Literatures.
Nashville: Vanderbilt U. Pr., 1971. 225 pp.
Transl. by Richard Noel Porter and Martin P. Rice of German ed., Berlin:
de Gruyter, 1968, 2 vols. All quotations in orig. and transl.
Bibl., paralleling text, of books and arts. in various langs.
Note also his Outline of Comparative Slavic Literatures, Boston:
Amer. Academy of Arts and Sciences, 1952, 143 pp.
YWMLS 71:905; SEEJ ns 16 (1972):84-89--notes omissions and is severely
critical of transl. of the 2nd half of book; CASS 7 (1973):422

● ● RUSSIAN LITERATURE ● ●

● BIBLIOGRAPHIES ●

9/43 Zenkovsky, Serge A. and David L. Armbruster. A Guide to the Bibliographies of Russian Literature. Nashville, Tenn.: Vanderbilt
U. Pr., 1971. 62 pp.
Part II: Literary Bibliography, pp. 26-54, by period and form. Incl.
encyclopedias and handbooks.

9/44 Skoric, Sofija. Russian Reference Aids in the University of Toronto Library. Toronto: the Library, 1973. 93 pp.
325 entries, listing language dictionaries, literary histories, bibls.,
handbooks, etc., in Russian, English, occasionally French or German. Annotated.

9/45 Kandel, Boris L., ed. Russkaia khudozhestvennaia literatura i

literaturovedenie: Ukazatel' spravochnobibliograficheskikh posobii
s kontsa XVIII veka po 1974 god. Moskva: Kniga, 1976. 492 pp.
More than 2500 entries, in the Cyrillic alphabet, by subject. Authors,
    alphabetically, pp. 146-428. Index, chiefly of names.
YWMLS 76:860--"carefully annotated and incl. journal and sbornik arts.";
    76:890

9/46 Wytrzens, Günther. Bibliographie der russischen Autoren und ano-
    nymen Werke. Frankfurt am Main: Klostermann, 1975. (Zeitschrift
    für Bibliothekswesen und Bibliographie, Sonderheft 19) 267 pp.
Cites bibls., eds., transls. into German, sometimes into English, and
    studies in Russian and other langs. Index of names, incl. sub-
    jects.
RLJ 110 (1977):204; YWMLS 75:804--"emphasizes latest eds. and recent
    secondary lit., incl. diss. but few journal arts."; 75:836

● TRANSLATIONS ●

9/47 Bibliography of Russian Literature in English Translation to 1945.
    Totowa, N. J.: Rowman and Littlefield/London: Methuen, 1972.
Reprints a bibl. covering to 1900 by Maurice B. Line, first publ. in
    1963, and a bibl. for 1900-1945 by Amrei Ettlinger and Joan M.
    Gladstone, orig. publ. in 1947.

● HANDBOOKS ●

9/48 Auty, Robert and Dimitri Obolensky, eds. A Companion to Russian
    Studies. Cambridge, etc.: Cambridge U. Pr., 1976-80.
3 vols. I: Introduction to Russian History. 1976. 403 pp. II: Intro-
    duction to Russian Language and Literature. 1977. 300 pp. III:
    Introduction to Russian Art and Architecture. 1980. 194 pp.
Vol. 2: literature, 1000-1975, chapters 3-7, pp. 56-230; theater (drama
    as literature and on the stage), chapters 8-10, pp. 231-85. Leng-
    thy bibls. with each chapter. Detailed index of names and other

subjects, incl. terms, etc.

YWMLS 77:890-91, 913, 917; CSP 21 (1979):415-16; RLJ 110 (1977):185-86;
SEEJ ns 24 (1980):435-36; CASS 12 (1978):418-19--all with ref. to
vol. 2

9/49   Weber, Harry B., ed. The Modern Encyclopedia of Russian and Soviet
Literatures. Gulf Breeze, Fla.: Academic International Pr.,
1977--.

4 vols. to date, through Cosmism. **Vol. 4,** publ. 1981: appr. 60 arts.,
more than half written for this work, the others adapted from
various Russian sources. Incl. arts. on writers (Chekhov: 10 1/2
pp., plus bibl.) languages, schools (3 arts. on literary circles,
1800-1917), etc. Vol. 4 adds the phrase "including Non-Russian
and Emigré Literatures" to the title.

SEER 59 (1981):80-81; SEEJ ns 23 (1979):137-39--both v fav

9/50   Harkins, William Edward. Dictionary of Russian Literature.
London: Allen & Unwin, 1957. 439 pp.

Mostly brief entries on writers, schools, and other topics. Dostoyevsky:
18+ pp., mostly biography and plot summaries.

● HISTORIES ●

9/51   Mirskij, Dmitrii P. A History of Russian Literature, Comprising A
History of Russian Literature and Contemporary Russian Literature.
N. Y.: Knopf, 1949. 518 pp.

Ed. and abridged by Francis J. Whitfield. **Pp. 3-70, chapters** 1-3, cover
literature through the 18th c.; the remaining chapters cover
through the early 1920s. Index of names, titles in English and
other subjects.

9/52   Lindstrom, Thaïs S. A Concise History of Russian Literature.
N. Y.: New York U. Pr., 1966-78.

I: From the Beginnings to Chekhov. 233 pp. II: From 1900 to the Present.

Day. 314 pp. Most of vol. 1 is on Pushkin and after. Vol. 2
covers through Solzhenitsyn. Bibl. in each vol. of books in English. Index of names, titles in English and a few other subjects.
RLJ 116 (1979):241-44--v fav, praising the comparisons with W. European
literatures, and the bibl.

● 19th CENTURY ●

• HISTORIES •

9/53 Düwel, Wolf, ed. Geschichte der klassischen russischen Literatur.
      Berlin: Aufbau, 1973. 1012 pp.
2nd ed. 1st ed. 1965. Literature from 1790 to 1905. Bibl., paral-
      leling text, largely of titles in Russian. Index of authors and
      their works (by Russian and German titles).
YWMLS 66:675--v fav

9/54 Chyzhevs'kyi, Dmytro. History of Nineteenth-Century Russian Liter-
      ature. Nashville, Tenn.: Vanderbilt U. Pr., 1974.
2 vols. Transl. by Richard N. Porter of Russische Literaturgeschichte
      des 19. Jahrhunderts. Vol. I: The Romantic Period. 236 pp. II:
      The Age of Realism. 218 pp. Index in each vol. of names, titles
      (in Russian and English) and other subjects. "Bibliography of
      Russian Romanticism," I:179-219, listing books in Russian and En-
      glish. No bibl. or notes in vol. 2. Quotations in Russian and
      English.

• HANDBOOK •

9/55 Berry, Thomas E. Plots and Characters in Major Russian Fiction.
      Folkestone, Kent: Dawson, 1977-78.
2 vols. I: Pushkin, Lermontov, Turgenev, Tolstoi. 226 pp. II: Gogol,
      Goncharov, Dostoyevskii. 265 pp.
YWMLS 77:899; RLJ 114 (1979):212-13

• AUTHORS •

9/56 Shaw, Joseph Thomas. <u>Baratynskii</u>: <u>A</u> <u>Dictionary</u> <u>of</u> <u>the</u> <u>Rhymes</u> <u>and</u>
<u>a</u> <u>Concordance</u> <u>to</u> <u>the</u> <u>Poetry</u>. Madison: U. of Wisconsin Pr., for
the Dept. of Slavic Langs. and Lits., 1975. 434 pp.

9/57 Shaw, Joseph Thomas. <u>Batiushkov</u>: <u>A</u> <u>Dictionary</u> <u>of</u> <u>the</u> <u>Rhymes</u> <u>and</u> <u>a</u>
<u>Concordance</u> <u>to</u> <u>the</u> <u>Poetry</u>. Madison: U. of Wisconsin Pr., for the
Dept. of Slavic Langs. and Lits., 1975. 358 pp.

9/58 "Current Bibliography." In <u>Dostoevsky</u> <u>Studies</u>: <u>Journal</u> <u>of</u> <u>the</u> <u>In-</u>
<u>ternational</u> <u>Dostoevsky</u> <u>Society</u>, 1 (1980)--.
Annual. 1 (1980):169-82. Previously in the <u>Bulletin</u> of the International Dostoevsky Society, 1 (1971)-9 (1979). Meant to be "as
nearly inclusive as possible of all material published from 1970."
In 3 sections, listing publs. in the Western langs., in the langs.
of the Soviet Union, and in the other E. European langs.
YWMLS 73:799; 77:907

9/59 Wreath, Patrick J. and April I. Wreath. "Alexander Pushkin: A
Bibliography of Criticism in English, 1920-1975." In <u>Canadian-</u>
<u>American</u> <u>Slavic</u> <u>Studies</u> 10 (1976):279-304.
Books, arts., passages in books and U. S. diss., by year of publ. Occa-
sional brief notes.

9/60 Bilokur, Borys. <u>A</u> <u>Concordance</u> <u>to</u> <u>the</u> <u>Russian</u> <u>Poetry</u> <u>of</u> <u>Fedor</u> <u>I</u>.
<u>Tiutchev</u>. Providence, R. I.: Brown U. Pr., 1975. 343 pp.
YWMLS 75:851; CASS 10 (1976):605-06

9/61 Egan, David R. and Melinda A. Egan. <u>Leo</u> <u>Tolstoy</u>: <u>An</u> <u>Annotated</u>
<u>Bibliography</u> <u>of</u> <u>English-Language</u> <u>Sources</u> <u>to</u> <u>1978</u>. Metuchen, N. J.:
Scarecrow, 1979. 267 pp.
<u>War</u> <u>and</u> <u>Peace</u>: appr. 140 entries, plus 8 lines of cross-refs., by entry
number only. Many annotations, to several sentences long. Subject

index, pp. 256-67; <u>War</u> <u>and</u> <u>Peace</u>: 2 cols., subdivided by specific
topic (filming of, future tense in, Napoleon).
SEER 59 (1981):84-85; N&Q ns 28 (1981):477-79

9/62 Terry, Garth M. "Tolstoy Studies in Great Britain: A Bibliographic
      Survey." In Malcolm Jones, ed., <u>New</u> <u>Essays</u> <u>on</u> <u>Tolstoy</u>, N. Y.: Cam-
      bridge U. Pr., 1978, pp. 223-50.
By year of publ., 1946-77. Index of scholars.

● 20th CENTURY ●

• TRANSLATIONS •

9/63 Gibian, George. <u>Soviet</u> <u>Russian</u> <u>Literature</u> <u>in</u> <u>English</u>: <u>A</u> <u>Checklist</u>
      <u>Bibliography</u>: <u>A</u> <u>Selective</u> <u>Bibliography</u> <u>of</u> <u>Soviet</u> <u>Russian</u> <u>Literary</u>
      <u>Works</u> <u>in</u> <u>English</u> <u>and</u> <u>of</u> <u>Articles</u> <u>and</u> <u>Books</u> <u>in</u> <u>English</u> about <u>Soviet</u>
      <u>Russian</u> <u>Literature</u>. Ithaca, N. Y.: Center for International Stu-
      dies, Cornell U., 1967. 118 pp.
Transls. publ. as books or in books and journals.
CSP 21 (1979):252-53

• HANDBOOKS •

9/64 Kasack, Wolfgang. <u>Lexikon</u> <u>der</u> <u>russischen</u> <u>Literatur</u> <u>ab</u> <u>1917</u>.
      Stuttgart: Kröner, 1976. 457 pp.
Brief arts., chiefly on writers, movements, literary journals and other
      topics. Bulgakov: 3 3/4 cols., plus 3/4 col. bibl., citing works
      and criticism. Sozialistischer Realismus: 5+ cols., incl. bibl.
      Index of names.
YWMLS 77:913--"remarkably comprehensive and accurate"

9/65 Ludwig, Nadeshda, ed. <u>Handbuch</u> <u>der</u> <u>Sowjetliteratur</u> (<u>1917</u>-<u>1972</u>).
      Leipzig: VEB Bibliographisches Inst., 1975. 616 pp.
Historical survey, pp. 11-133, followed by a section of biographies with

plot-summaries of major works, pp. 135-558.   Index to names and
titles (in German).

• HISTORIES •

9/66   Struve, Gleb. Russian Literature under Lenin and Stalin, 1917-
       1953. Norman: U. of Oklahoma Pr., 1971. 454 pp.
Lengthy bibl. (pp. 396-432) of transls. and studies (mostly books, and
       some arts.) in English and Russian. Index of names and other sub-
       jects. All quotations in English only.

9/67   Brown, Deming. Soviet Russian Literature since Stalin. Cambridge:
       Cambridge U. Pr., 1978. 394 pp.
Index of names and a few other subjects. All quotations in English only.
YWMLS 78:1016--"detailed and readable"; SEEJ ns 22 (1978):544-45; RLJ
       113 (1978):235-36

9/68   Segel, Harold B. Twentieth-Century Russian Drama: From Gorky to
       the Present. N. Y.: Columbia U. Pr., 1979. 502 pp.
Bibl., chiefly of plays in transl. Index of names, titles in English
       and a few other subjects. Lengthy plot summaries, with quotations
       in English only.

• AUTHORS •

9/69   Proffer, Ellendea. International Bibliography of Works by and
       about Mikhail Bulgakov. Ann Arbor, Mich.: Ardis, 1976. 133 pp.
1283 entries, by language. English: pp. 81-105, incl. transls., revs.
       of transls. and 125+ studies, incl. passages in books and U. S.
       diss. Suppl. for 1976-81 in Canadian-American Slavic Studies 15
       (1981):457-61, by Nadine Natov.

9/70   Koubourlis, Demetrius J. A Concordance to the Poems of Osip
       Mandelstam. Ithaca, N. Y.: Cornell U. Pr., 1974. 678 pp.

CASS 9 (1975):104-05

9/71   Sendich, M.   "Pasternak's Doktor Živago: An International Bibliog-
       raphy of Criticism."   In Russian Language Journal 105 (Winter,
       1976):109-52
Suppl., 113 (Fall, 1978):193-205. By year of publ. Index of scholars.
YWMLS 78:1025; 79:1082

9/72   Fiene, D. Alexander Solzhenitsyn: An International Bibliography
       of Writings by and about Him, 1962-1973. Ann Arbor, Mich.: Ardis,
       1973. 154 pp.
Arranged by lang. Lists eds. or transls. and studies, biographies, etc.
       English: pp. 35-83; studies in English, pp. 42-83, by type of publ.
       (books, arts., diss., book revs., etc.).

● ● POLISH LITERATURE ● ●

● BIBLIOGRAPHIES ●

9/73   Polska Akademia Nauk. Instytut Badań Literackich. Bibliografia
       literatury polskiej "Nowy Korbut." Warszawa: Państwowy Instytut
       Wydawniczy, 1963--.
17 vols. to date. By period. Romantic period: vols. 7-9; index of
       names as subjects, vol. 9, pp. 559-698. Vol. 17, pt. 1, publ.
       1981, 201 pp., on Bolesław Prus (Aleksander Głowacki), citing eds.,
       transls. and studies (pp. 79-156, in classified order).

9/74   Polska bibliografia literacka za lata [years]. Wrocław: Zakład
       Narodowy Imienia Ossolińskich, 1957--.
Vol. for 1974-75, publ. 1979. 2 vols. Vol. 1, pp. 26-758, entries 232-
       9806: studies of Polish literature, by topic, incl. genres, or by
       author (pp. 216-758). Vol. 2 lists studies of world literature
       in Polish and of transls. Covers from 1944/45.

● TRANSLATIONS ●

9/75 Hoskins, Janina W. Polish Books in English, 1945-1971. Washing-
      ton, D. C.: Library of Congress, 1974. 163 pp.

9/76 Coleman, Marion Moore. Polish Literature in English Translation:
      A Bibliography. Cheshire, Conn.: Cherry Hill Books, 1963. 180 pp.
Incl. transls. publ. in journals and anthologies.

9/77 Maciuszko, Jerzy J. The Polish Short Story in English: A Guide and
      Critical Bibliography. Detroit, Mich.: Wayne St. U. Pr., 1968.
      473 pp.
Gives plot summaries.

9/78 Taborski, Bolesław. Polish Plays in English Translations: A Bibli-
      ography. N. Y.: Polish Inst. of Arts and Sciences in America,
      1968. 79 pp.

● HISTORIES ●

9/79 Miłosz, Czesław. History of Polish Literature. N. Y.: Macmillan/
      London: Collier-Macmillan, 1969. 570 pp.
Covers through the 1950s, with emphasis on the 19th and 20th centuries.
      Bibl. of eds. and transls. (books only) and a few studies, incl.
      some journal arts. Index of names and titles in English. All
      quotations in English and Polish.

9/80 Kridl, Manfred. A Survey of Polish Literature and Culture. N. Y.:
      Columbia U. Pr., 1956. 525 pp.
Transl. by Olga Scherer-Virski. Covers through the 1930s, and esp. the
      19th and 20th cs. Index of names. All quotations in English only.

9/81 Krzyżanowski, Julian. A History of Polish Literature. Warszawa:
      PWN--Polish Scientific Publs., 1978. 807 pp.

Transl. by Doris Ronowicz of the 1972 Polish ed. Bibl., pp. 671-737,
     paralleling text, listing books only. Polish Literature in English
     Translation: pp. 739-52, by period and author, incl. transls. publ.
     in journals. Index, chiefly of names.
YWMLS 78:950-51--"would have made an excellent ref. book, were it not for
     the poor transl."

X

ORIENTAL LITERATURES

OUTLINE

ORIENTAL LITERATURES
    Bibliographies 10/1-10/3
    Handbooks 10/4-10/6
    History 10/7

NEAR EASTERN LITERATURES
    Bibliography 10/8
ISLAMIC LITERATURES
    Bibliographies 10/9-10/11
    Handbook 10/12
ARABIC LITERATURE
    Bibliography 10/13
    Translations 10/14
    Histories 10/15-10/17
IRANIAN and PERSIAN LITERATURES
    Bibliographies 10/18-10/19
    Histories 10/20-10/22
TURKISH LITERATURE
    Bibliography 10/23
    Histories 10/24-10/26

● ● ORIENTAL LITERATURES ● ●

● BIBLIOGRAPHIES ●

10/1 Nunn, G. Raymond. Asia: Reference Works: A Select Annotated Guide.
       London: Mansell, 1980. 365 pp.
2nd ed. 1st ed. 1971. Lists bibls., dictionaries, general and biogra-
       phical encyclopedias, etc., on the countries of S. C., S. E. and E.
       Asia, by country, from Pakistan to the Philippines. Most sections
       incl. a few bibls. of literature and literary research. Incl.
       works in English, the other European langs., and the Asian langs.

10/2 Bibliography of Asian Studies. 1973--.
Covers 1971--. Annual. Geographic arrangement, divided and subdivided
       by topic. Lists books, arts. and reports in W. European langs.
       Vol. for 1977, publ. 1980: 682 pp., 16205 entries. Sections on
       more than 30 nations or regions of S. C., S. E. and E. Asia, in up
       to 16 divisions covering all aspects of culture and society, incl.
       literature; the literature section is itself sometime subdivided by
       form (Poetry, Prose, Drama) but never further divided. No cross-
       refs., no subject index. Index of scholars.
In addition to covering all aspects of Asian culture, incl. art, history
       and philosophy, this offers references to a number of studies of
       literature not to be found in the MLA Bibl. (1/9), esp. studies
       publ. in books, many in English. The MLA, on the other hand, lists
       diss. from DAI and arts. from some journals not covered by this.

10/3 Cumulative Bibliography of Asian Studies. Boston: Hall, 1969-73.
I: Subject Bibliography, 1941-1965. 4 vols. 1970. Suppl., 1966-1970.
       3 vols. 1972. II: Author Bibliography, 1941-1965. 4 vols. 1969.
       Suppl., 1966-1970. 3 vols. 1973. Cumulates the bibls. orig.
       publ. in Journal of Asian Studies, which preceded 10/2.

● HANDBOOKS ●

10/4 Průšek, Jaroslav, gen. ed. Dictionary of Oriental Literatures.
      London: Allen & Unwin, 1974.
I: East Asia, ed. by Zbigniew Słupski. 262 pp.
II: South and South-East Asia, ed. by Dusan Zbavitel. 191 pp.
III: West Asia and North Africa, ed. by Jiří Bečka. 213 pp.
Brief signed arts., up to about 2 pp., with bibls., on authors, works,
      characters, forms, etc. Vol. I: monogatori: nearly 2 cols., bibl.
      of 3 transls.; Li Po: 4 cols., plus bibl. of transls. and studies.
      Vol. II: Kalidasa: 4 1/2 cols.
LE&W 19 (1975):254-57--mixed, with ref. to coverage of Chinese literature

10/5 Lang, David Marshall, ed. A Guide to Eastern Literatures. London:
      Weidenfeld & Nicolson, 1971. 501 pp.
15 chapters. Literature in Arabic: appr. 35 pp., incl. a survey and en-
      tries on 36 writers. Persian Literature: 32 pp., incl. entries on
      40 writers. Bibls. of books only. Index of names, titles and
      other subjects.

10/6 DeBary, William Theodore and Ainslie T. Embree, eds. A Guide to
      Oriental Classics. N. Y.: Columbia U. Pr., 1975. 257 pp.
2nd ed. 1st ed. 1964. Sections on Islamic, Indic, Chinese and Japanese
      literature, listing transls., usually into English, and studies
      (books and arts., usually in English). Incl. religious and philo-
      sophical texts. Many brief evaluative annotations.

● HISTORY ●

10/7 Botto, Oscar, ed. Storia delle letterature d'Oriente. Milano:
      Vallardi, 1969.
4 vols. Covers W., S. S. E. and E. Asia, incl. the ancient Near East.
      Chinese literature: vol. 4, pp. 3-210, by period, then form. Japa-
      nese literature: vol. 4, pp. 415-756. "Indice dei nomi" in each

vol., incl. names, titles and technical terms.

● ● NEAR EASTERN LITERATURE ● ●

● BIBLIOGRAPHY ●

10/8 "Bibliography of Periodical Literature." In Middle East Journal,
      (1947)--.
In each issue (4/yr.). Selective, but attempts to cover "all important
      periodicals." Appr. 300 covered in 1980. Covers the Near East
      since the rise of Islam. 35:1 (Winter, 1981):109-34, entries
      52557-53511. Classified arrangement. "Language, Literature,
      Arts": 65 entries. Arabic, Hebrew and Russian studies cited by an
      English title only.

● ISLAMIC LITERATURES ●

· BIBLIOGRAPHIES ·

10/9 Quarterly Index Islamicus: Current Books, Articles and Papers on
      Islamic Studies. 1977--.
Covers 1976--. Arranged by region. The longer sections (Islam, Arabic,
      Iran, Turkey) are divided by broad subjects, incl. literature.
      Lists books and arts. in English, French, German, Russian, etc.,
      but not the Near Eastern langs. No indexes.

10/10 Index Islamicus, 1906-1955: A Catalogue of Articles on Islamic
      Subjects in Periodicals and Other Collective Publications. Cam-
      bridge, Engl.: Heffer, 1958. 897 pp.
Suppls., 1956-1960, 1962, 316 pp.; 1961-1965, 1967, 342 pp.; 1966-1970,
      (publ. by London: Mansell) 1972, 384 pp.; 1971-1975, 1977, 429 pp.
      Arranged by subject or region. Regional sections cover geography,
      sociology and history. Subject sections subdivided by region or
      language. Sections 36-42: Languages and Literatures; 37: Arabic

Literature, by period.

10/11 Abstracta Islamica: Bibliographie sélective des études islamiques.
       1927--.
Annual. Suppl. to Revue des études islamiques, 1 (1927)--. 29 (1975),
       publ. 1980. Section 3: Langues et littératures, pp. 82-105, 70 en-
       tries, subdivided by lang. (Arabic, Persian, Turkish, other). Ab-
       stracts in French. Lists books and arts. in various langs., incl.
       the Near Eastern langs. Index of scholars.

· HANDBOOK ·

10/12 The Encyclopaedia of Islam. Leiden, Brill, 1960--.
New ed. H. A. R. Gibb, et al., eds. 1st ed. 1913-36, in 4 vols. and
       suppl., 1938. Vols. 1-3 and fasc. 4 of vol. 4 (fasc. 85/86) to
       date, through al-Ḵurṭubī. Arts. on people, places and other sub-
       jects, incl. literary terms, forms, etc. Ḵiṣṣa [fiction, novel]:
       43 cols. Firdawsī: 5 cols., plus 1 col. bibl. Index to vols. 1-
       3, 1979, of names, titles, etc. Suppl., 1980--. Also publ. in
       French (Encyclopédie de l'Islam, Paris: Maisonneuve & Larose).
       The Shorter Encyclopaedia of Islam, H. A. R. Gibb and J. H.
       Kramers, eds., Ithaca, N. Y.: Cornell U. Pr., 1953, 671 pp., con-
       tains arts. on law and religion only, from the orig. Encyclopaedia.

· ARABIC LITERATURE ·

· BIBLIOGRAPHY ·

10/13 Altoma, Salih J. Modern Arabic Literature: A Bibliography of
       Articles, Books, Dissertations and Translations in English.
       Bloomington: Indiana U. Asian Studies Research Inst., 1975., 73
       pp.
850 entries on literature since 1800, by genre or author. Suppl. list of
       U. S. and British diss., pp. 63-67. Index of scholars.

RAL 7 (1976):300-01

• TRANSLATIONS •

10/14 Anderson, Margaret. Arabic Materials in English Translation: A
    Bibliography of Works from the Pre-Islamic Period to 1977. Boston:
    Hall, 1980. 249 pp.
Literature: pp. 150-207. Lists transls. publ. as books and in books and
    periodicals. Brief annotations.

• HISTORIES •

10/15 Nicholson, Reynold Alleyne. A Literary History of the Arabs.
    Cambridge: The University Pr., 1966. 506 pp.
Reprint of the 2nd, 1930 ed. 1st ed. 1907. Emphasis is on the period
    through the 10th c. Index of names and other subjects, incl. tech-
    nical terms.

10/16 Gibb, Sir Hamilton A. R. Arabic Literature: An Introduction. Ox-
    ford: Clarendon Pr., 1963. 182 pp.
2nd rev. ed. 1st ed. 1926. Covers to 1800, but particularly through
    the 10th c.

10/17 Brockelmann, Carl. Geschichte der arabischen Literatur. Leiden:
    Brill, 1943-49.
2nd ed. 2 vols. Suppl., 3 vols., 1937-42. Cumulative indexes of au-
    thors and titles in all 5 vols. in vol 3 of suppl. Covers into the
    20th c. Dense with facts and bibl.

• IRANIAN and PERSIAN LITERATURE •

• BIBLIOGRAPHIES •

10/18 Ricks, Thomas, Thomas Gouttierre and Denis Egan. Persian Studies:

A Selected Bibliography of Works in English. Bloomington: Indiana
U., 1969. 266 lv.
Section X: Literature: lv. 185-210, incl. transls. of poetry and prose
as books or in journals, and studies, lv. 198-210, by scholar.

10/19 Nawabi, Y. M. A Bibliography of Iran: A Catalogue of Books and
Articles on Iranian Subjects, Mainly in European Languages.
Tehran: Khajeh Pr., 1969.
3 vols. Vol. 2: Persian Language and Literature. 479 pp.

• HISTORIES •

10/20 Browne, Edward Granville. Literary History of Persia. Cambridge:
The University Pr., 1928.
4 vols. Reprint of the 1908-24 ed. Covers through 1924. Lengthy quotations in Persian, not always translated. Index of names and some
other subjects in each vol.

10/21 Rypka, Jan, et al. History of Iranian Literature. Dordrecht:
Reidel, 1968. 928 pp.
Rev. and transl. from the Czech. Covers Persian and Tajik literatures
to the present. Lengthy bibl. of studies in various langs., paralleling text.

10/22 Arberry, Arthur John. Classical Persian Literature. London:
Allen & Unwin, 1958. 464 pp.
Covers from the beginning of the 9th to the end of the 15th c. Brief
index. Extensive quotations in transl. only.

• TURKISH LITERATURE •

• BIBLIOGRAPHY •

10/23 "Turkologischer Anzeiger." In Wiener Zeitschrift für die Kunde des Morgenlandes, 67 (1975)--.

Lengthy separately paged annual suppl., in classified order. 72 (1980).
     295 pp. Literature: pp. 53-77, entries 398-746.

• HISTORIES •

10/24 Philologiae Turcicae Fundamenta. Aquis Mattiacis [i. e., Wies-
       baden]: Steiner, 1959-64.

2 vols. Vol. 2: Turkish literatures, 963 pp. Chapters, chiefly in Ger-
     man, on folk literature, ancient and modern Turkish literature,
     and other literatures of Turkey. Bibls. with each chapter. Index
     of names and subjects.

10/25 Gibb, Elias J. W. History of Ottoman Poetry. London: Luzac,
       1900-1909.

6 vols., ed by E. G. Browne. Covers through the late 19th c.

10/26 Bombaci, Alessio. La letteratura turca. Con un profilo della
       letteratura mongola. Firenze: Sansoni/Milano: Accademia, 1969.
       528 pp.

New ed. 1st ed. 1963. Transl. into French: Histoire de la littérature
     turque, Paris: Klincksieck, 1968, 435 pp.

● HEBREW and YIDDISH LITERATURES ●

• BIBLIOGRAPHIES •

10/27 Shunami, Shlomo. Bibliography of Jewish Bibliographies. Jeru-
       salem: Magnes Pr., Hebrew Univ., 1965. 992 pp.

2nd ed. 1st ed. 1936. Suppl., 1975, 464 pp. Covers all aspects of
     Jewish culture and history, through the mid 20th c. Chapter 14:
     Jewish literature, pp. 201-17, entries 1146-1240. Also sections on
     the Bible, the Talmud, and Yiddish, Judeo-Spanish and Portuguese
     literatures, and a section of author bibls.

Because this cites bibls. which are attached to studies, incl. periodical
and encyclopedia arts. in various langs., it may also serve as a
partial subject index to studies on Jewish topics.

10/28 Index of Articles on Jewish Studies. 1969--.
Covers 1966--. Annual. Lists arts. in Hebrew, English and other langs.
Classified arrangement. Section 8: literature, incl. Hebrew literature, divided into 3 periods, Yiddish literature, other literatures, and "Jews and Judaism in World Literature." Subject index,
of names (people and places) and titles only, in English and Hebrew. 16 (1979): Section 8: pp. 51-66, entries 809-1072. The
Index to Jewish Periodicals: An Author and Subject Index to Selected English Language Journals of General and Scholarly Interest,
1963/64--, covers 40 journals, none much concerned with literature.

• TRANSLATIONS •

10/29 Goell, Yohai. Bibliography of Modern Hebrew Literature in English
Translation. Jerusalem: Israel U. Pr., 1968. 110 + 22 pp.
More than 3150 entries, from books, journals and newspapers. Covers
literature from the latter part of the 19th c. and after. See also
his Bibliography of Modern Hebrew Literature in Translation, Tel
Aviv: Inst. for the Translation of Hebrew Literature, 1975, 117
pp., which covers literature since 1917, in book-length transl.,
chiefly, into 25 langs., Arabic to Yiddish.

• HISTORIES •

10/30 Waxman, Meyer. A History of Jewish Literature. N. Y.: Yoseloff,
1960.
5 vols. in 6. 3rd ed. 1st ed. 1930-33, in 4 vols. Covers through 1960.

10/31 Zinberg, Israel. A History of Jewish Literature. Cleveland &
London: Case Western Reserve U. Pr., 1972-78.

12 vols. From vol. 4 publ. by Cincinnati: Hebrew Union College/N. Y.:
    Ktav. Ed. and transl. by Bernard Martin from the Yiddish orig.,
    1929-66. Brief index in each vol. Bibl. essay in each vol.

10/32 Silberschlag, Eisig. From Renaissance to Renaissance: Hebrew
    Literature from 1492-1970. N. Y.: Ktav, 1973-77.
2 vols. 1: Hebrew Literature from 1492-1970. 1973. 431 pp. 2: Hebrew
    Literature in the Land of Israel, 1870-1970. 1977. 427 pp. In-
    dex of names in each vol. No bibls., but many notes, occasionally
    citing English transls. All quotations in English only.

● ● INDIC LITERATURES ● ●

● BIBLIOGRAPHIES ●

10/33 South Asian Bibliography: A Handbook and Guide. Sussex, Engl.:
    Harvester Pr., 1979. 381 pp.
J. D. Pearson, gen. ed. Covers India and Pakistan and neighboring coun-
    tries from Tibet to Ceylon. Language and Literature, by Albertine
    Guar and others, pp. 166-201.
JASt 39 (1979/80):375-76--mixed, but no mention of literature section

10/34 Gidwani, N. N. and K. Navalani. A Guide to Reference Materials
    on India. Jaipur: Sarasivati, 1974.
2 vols. 1536 pp. Literature: pp. 857-96. Cites books and arts., incl.
    a few encyclopedia arts., in English and the Indian langs. Sec-
    tions on the various literatures of India, Assamese-Urdu. Index,
    incl. names and other subjects.
JASt 35 (1975/76):528x--v fav

● HISTORIES ●

10/35 Dimock, Edward C., et al. The Literatures of India: An Intro-
    duction. Chicago: U. of Chicago Pr., 1974. 265 pp.

Chapters on the epic, classical drama, poetics, lyric, "story litera-
    ture," and on Bengali novels and Hindi short stories. Index of
    names and other subjects.
JASt 35 (1975/76):158-59--v fav

10/36 A History of Indian Literature. Wiesbaden: Harrassowitz, 1973--.
10 vols. projected, all in several parts. Jan Gonda, ed. The vols. incl:
1:   Veda and Upanishads. 3 parts projected.
2:   Epics and Sanskrit Religious Literature. 3 parts projected.
3:   Classical Sanskrit Literature. 3 parts projected.
4-6: Scientific and Technical Literature.
     5:1 Edwin Gerow. Indian Poetics. 1977. pp. 217-301.
8-9: Modern Indo-Aryan Literature.
     8:1 Urdu and Hindi
     8:1:5 P. Gaeffke. Hindi Literature in the Twentieth Century.
            1978. 118 pp.
            BSOAS 44 (1981):186
     9:   Other literatures
     9:3 Dusan Zbavitel. Bengali Literature. 1976. pp. 119-307.
          Notes and index of names and titles. Most of the book covers
          lit. since the 18th c.
     9:4 Shankar Gopal Tulpule. Classical Marāthī Literature, from
          the Beginning to A. D. 1818. 1979. pp. 311-471.
10: Dravidian Literature.
     10:1 Kamil Veith Zvelebil. Tamil Literature. 1974. 316 pp.
          JASt 37 (1977/78):380-82x; JAsiat 267 (1977):461-64

10/37 History and Culture of the Indian People. Bombay: Bharatiya Vidya
       Bhavan, 1951-77.
11 vols. Most vols. have lengthy chapters on the literatures of the
    major langs. of India, by various scholars. II: The Age of Impe-
    rial Unity, chapter 16, Language and Literature: appr. 60 pp. on
    Sanskrit and Dravidian. VII: The Mughal Empire, chapter 19, Liter-
    ature: nearly 80 pp., in 16 sections, each on a different lang.

10/38 A Cultural History of India. Oxford: Clarendon Pr., 1975. 585
     pp.
A. L. Basham, ed. Incl. 3 brief chapters on literature.

10/38a Winternitz, Moriz. A History of Indian Literature. N.Y.: Rus-
     sell & Russell, 1971.
Reprint of the 1927-33 ed. 2 vols. I: Introduction, Veda, National
     Epics, Purāṇas and Tantras. 634 pp. II: Buddhist Literature and
     Jaina Literature. 673 pp. Transl. by S. Ketkar and H. Kohn from
     the German.

10/39 Winternitz, Moriz. History of Indian Literature. Delhi, etc.:
     Motilal Banarsidass, 1963.
Transl. "with additions" by Subhadra Jhā of vol. 3 of Winternitz's his-
     tory. In 2 parts, 720 pp. I: Classical Sanskrit Literature. II:
     The Scientific Literature.

● ● SOUTH-EAST ASIAN LITERATURES ● ●

● BIBLIOGRAPHIES ●

10/40 Johnson, Donald Clay. A Guide to Reference Materials on South-
     east Asia, Based on the Collections in the Yale and Cornell Univer-
     sity Libraries. New Haven: Yale U. Pr., 1970. 160 pp.
Section O: Language and literature, pp. 69-72.

10/41 Johnson, Donald Clay. Index to Southeast Asian Journals, 1960-
     1974: A Guide to Articles, Book Reviews, and Composite Works. Bos-
     ton: Hall, 1977. 811 pp.
Covers all aspects of culture and society, incl. literature. Alphabet-
     ical subject arrangement. Lists arts. from 44 journals, none
     specifically devoted to literature, and from a number of books,
     mostly in English.

10/42 Nemenzo, Catalina A. "Southeast Asian Languages and Literatures
       in English: An Annotated Bibliography." In Philippine Social
       Sciences and Humanities Review 34 (1969):1-984.
Not seen. Said by Jenner (10/43) to contain nearly 7500 entries, from
       1624 to 1966, incl. 3800 on Philippine literature.

● TRANSLATIONS ●

10/43 Jenner, Philip N. Southeast Asian Literatures in Translation: A
       Preliminary Bibliography. Honolulu: U. Pr. of Hawaii, 1973.
       (Asian Studies at Hawaii, 9) 198 pp.
Lists transls. publ. as books or in books and journals, covering 9 na-
       tions, Burma to Vietnam, incl. the Philippines. Each section also
       incl. a brief list of general literary studies.

● ● EAST ASIAN LITERATURES ● ●

● JAPANESE LITERATURE ●

● TRANSLATIONS ●

10/44 Kokusai Bunka Kaikan, Tokyo. Toshoshitsu. Modern Japanese Liter-
       ature in Translation: A Bibliography. Tokyo: Kodansha, 1979. 311
       pp.
New ed. 1st ed. 1972. Transls. into English and other langs., incl.
       Russian, Arabic, Chinese, etc., of literature since 1868, and
       publ. as books or in books and journals.
BSOAS 43 (1980):628-29

● HANDBOOK ●

10/45 Hisamatsu, Sen'ichi. Biographical Dictionary of Japanese Liter-
       ature. Tokyo: Kodansha, 1976. 437 pp.
By period. Brief entries, few more than 1 p. "Selected Glossary," pp.

363-75, incl. forms and a few anonymous works. Index of names, as
well as titles and technical terms in Japanese.

JASt 36 (1976/77):760-61--**fav**, but questions whether well adapted for
use by people without knowledge of Japanese; also notes omissions
in modern section.

• HISTORIES •

10/46 Katō, Shūichi. A History of Japanese Literature. Tokyo & N. Y.:
Kodansha, 1979--.

Transl. by David Chibbett. I: The First Thousand Years. 319 pp. Covers through the mid 16th c. Glossary of technical terms.

10/47 Keene, Donald. World Within Walls: Japanese Literature of the
Pre-Modern Era, 1600-1867. N. Y.: Holt, Rinehart Winston, 1976.
606 pp.

Bibls. with each chapter. Index of names, titles and other subjects.
"Glossary of Japanese Terms and of Certain Japanese and Chinese
Names," pp. 571-80. Quotations in Japanese (transliterated) and
English.

10/48 Martins Janeira, Armando. Japanese and Western Literature: A
Comparative Study. Rutland, Vt.: Tuttle, 1970. 394 pp.

Most of book deals with lit. from the 17th c., and esp. since 1868. Index of names and other subjects.

YWMLS 74:371

• PLOTS •

10/49 Kokusai Bunka Shinkōkai, Tokyo. Introduction to Classic Japanese
Literature. Tokyo: N. p., 1948. 443 pp.

10/50 Kokusai Bunka Shinkōkai, Tokyo. Introduction to Contemporary
Japanese Literature. Tokyo: KBS, 1939. 485 pp.

Plot summaries and biographies, 1902-1935.

10/51 Kokusai Bunka Shinkōkai, Tokyo. Introduction to Contemporary
       Japanese Literature, 1936-1955: Part II. Tokyo: KBS, 1959. 296
       pp.

10/52 Kokusai Bunka Shinkōkai, Tokyo. Introduction to Contemporary
       Japanese Literature, 1956-1970: Synopses of Major Works. Tokyo:
       U. of Tokyo Pr., 1972. 313 pp.

• POETRY •

10/53 Rimer, J. Thomas and Robert E. Morrell. Guide to Japanese Poetry.
       Boston: Hall, 1975. 151 pp.
Annotated bibl. of transls. and criticism, books and arts., in English.

• FICTION •

10/54 Marks, Alfred H. and Barry D. Bort. Guide to Japanese Prose.
       Boston: Hall, 1975. 150 pp.
Mostly plot summaries.

10/55 Rimer, J. Thomas. Modern Japanese Fiction and Its Traditions: An
       Introduction. Princeton: Princeton U. Pr., 1978. 313 pp.
Chapters on 20th c. novelists and their "antecedents" and sources.
JASt 40 (1980/81):140-42; BSOAS 42 (1979):398-400x--v fav

• DRAMA •

10/56 Pronko, Leonard C. Guide to Japanese Drama. Boston: Hall, 1973.
       125 pp.
Annotated bibl. of transls. and criticism, publ. as books in English.
JASt 34 (1974/75):533-34--v fav

10/57 Leiter, Samuel L. Kabuki Encyclopedia: An English-Language Adaptation of Kabuki Jiten. Westport, Conn. & London: Greenwood Pr.,
1979. 572 pp.
Rev., reorganized and expanded transl. of Kabuki Jiten, by Jirō Yamamoto,
et al. Biographies, plot-summaries and technical terms. Chronology. Classified bibl. Index of names, titles and technical
terms.

● CHINESE LITERATURE ●

• BIBLIOGRAPHIES •

10/58 Lust, John and Werner Eichhorn. Index Sinicus: A Catalogue of
Articles Relating to China in Periodicals and Other Collective
Publications, 1920-1955. Cambridge, Engl.: Heffer, 1964. 663 pp.
Section 15: Literature: pp. 336-58, entries 11609-12397, in 5 sections,
incl. poetry (subdivided by period), drama and fiction. Lists
arts. from journals and books in various langs. Indexes of scholars and subjects. Continues Cordier (10/59) and suppls. Yuan
(10/60).

10/59 Cordier, Henri. Bibliotheca Sinica. Paris: Libraire orientale
et americaine, 1904-24.
2nd ed., rev., corrected and enlarged. 3 vols. and 2 vol. suppl. Section 13, vol. 3: Langue et littérature, cols. 1577-1834; literature, cols. 1753-1834. Some annotations.

10/60 Yuan, T'ung-Li. China in Western Literature: A Continuation of
Cordier's Bibliotheca Sinica. New Haven, Conn.: Far Eastern
Publs., Yale U., 1958. 802 pp.
Lists books in English, French and German, 1921-57. No annotations.

10/61 Li, Tien-Yi. The History of Chinese Literature: A Selected Bibliography. New Haven, Conn.: Far Eastern Publs., Yale U., 1970.

98 pp.
2nd ed. 1st ed. 1968. Books only, in English, French, German, Chinese
    and Japanese.

10/62 Gibbs, Donald A., Yun-Chen Li and Christopher C. Rand. A Bibli-
    ography of Studies and Translations of Modern Chinese Literature,
    1918-1942. Cambridge, Mass.: East Asian Research Center, Harvard
    Univ., 1975. 239 pp.
Lists transls. into English and studies in English and other langs.,
    incl. books, arts. and diss.
JASt 36 (1976/77):140-41; BSOAS 39 (1976):511

● TRANSLATIONS ●

10/63 Davidson, Martha. A List of Published Translations from Chinese
    into English, French and German. New Haven: Far Eastern Publs.,
    Yale Univ., for the American Council of Learned Societies, 1952-57.
2 vols. 462 pp. Covers fiction, plays, poetry, etc.

● HISTORIES ●

10/64 Liu, Wu-chi. An Introduction to Chinese Literature. Bloomington
    & London: U. of Indiana Pr., 1966. 321 pp.
Covers to the 1930s. Bibl. of books in English, with occasional notes.
    Index of names, titles in English and other subjects.

10/65 Ch'ên, Shou-Yi. Chinese Literature: A Historical Introduction.
    N. Y.: Ronald Pr., 1961. 665 pp.
To the early 20th c. No bibl. or notes. Index of names, titles and
    other subjects.

10/66 Margouliès, Georges. Histoire de la littérature chinoise. Paris:
    Payot, 1949-51.
2 vols., covering prose and poetry separately.

10/67 Watson, Burton. <u>Early Chinese Literature</u>. N. Y. & London: Columbia U. Pr., 1962. 304 pp.
Sections on history, philosophy and poetry, to about 100 A. D. Brief
bibls., of books only, in English. Index of names and Chinese titles, with cross-refs. from English titles.

• POETRY •

10/68 Bailey, Roger B. <u>Guide to Chinese Poetry and Drama</u>. Boston:
Hall, 1973. 100 pp.
Annotated bibl. of transls. and studies in English, mostly books.
Poetry: pp. 1-75.

• DRAMA •

10/69 Dolby, William. <u>A History of Chinese Drama</u>. N. Y.: Harper & Row/
London: Elek, 1976. 327 pp.
Covers to the present. Lengthy quotations, in English. Bibls. of eds.,
of studies, chiefly in English, Chinese and Japanese, and of
transls. into English, French, German, etc. Index of names, titles
in Chinese and English, technical terms and other subjects.
TLS June 3, 1977, p. 673

• FICTION •

10/70 Li, Tien-Yi. <u>Chinese Fiction: A Bibliography of Books and Arti-
cles in Chinese and English</u>. New Haven, Conn.: Far Eastern Publs.,
Yale U., 1968. 356 pp.
By period, then by genre, or, for modern period, by work.

10/71 Chou, Shu-Jên. <u>A Brief History of Chinese Fiction</u>. Peking: Foreign Langs. Pr., 1959. 462 pp.

"By Lu Hsun."   Transls. by Yang Hsien-Yi and Gladys Yang of the 1930
     Chinese ed.   Covers to about 1900.   Index of names and titles in
     English.

10/72   Yang, Winston L. Y., Peter Li and Nathan K. Mao.   Classical Chin-
     ese Fiction: A Guide to Its Study and Appreciation: Essays and
     Bibliographies.   Boston: Hall, 1978.   302 pp.
Bibls., pp. 119-278, listing eds., transls., and studies, incl. books,
     arts. and diss., mostly in English.
JASt 39 (1979/80):339-40--v fav

10/73   Paper, Jordan D.   Guide to Chinese Prose.   Boston: Hall, 1973.
     137 pp.
Annotated bibl. of transls., with some refs. to studies in English.

XI

RELATED FIELDS

OUTLINE

ARTS AND HUMANITIES

GENERAL
    Bibliographies 11/1-11/2

ART
    Bibliographies 11/3-11/6
    Handbooks and Encyclopedias 11/7-11/9
    Themes 11/10-11/13
    Histories 11/14-11/15

FILM
    Bibliographies 11/16-11/22
    Dissertations 11/23
    Handbooks 11/24-11/29
    Histories 11/30-11/31

FOLKLORE
    Bibliographies 11/32-11/36
    Handbooks 11/37-11/38
    Themes 11/39-11/40

Mythology
  Bibliography 11/41
  Handbooks 11/42-11/43

HISTORY
  Bibliographies 11/44-11/45
  Handbook 11/46
  Chronology 11/47

LINGUISTICS
  Bibliographies 11/48-11/52
  Dictionaries 11/53-11/54

MUSIC
  Bibliographies 11/55-11/57
  Handbooks 11/58-11/59
  Histories 11/60-11/61
  Special Topics
    Opera
      Handbooks 11/62-11/63
      History 11/64
    Song
      History 11/65
    Dance
      Bibliography 11/66
      Handbooks 11/67-11/68

PHILOSOPHY
  Bibliographies 11/69-11/72
  Handbooks, Encyclopedias 11/73-11/74
  Special Topics
    Aesthetics
      Bibliography 11/75
      Histories 11/76-11/77

● ● RELATED FIELDS ● ●

● ● ARTS and HUMANITIES ● ●

● GENERAL ●

● BIBLIOGRAPHIES ●

⸢The best general indexes of studies on the other arts and humanities
     have already been cited, for their coverage of literary research:
     Humanities Index (1/12); Arts and Humanities Citation Index (1/13);
     Current Contents: Arts and Humanities (1/14); Essay and General
     Literature Index (1/15) and Index to Social Sciences and Humanities
     Proceedings (1/16).⸥

11/1 Modern Language Assn. of America. General Topics 9. Bibliography
     Committee. A Bibliography on the Relations of Literature and the
     Other Arts, 1952-1967. N. Y.: AMS, 1968.
Reprints the 1952-58 bibl. and the annual bibls. for 1959-67, uncumulated
     and paginated separately. In 3 sections: I: Theory and General;
     II: Music and Literature; III: Visual Arts and Literature.

11/2 "A Bibliography for ⸢year⸥ on the Relations of Literature and the
     Other Arts." In Hartford Studies in Literature, 6 (1974)-8 (1976).
Installments 21-23, for 1973-75. The intervening installments were not
     formally published.

● ART ●

● BIBLIOGRAPHIES ●

11/3 Arntzen, Etta and Robert Rainwater. Guide to the Literature of
     Art History. Chicago: American Library Assn./London: Art Book
     Co., 1980. 616 pp.

Annotated list of bibls., indexes, dictionaries and encyclopedias, sur-
     veys, etc., incl. a few items publ. in journals. Sections A-I:
     general sources, by form or topic. F: Iconography, pp. 60-71, 86
     entries. Sections J-P: the particular arts, subdivided by topic,
     by nation or by form. M: Painting, pp. 279-351, 583 entries, incl.
     sections on general bibl., biographical collections, handbooks,
     and on periods, regions and nations. Author-title index and sub-
     ject index. Incl. photography, but not film.
This is a revision of Mary W. Chamberlin, Guide to Art Reference Books,
     Chicago: A. L. A., 1959, 418 pp. Note also Donald L. Ehresmann,
     Fine Arts: A Bibliographic Guide to Basic Reference Works, Histo-
     ries and Handbooks, Littleton, Colo.: Libraries Unlimited, 1979.
     2nd ed. 1st ed. 1975. Classified arrangement. Annotated, with
     evaluative comments.
Art Bull 59 (1977):300-03--Ehresmann, the 1st ed.

11/4 Art Index. 1929--.
4/yr., with an annual cumulation. Covers journals in English and other
     W. European langs. Alphabetical list of subjects and scholars,
     with cross-refs. 28 (1979/80):Art-Themes: 1 3/4 cols. of cross-
     refs., incl. Melancholy, Monkeys and Sphinxes; Art and Literature:
     3/4 col. of entries, incl. arts. on Melville, Tasso and Zola.
     Also covers film and photography.

11/5 RILA: Répertoire international de la littérature de l'art. Inter-
     national Bibliography of the Literature of Art. 1975--.
2/yr. Classified arrangement, in 7 sections, most covering a period,
     medieval to modern, in "post-classical European and post-Columbian
     American art." (Pref.) Subject index, incl. specific themes;
     also "Literature and Art" and "Poetry and Art."
TLS 18 March, 1977, 301

11/6 Artbibliographies: Modern. 1969--.
2/yr. Covers art since 1800. Gives abstracts. Vols. 1-3 called LOMA:

Literature on Modern Art. This bibl. can be searched through a
computer service.

• HANDBOOKS •

11/7 Encyclopedia of World Art. Enciclopedia universale dell'arte.
        N. Y.: McGraw-Hill, 1959-68.
14 vols. and index vol. Long, detailed arts. on major topics and art-
        ists, with bibls. Myth and Fable: 50 cols., in a number of sec-
        tions, and 4 cols. bibl. Baroque Art: 118 cols. and 8+ cols. bibl.
        All arts. are in English; there is also an Italian version.

11/8 McGraw-Hill Dictionary of Art. N. Y.: McGraw-Hill, 1969.
5 vols. Bernard S. and Shirley Myers, eds. Brief arts. on artists,
        paintings, buildings, cities, and other topics, incl. much not
        covered in a separate entry in the Encyclopedia of World Art (11/7).

11/9 Osborne, Harold. The Oxford Companion to Art. Oxford: Clarendon
        Pr., 1970. 1277 pp.
Brief unsigned arts. covering artists, movements, periods (Baroque: 6
        3/4 cols.), and technical terms. "A non-specialist introduction
        to the fine arts" (Pref.).

• THEMES •

11/10 Iconclass: An Iconographic Classification System. Amsterdam:
        North-Holland, for the Netherlands Academy of Arts and Sciences,
        1973--.
"Devised by H. van de Waal; completed and edited by L. D. Couprie with R.
        H. Fuchs and E. Tholen." Publ. in sections.
1:    The Supernatural, God and Religion. Not yet publ.
2-3: Nature, Human Being, Man in General.
4:    Society, Civilization, Culture.
5-6: Abstract Ideas and Concepts. History.

7:    The Bible. Not yet publ.

8-9: Literature. Classical Mythology and Ancient History.

Sections 6-9 cover particular traditional, literary or historical instan-
    ces of general concepts covered in sections 1-5. In 2 "series."
    I: a classified list of themes and subjects; II: a bibl. of stud-
    ies, incl. books, arts. and passages in the standard reference
    works, arranged to parallel series I. 81A (i. e., subsection 1A
    of section 8): Arthurian subjects, by person and episode. 98C:
    Greek and Roman women, Artemesia through Zenobia Septimia.

11/11 Hall, James. Dictionary of Subjects and Symbols in Art. N. Y.,
    etc.: Harper & Row, 1975. 345 pp.

Characters and events, objects, etc., from Christian and classical myth-
    ology. Flora: 2/3 p., citing classical sources and 4 themes asso-
    ciated with her. Cross-refs. Does not cite particular works of
    art, or artists. Illus. with occasional sketches.

ArchR 157 (1975):184; Apollo ns 101 (1975):146--v fav; Studio 188 (1974):
    211--unfav

11/12 Tervarent, G. de. Attributs et symboles dans l'art profane,
    1450-1600: Dictionnaire d'un langage perdu. Genève: Droz, 1958-
    64. (Travaux d'Humanisme et Renaissance) 484 cols.

Cites themes from literature and mythology, etc., and examples of their
    use in art. Lyre: 6 significations; Miroir: 7 significations.

11/13 Ferguson, George Wells, Signs and Symbols in Christian Art, with
    Illustrations from the Painters of the Renaissance. N. Y.: Oxford
    U. Pr., 1954. 346 pp.

In 14 sections: Animals, Birds, Insects; Religious Objects; etc. Does
    not cite particular works of art in the text, but many full-page
    illus., some in color.

●   HISTORIES   ●

11/14 Hartt, Frederick. <u>Art</u>: <u>A</u> <u>History</u> <u>of</u> <u>Painting</u>, <u>Sculpture</u>, <u>Archi-
       tecture</u>. N. Y.: Abrams, 1976.
2 vols. Western art only. Vol. 1: Prehistory [incl. recent pre-liter-
       ate societies], Ancient World, Middle Ages. 468 pp. Vol. 2:
       Renaissance, Baroque, The Modern World. 527 pp. Chronological
       charts of political, cultural and artistic landmarks with each
       section. Glossary of technical terms, bibl. of books, paralleling
       text, and index of names, incl. titles of works of art, and other
       subjects in each vol.

11/15 Bland, David. <u>A</u> <u>History</u> <u>of</u> <u>Book</u> <u>Illustration</u>: <u>The</u> <u>Illuminated</u>
       <u>Manuscript</u> <u>and</u> <u>the</u> <u>Printed</u> <u>Book</u>. Berkeley: U. of Calif. Pr.,
       459 pp.
2nd ed. 1st ed, 1958. Chapters 1-3 cover western and oriental manu-
       scripts. Index of names, titles and other subjects.

●   FILM   ●

●   BIBLIOGRAPHIES   ●

11/16 **Vincent, Richard C.** "An Introduction to Film Bibliographies" and
       "Bibliography of Film Reference Sources." In <u>Journal</u> <u>of</u> <u>the</u> <u>Uni-
       versity</u> <u>Film</u> <u>Assn.</u> 28:3 (Summer, 1976):39-43 and 29:3 (Summer,
       1977):43-56.
Annotated lists of bibls., handbooks, lists of films and film revs., etc.

11/17 Welch, Jeffrey Egan. <u>Literature</u> <u>and</u> <u>Film</u>: <u>An</u> <u>Annotated</u> <u>Bibliog-
       raphy</u>, <u>1909</u>-<u>1977</u>. N. Y. & London: Garland, 1981. 315 pp.
1102 entries for books and arts., by year of publ. Indexes.

11/18 <u>International</u> <u>Index</u> <u>to</u> <u>Film</u> <u>Periodicals</u>: <u>An</u> <u>Annotated</u> <u>Guide</u>.
       1973--.

Now an annual. Covers from 1972--. 1979: 593 pp., in 11 sections, incl.
 Aesthetics, Theory, Criticism; and Individual Films (by title in
 orig. lang., without transl.: 150 pp.). Covers about 70 film
 journals, in English and other langs. Indexes incl. directors and
 other subjects.

11/19 Film Literature Index. 1973--.
4/yr., and annual cumulation. Slow to appear. Covers about 250 journals
 in film and the humanities, in English and other langs., as well as
 some popular magazines. Subjects and scholars, alphabetically.
 The cumulated vol. of 4 (1976) was never publ.

11/20 The Film Index: A Bibliography. N. Y.: Museum of Modern Art Film
 Library and the H. W. Wilson Co., 1941.
I: The Film as Art. 723 pp. No more publ. Books and arts.

11/21 MacCann, Richard Dyer and Edward S. Perry. The New Film Index: A
 Bibliography of Magazine Articles in English, 1930-1970. N. Y.:
 Dutton, 1975. 522 pp.
Classified arrangement. Relations with the Other Arts: pp. 140-50.

11/22 Eschbach, Achim and Wendelin Rader. Film Semiotik: Eine Bibliographie. Semiotics of Film: A Bibliography. Sémiologie du cinéma:
 Une bibliographie. München, N. Y., etc.: Saur, 1978. 203 pp.
2480 entries for books, arts. and chapters in books, by author. Index of
 names and other subjects. See also their Semiotik-Bibliographie
 (1/77), which contains a chapter on film.

· DISSERTATIONS ·

11/23 Fielding, R. A Bibliography of Theses and Dissertations on the
 Subject of Film, 1916-1979. Houston, Texas: University Film Assn.
 at the School of Communication, U. of Houston, 1979. (Univ. Film
 Assn. Monograph, 3) 72 pp.

1420 entries, by scholar, with a subject index using very broad cate-
     gories.

● HANDBOOKS ●

11/24 Katz, Ephraim. The Film Encyclopedia. N. Y.: Crowell, 1979.
       1266 pp.
Biographies, with list of films, 1/2 col. to several pp. Technical
     terms, briefly defined. No entries on films.
FLQ 13:2/3 (1980):46

11/25 Bawden, Liz-Anne. Oxford Companion to Film. N. Y. & London: Ox-
       ford U. Pr., 1976. 767 pp.
Brief arts. Biographies, films, national histories, technical terms.
FilmC 12:6 (Nov.-Dec., 1976):62-64--v unfav, esp. as regards accuracy
     and criticism, but praises technical entries; QJFS 3 (1978):97-
     98x--v unfav, esp. as regards accuracy; NYRB Sept. 16, 1976, pp.
     38-39x--v unfav

11/26 Sadoul, Georges. Dictionary of Films. Berkeley & Los Angeles: U.
       of California Pr., 1972. 432 pp.
Transl., ed. and updated by Peter Morris from 1965 French ed. Brief sum-
     maries, under title in orig. lang. Cross-refs. from English title.
Films in Rev 24 (1973):46-47

11/27 Sadoul, Georges. Dictionary of Film Makers. Berkeley: U. of
       California Pr., 1972. 288 pp.
Transl., ed. and updated from 1965 French ed. by Peter Morris. Brief en-
     tries on directors, screenwriters, producers, cameramen, etc., but
     not actors.
Films in Rev 24 (1973):46-47

11/28 Filmlexicon degli autori e delle opere. Roma: Bianco e Nero,
       1958-67.

7 vols. <u>Aggiornamento</u>, <u>1958</u>-<u>1971</u>, 2 vols., 1973-74. Biographical arts.
only, with bibls. of books and arts. and lists of films. The plan-
ned vols. on films have not been publ.

11/29 Thiery, Herman. <u>Dictionnaire</u> <u>filmographique</u> <u>de</u> <u>la</u> <u>littérature</u>
<u>mondiale</u>. <u>Filmographic</u> <u>Dictionary</u> <u>of</u> <u>World</u> <u>Literature</u>. Ghent:
Story-Scientia/N. Y.: Humanities, 1971-75.
2 vols. "By Johan Daisne." Arranged by name of novelist or playwright.
O'Neill: 9 works, giving year, director, cast and roles. Note also
A. G. S. Enser, <u>Filmed</u> <u>Books</u> <u>and</u> <u>Plays</u>: <u>A</u> <u>List</u> <u>of</u> <u>Books</u> <u>and</u> <u>Plays</u>
<u>from</u> <u>which</u> <u>Films</u> <u>Have</u> <u>Been</u> <u>Made</u>, <u>1928</u>-<u>1974</u>, N. Y.: Academic Pr.,
1975, 549 pp., a bare list of titles and year of production.

• HISTORIES •

11/30 Robinson, David. <u>The</u> <u>History</u> <u>of</u> <u>World</u> <u>Cinema</u>. N. Y.: Stein and
Day, 1981. 494 pp.
Rev. and updated. 1st ed. 1973. Selected Filmographies, pp. 401-71.
Indexes of general topics, of films, and of persons.

11/31 Rhode, Eric. <u>A</u> <u>History</u> <u>of</u> <u>the</u> <u>Cinema</u>: <u>From</u> <u>Its</u> <u>Origins</u> <u>to</u> <u>1970</u>.
N. Y.: Hill & Wang, 1976. 674 pp.
Bibl. of books only, paralleling text. Index of names and films.
QJFS 3 (1978):95-97--v fav

• FOLKLORE •

• BIBLIOGRAPHIES •

11/32 Brunvand, Jan Harold. <u>Folklore</u>: <u>A</u> <u>Study</u> <u>and</u> <u>Research</u> <u>Guide</u>.
N. Y.: St. Martin's, 1976. 144 pp.
Ch. 1: history of theories of folklore, pp. 7-33; ch. 2: "Reference
Guide," pp. 35-84. Also a lengthy section on writing a research
paper.

JAF 91 (1978):872-74

11/33   Internationale Volkskundliche Bibliographie. International Folk-
        lore and Folklife Bibliography. Bibliographie internationale des
        arts et traditions populaires. 1949--.
Covers 1939/41--. Recently this has appeared every 2 years. 1975/76,
        publ. 1979: 727 pp., 8637 numbered entries, on the traditional cul-
        ture of W. and E. Europe, incl. the Americas. Classified arrange-
        ment, incl. appr. 60 pp. on poetry and 45 pp. on narrative, both
        subdivided by lang. or culture. Occasional brief annotations.
        Indexes of scholars and of subjects, incl. names. Continues sever-
        al earlier bibls.

11/34   MLA International Bibliography. (See 1/9).
In recent years there has been a lengthy section on folklore in "vol." 1,
        covering all aspects of traditional culture, incl. music, dance,
        games and objects, as well as folk literature. The items con--
        cerned with African and E. European traditional culture are re-
        peated in the folklore subsections of those sections of "vol." 2.
        1980: more than 3350 entries in 9 sections. II: Prose narratives,
        500 entries in 5 sections, incl. Myths and Legends, and Folktales,
        each subdivided by continent.

11/35   Folklore Bibliography for [year]. 1975--.
Covers from 1973. Compiled by Merle E. Simmons. Follows the regrettable
        schedule of publ. an annual vol. every other year. 1975, publ.
        1979. Continues his bibl. in Southern Folklore Quarterly, 2
        (1938)-37 (1973). Both are annotated classified bibls., chiefly on
        the folk culture of the Iberian peninsula and of the Americas,
        incl. the U. S. and the Caribbean. No indexes.

11/36   Abstracts of Folklore Studies. 1 (1963)-13 (1975).
Arranged by journal. Annual index of authors and subjects. Note also
        the "Annual Folklore Bibliography" in the Journal of American

Folklore, 69 (1956)-76 (1963), which cited books and arts. from appr. 150 journals, under 12 broad subject headings.   No indexes.

• HANDBOOKS •

11/37 Funk and Wagnalls Standard Dictionary of Folklore, Mythology and Legend.   N. Y.: Funk and Wagnalls, 1972.   1236 pp.

Rev. ed.   1st ed. in 2 vols., 1949-50.   Maria Leach, ed.   Mostly brief arts., sometimes with bibls., some signed.   Arthur: 2 1/2 cols.; Leprosy: 1 2/3 cols.; Letter of Death: 3/4 col., incl. ref. to its use in Hamlet.

11/38 Enzyklopädie des Märchens: Handwörterbuch zur historischen und vergleichenden Erzählforschung.   Berlin & N. Y.: de Gruyter, 1977--.

Kurt Ranke, ed.   2+ vols. to date, through Drei, each with 1400+ cols. Signed arts., generally 3-5 cols., with bibls., on folk tales (citing Aarne-Thompson number [see 11/39]), characters (Don Juan: 3 1/2 cols., plus 1+ col bibl.), countries (Brazil: 10 cols., in 5 sections, with bibls.), and writers who have drawn upon folk sources (Boccaccio: 10 cols. of text, 1 col. listing motifs used, and 1 col. bibl.).   Emphasis is on Europe and "those countries most heavily influenced by the European tradition" (publisher's advertisement).

JEGP 76 (1977):71-72; GQ 51 (1978):96-97x and 414-15; Folklore 187 (1976):242; 188 (1977):244-45; 191 (1980):199-20

• THEMES •

11/39 Aarne, Antti A.   The Types of the Folktale: A Classification and Bibliography.   Helsinki: Suomalainen Tiedeakatemia, 1961.   588 pp.

2nd rev. ed.   Transl. by Stith Thompson.

11/40 Thompson, Stith.   Motif-Index of Folk-Literature: A Classification

of Narrative Elements in Folktales, Ballads, Myths, Fables, Medieval Romances, Exempla, Fabliaux, Jest-books and Local Legends.
Bloomington: Indiana U. Pr., 1955-58.

Rev. and enl. ed. A "type" is a "narrative capable of maintaining an
independent existence in tradition" (S. Thompson, Funk and Wag-
nall's Standard Dict. [11/38]); a "motif" is a plot-element or epi-
sode found in a folk narrative. Cinderella represents a tale-type;
the wicked step-mother or the talking mirror would be motifs. Both
these books are systematic indexes to published collections of
materials in various European langs. There are also a number of
indexes to "types" or "motifs" in a national tradition or a body of
literature close to folk sources, many of which follow the Aarne-
Thompson or Thompson classification system. J. Wesley Childers,
Tales from Spanish Picaresque Novels: A Motif Index, Albany: SUNY
Pr., 1977, 262 pp. (Thompson system). Frederic C. Tubach, Index
Exemplorum: A Handbook of Medieval Religious Tales, Helsinki:
Suomalainen Tiedeakatemia, 1969, 530 pp. (alphabetical). Ernest
Warren Baughman, Type- and Motif-Index of the Folktales of England
and North America, The Hague: Mouton, 1966, 607 pp. And others.

• MYTHOLOGY •

BIBLIOGRAPHY

11/41 Peradotto, John. Classical Mythology: An Annotated Bibliographical Survey. Urbana, Ill.: Amer. Philological Assn., 1973. 76
pp.

Brief bibl. essays, incl. sections on Myth and Art and The Structural
Study of Myth, etc. Total of 212 references, mostly books, most in
English.

G&R 2 ser. 21 (1974):213

HANDBOOKS

11/42 Mayerson, Philip. Classical Mythology in Literature, Art and
       Music. Waltham, Mass.: Xerox College Publs., 1971. 509 pp.
Relates the myths and notes their use by writers and in classical and
       western art, as well as in opera and other forms of music. Or-
       pheus and Eurydice: 10 pp., citing works by Shakespeare, Poliziano,
       Cocteau, Rilke, Williams and others, and compositions from Monte-
       verdi to Milhaud. Illus.
ClassW 65 (1971/72):205-06; ClassP 67 (1972):152-53x--v fav

11/43 Tripp, Edward. Crowell's Handbook of Classical Mythology. N. Y.:
       Crowell, 1970. 631 pp.
Brief entries, chiefly on names of gods and other figures. Some entries
       for places and on writers and anonymous works which record the
       myths. Perseus: nearly 4 pp., citing 3 classical sources.
ClassW 67 (1973/74):404-05--v fav

● HISTORY ●

● BIBLIOGRAPHIES ●

11/44 International Bibliography of Historical Sciences. 1930--.
Annual. Slow to appear. Covers 1926--. Cites books and arts. in vari-
       ous W. and E. European Langs., from prehistory to the present,
       worldwide. Cites book revs. Classified arrangement.

11/45 Historical Abstracts. 1 (1955)--.
From 17 (1971) in 2 sections. A: Modern History Abstracts (1450-1914).
       B: Twentieth Century Abstracts (1914-[current year]). Each section
       publ. quarterly. Geographic and chronological arrangement.
       Lengthy subject indexes in each issue, cumulated annually and at
       5-year intervals. The current vols. are 1 (1955)-25 (1979) and
       31 (1980)--. The missing 5 vol. numbers have been set aside for

supplemental retrospective indexing, 1954-78, to be publ. at 1-yr.
intervals. This bibl. can be searched through a computer service.
Excludes the U. S. and Canada, which are covered by a companion publ.,
America: History and Life: A Guide to Periodical Literature,
1964--, which covers from 1955. In addition, there are annual
bibls. listing research on a number of countries, particularly
of W. Europe, which cannot be listed here.

• HANDBOOK •

11/46 Dictionary of World History. London: Nelson, 1973. 1720 pp.
Gerald Malcolm David Howat, gen. ed. A. J. P. Taylor, advisory ed.
    Mostly brief entries, few as long as 1 col., on people, events,
    organizations and groups, and some general topics.

• CHRONOLOGY •

11/47 Langer, William L. An Encyclopedia of World History: Ancient,
    Medieval, and Modern, Chronologically Arranged. Boston: Houghton
    Mifflin, 1972. 1569 pp.
5th ed. 1st ed. 1940. Chronological arrangement is subdivided into
    chapters on regions and sometimes subjects, e. g., Science and
    Learning, 1450-1700. Dates followed by a paragraph or more of
    narrative. Index of names, pp. 1379-569, incl. people, places,
    events, etc.

• LINGUISTICS •

• BIBLIOGRAPHIES •

11/48 Bibliographie linguistique de l'année. 1949--.
Now an annual. Covers from 1939. 1978, publ. 1981. Classified arrange-
    ment with cross-refs. Some brief annotations. Cites book revs.
    The sections on the major European langs. (English, Spanish,

Russian, Polish, etc.) are subdivided by topic, incl. section 7:
Stylistics, Literary Language and section 8: Prosody, Metre, Versification. Index of scholars.

11/49 Bibliographie linguistischer Literatur (BLL). Bibliographie zur
allgemeine Linguistik und zur anglistischen, germanistischen und
romanistischen Linguistik. 1976--.

Now an annual. Vol. 1 covered 1971-75. Cites books and arts. Sections
on the language groups and languages, all subdivided in great detail, incl. sections on translation, stylistics and rhetoric.
Vols. 1-3 were called Bibliographie unselbständiger Literatur-
Linguistik (BUL-L) and listed only arts.

11/50 LLBA: Language and Language Behavior Abstracts. 1967--.
4/yr. Lists books, arts., research reports, etc., in various langs.
Lists esp. research taking an interdisciplinary approach. Incl.
brief sections on poetics and stylistics, literary criticism and
literary theory. Indexes of scholars on subjects.

11/51 MLA International Bibliography. (See 1/9).
"Vol." 3 covers linguistics and the languages of the world. By language
family and language, with broad subject subdivisions. The sections
on many langs. have a subdivision "Stylistics."

11/52 Stankiewicz, E. "Bibliography of the History of Linguistics."
In Current Trends in Linguistcs, Thomas A. Sebeok, ed., vol. 13,
pt. 2, pp. 1381-446, The Hague: Mouton, 1975.
Books and arts. in various langs., in classified order, incl. sections on
periods, theorists (pp. 1406-39, incl. Aristotle, Dante and Rousseau) and countries.

• DICTIONARIES •

11/53 Crystal, David. A First Dictionary of Linguistics and Phonetics.

Boulder, Colo.: Westview Pr., 1980. 390 pp.
Brief entries on technical terms, a few with refs. to a bibl. of 22
    books. A few entries on schools and theorists. Entries may be so
    brief and dense with cross-refs. to other entries as to be diffi-
    cult to absorb. Sibilant: 7 lines, 8 cross-refs.
TLS 27 Feb., 1981, p. 235--v fav

11/54 Ducrot, Oswald. Encyclopedic Dictionary of the Sciences of Lan-
    guage. See 1/40.

• MUSIC •

• BIBLIOGRAPHIES •

11/55 Duckles, Vincent. Music Reference and Research Materials: An An-
    notated Bibliography. N. Y.: The Free Pr./London: Collier-Macmil-
    lan, 1974. 526 pp.
3rd ed. 1st ed. 1964. Classified list of bibls., encyclopedias, histo-
    ries, etc. Evaluative annotations, usually 2-3 sentences. Covers
    folk music, jazz, etc., as well as the European classical tradition.

11/56 Music Index. 1950--.
Covers 1949--. 12/yr., and belated annual cumulations. Monthly issues
    also slow to appear. Covers appr. 200 journals in the langs. of W.
    and E. Europe, incl. ones devoted to jazz, folk, and popular music,
    etc., and some general popular magazines and folklore journals.
    Subjects and scholars, alphabetically. Some brief notes. 26
    (1974) had headings Literary Texts, Musical Settings of (9 en-
    tries); Literature (13 cross-refs. to other subject headings, incl.
    Bible; Legends and Myths; and Poetry, but not incl. personal names,
    and 32 entries); also entries for authors, incl. Brecht (2 en-
    tries), T. Mann (6) and Blind Lemon Jefferson (2). 27 (1975) publ.
    1981. 33:2 (Feb. 1981) publ. early 1982.

11/57 <u>RILM</u> Abstracts <u>of</u> <u>Music</u> <u>Literature</u>. 1967--.
3/yr. and index. Slow to appear. Classified arrangement. Sections 75-
    79: Music and the Other Arts; Poetry and Literature: section 78 (35
    entries in 9 [1975] and many cross-refs. Lists books and arts. in
    various langs. 11:1 (Jan.-April, 1977) publ. 1981. This bibl. can
    be searched through a computer service.

• HANDBOOKS •

11/58 The <u>New</u> <u>Grove</u> <u>Dictionary</u> <u>of</u> <u>Music</u> <u>and</u> <u>Musicians</u>. London: Macmil-
    lan, 1980.
20 vols. Stanley Sadie, ed. Arts. on all aspects of music and music
    history, incl. poets (Shakespeare: 7 2/3 cols., plus bibl., incl.
    discussion of his use of music as symbol), Lieder writers, folk
    singers, popular composers and lyricists, and jazz musicians. No
    entries on literary themes as subjects of compositions. The orig.
    Grove's was publ. in 1878-89; 5th ed., 10 vols., 1954.
Opera 32 (1981):1000-03; Notes 38 (1981/82):45-49

11/59 Scholes, Percy A. The <u>Oxford</u> <u>Companion</u> <u>to</u> <u>Music</u>. London, etc.:
    Oxford U. Pr., 1970. 1189 pp.
10th ed., rev. by John Owen Ward. 1st ed. 1938. Brief entries on com-
    posers, technical terms, etc.
MusicalT 112 (1971):346-47

• HISTORIES •

11/60 Abraham, Gerald. The <u>Concise</u> <u>Oxford</u> <u>History</u> <u>of</u> <u>Music</u>. London,
    etc.: Oxford U. Pr., 1979. 968 pp.
Mainly on W. European music. Chapters on oriental music and the music of
    black people in Africa and the U. S. Annotated bibl., pp. 864-912.
    Index of names and other subjects.
TLS 24 Nov., 1980, p. 1207--v fav, except as regards the bibl.

11/61 Winn, James Anderson. Unsuspected Eloquence: A History of the
     Relations between Poetry and Music. New Haven, Conn.: Yale U. Pr.,
     1981. 381 pp.
Covers from classical Greece to Stravinsky. Gives musical quotations.

· OPERA ·

HANDBOOKS

11/62 Rosenthal, Harold and John Warrack. Concise Oxford Dictionary of
     Opera. London, etc.: Oxford U. Pr., 1964. 446 pp.
Brief arts. on composers, librettists, performers, operas, arias, etc.
     Goethe: 3/4 col., chiefly a list of operas based on his works.
     Don Juan: 2/3 col., mainly a list of operas on the theme, several
     of which are described in separate arts. 2nd ed., 1979, 561 pp.

11/63 Kobbé, Gustave. Kobbé's Complete Opera Book. London: Putnam,
     1976. 1694 pp.
9th ed., ed. and rev. by the Earl of Harewood. 1st ed. 1919. Plots,
     with comments on arias, often non-technical, but also many sup-
     ported with a musical quotation. Index of names and titles and a
     few subjects (Faust, Troy, etc.). Mozart: 8 operas, 75 pp.; Stra-
     vinski: 6 operas, 22 pp.

HISTORY

11/64 Grout, Donald Jay. A Short History of Opera. N. Y. & London:
     Columbia U. Pr., 1965. 852 pp.
2nd ed. 1st ed. 1947. Many musical quotations. Covers through 1960.
     Bibl., pp. 585-768. Index of names, titles and other subjects
     (Comic opera, Faust, Symbolism).

● SONG ●

HISTORY

11/65 Stevens, Denis W., ed. A History of Song. London: Hutchinson,
       1960. 491 pp.
Concerned with "secular art song" (Foreword). Indexes of names and
       titles.
MusicalQ 47 (1961):549-52--"its emphasis is altogether on [the] music";
       MusicR 23 (1962):65-67; M&L 42 (1961):67-70

● DANCE ●

BIBLIOGRAPHY

11/66 New York Public Library. Dance Collection. Dictionary Catalog
       of the Dance Collection: A List of Authors, Titles and Subjects of
       Multi-Media Materials. Boston: Hall, 1974.
10 vols. Incl. subject cataloguing of arts. from the major dance jour-
       nals, as well as films, videotapes and photographs.

HANDBOOKS

11/67 Koegler, Horst. The Concise Oxford Dictionary of Ballet. London,
       etc.: Oxford U. Pr., 1977. 583 pp.
Transl. and rev. of his Friedrichs Balletlexikon von A-Z, Velber: Fried-
       rich, 1972. Very brief arts. on choreographers, dancers, compa-
       nies, ballets, technical terms, etc. Faust ballets: 3/4 col.;
       Shakespeare ballets: 1 1/4 cols.

11/68 The Simon and Schuster Book of the Ballet: A Complete Reference
       Guide--1581 to the Present. N. Y.: Simon and Schuster, 1980. 323
       pp.
Ed. by Riccardo Mezzanotte. Transl. by Olive Ordish of the Italian ed.

(Il Balletto: Repertorio del teatro di danza dal 1581, Milano:
Mondadori, 1979). Brief signed arts. on ballets, arranged chronologically, giving plot, sometimes also commentary on music or a
literary source, or on other versions, or an evaluation.

● PHILOSOPHY ●

● BIBLIOGRAPHIES ●

11/69 De George, Richard T. The Philosopher's Guide to Sources, Re-
       search Tools, Professional Life and Related Fields. Lawrence:
       Regents Press of Kansas, 1980. 261 pp.
Rev. ed. of Guide to Philosophical Bibliography. . . , 1971. Classified,
    with evaluative notes. Lists histories, bibliographies, diction-
    aries and encyclopedias, and the standard eds. and reference works
    on individual philosophers. Section 7.1: Aesthetics: pp. 90-92, 23
    entries and cross-refs.; 9.5 and 9.6: Asian philosophies: 42 en-
    tries.

11/70 The Philosopher's Index: An International Index to Philosophical
       Periodicals. 1967--.
4/yr., with annual cumulation. Alphabetical subject index to an author
    listing. Gives abstracts, from 3 (1969). Cites book revs., from
    4 (1970). Increasing coverage of foreign lang. periodicals.
    Suppl. retrospective bibls. of English lang. publs. from 1940, 6
    vols., 1978-80. 14 (1980) has listing under Literary Criticism,
    Literature (1/2 col.), Poetics, Poetry, as well as writers (Dante,
    T. S. Eliot, Goethe).

11/71 Répertoire bibliographique de la philosophie. 1949--.
4/yr. Issues 1-3 list books and arts. in various langs., in classified
    order, unindexed, but with many cross-refs. Issue 4 is an index of
    names only, as subject and scholar, and a list of book revs. Brief
    sections in issues 1-3 on the philosophy of art and aesthetics.

11/72 Totok, Wilhelm. Handbuch der Geschichte der Philosophie. Frank-
    furt am Main: Klostermann, 1964--.
4 vols. in 5, to date, covering through the 17th c. Mainly bibls., with
    indexes of names and subjects in each vol.

• HANDBOOKS •

11/73 The Encyclopedia of Philosophy. N. Y.: Macmillan, 1967.
8 vols. Paul Edwards, ed.-in-chief. Arts. on philosophers and philo-
    sophical topics, movements, schools, national histories, etc.
    Nietzsche: 10 pp. Thoreau: 1+ pp. Stoicism: 3 pp. Aesthetics,
    History of: 17 pp., incl. 3 cols. on Plato and 2 pp. bibl. Aes-
    thetics, Problems of: 21 pp.
JAAC 27 (1968/69):463-65--v fav, with ref. to coverage of aesthetics

11/74 Flew, Antony, ed. A Dictionary of Philosophy. London: Macmillan,
    1979. 351 pp.
Usually brief unsigned arts. on technical terms and on major philosophers
    and schools of philosophy. Hegel: 7 1/2 cols.; Hegelianism: 1+
    col. Meaning: 3/4 col. Incl. some entries from oriental philos-
    ophy.
RelSt 15 (1979):582; PhilosB 22 (1981):25-27

• SPECIAL TOPICS •

• AESTHETICS •

BIBLIOGRAPHY

11/75 "Selective Current Bibliography for Aesthetics and Related
    Fields." In Journal of Aesthetics and Art Criticism, 1 (1941/42)-
    31 (1973).
In broad subject sections.

HISTORIES

11/76 Beardsley, Monroe C. Aesthetics from Classical Greece to the
    Present: A Short History. N. Y.: Macmillan, 1966. 414 pp.
Chapter 12, pp. 317-88, on 20th c. approaches, incl. semiotics, pheno-
    menology, existentialism and empiricism, with a 9+ pp. bibl. of
    books and arts. in English.
Philosophy 43 (1968):63-65--praises documentation and handling of con-
    temporary period; JAAC 25 (1966/67):213-15

11/77 Tatarkiewicz, Władysław. History of Aesthetics. The Hague:
    Mouton, 1970-74.
3 vols. Transl. from the Polish. I: Ancient Aesthetics, ed. by J.
    Harrell, 1970, 352 pp.; II: Medieval Aesthetics, ed. by C. Barrett,
    1970, 315 pp.; III: Modern Aesthetics, ed. by D. Petsch, 1974, 481
    pp. Covers through about 1700. No more publ., but see his History
    of Six Ideas: An Essay in Aesthetics, The Hague, etc.: Nijoff,
    1980, 383 pp. for essays toward a continuation of the history.
JHI 37 (1976):549-55; BJA 21 (1981):271-72--6 Ideas

• HISTORY of IDEAS •

11/78 Tobey, Jeremy L. The History of Ideas: A Bibliographical Intro-
    duction. Santa Barbara, Calif.: Amer. Bibl. Center, 1975--.
2 vols. to date. I: Classical Antiquity, 1975, 211 pp.; II: Medieval
    and Early Modern, 1977, 320 pp. Both vols. in 5 chapters: General
    (very similar in both vols.), Philosophy, Science, Religion and
    Aesthetics. Vol. I: Ancient Aesthetics, pp. 108-38, on literature,
    art and music, rather than aesthetic theory.
ClRev ns 27 (1977):293--dismissive of vol. 1; Isis 69 (1978):268-69--fav;
    Speculum 31 (1978):54-55; AHR 82 (1977):921-22--"serviceable"; all
    ref. to vol. 2

11/79 Dictionary of the History of Ideas: Studies of Selected Pivotal

Ideas. N. Y.: Scribner's, 1973-74.

Philip P. Wiener, ed.-in-chief. 4 vols. and index vol. Appr. 300 long
signed arts., with bibls., incl. more than 60 listed as concerned
with aesthetic theory and literary criticism. Baroque in Literature: 13 1/2 cols., and 1/2 col. bibl.

JHI 35 (1974):527-37--"The . . . category [of] ideas in literature and
the arts in aesthetic theory and literary criticism is immensely
rich." Isis 69 (1978):92-93; MLN 89 (1974):1076-81; AHR 79 (1974):
103-04

• HISTORY of SCIENCE •

11/80 "Relations of Literature and Science: A Bibliography of Scholarship." In Clio: An Interdisciplinary Journal of Literature, History and the Philosophy of History, 4 (1974)--.

In issue no. 1 (October). Covers 1972/73--. 10 (1980/81):59-84, for
1978/79). Arranged by period. Some brief annotations. No indexes. Previously in Symposium, 5 (1951)-21 (1967), but see next
entry.

11/81 Dudley, Fred Adair. The Relations of Literature and Science: A
Selected Bibliography, 1930-1967. Ann Arbor: UMI, 1968. 137 pp.

Rev. ed. 1st ed. 1949. Collects, combines and suppls. a series of annual bibls., incl. those in Symposium (see 11/80). By period,
subdivided chiefly by author. Lists studies chiefly in English,
French, German and Italian, on writers from W. Europe, the U. S.
and Russia, chiefly. Index of scholars.

11/82 "Critical Bibliography." In Isis: An International Review Devoted to the History of Science and Its Cultural Influences,
1912--.

Now an annual, in a suppl. issue. The 1980 bibl. listed publs. of 1979
and earlier, incl. a few to 1973, in 295 pp. Classified arrangement, in 4 main divisions and 39 subdivisions, incl. regions,

periods and disciplines; incl. a section on classical and Oriental
science and subsections under most periods on pseudo-science and
on travel and exploration. Brief annotations. Cites book revs.
Surveys a number of journals in history, philosophy, art and literature, as well as general humanities. Index of names only, as
subjects and scholars.
YWMLS 76:454--"invaluable for many aspects of Italian writing in the
   17th and 18th cs."

11/83 Isis Cumulative Bibliography: A Bibliography of the History of
   Science Formed from Isis Critical Bibliographies 1-90, 1913-1965.
   London: Mansell, 1971-78.
3 vols. I & II: Personalities and Institutions. 664 & 789 pp. III:
   Subjects, 678 pp. Continued by Isis Cumulative Bibliography:. . .
   Formed from Isis Critical Bibliographies 91-100, Indexing Liter-
   ature Published from 1965 to 1974. London: Mansell, 1980--. I:
   Personalities and Institutions. 483 pp. Dickens: 3 entries;
   Dante: 8 entries; Goethe: 6 cols., in 12 sections.

● RELIGION ●

• BIBLIOGRAPHIES •

11/84 Bollier, John A. The Literature of Theology: A Guide for Students
   and Pastors. Philadelphia: Westminster Pr., 1979. 208 pp.
Classified and annotated briefly. Covers the Christian traditions, with
   a brief section on Judaism.

11/85 Religion Index One: Periodicals. 1977--.
2/yr. and biennial cumulation. Continues Index to Religious Periodical
   Literature, 1949-76. Subject index to author list of arts. from
   journals in the W. European langs., but chiefly English, with abstracts. Cites book revs. 14 (1979-80), publ. 1981. Subject
   headings incl. Literature and Christianity, Literature and

Religion, Bible in Literature, etc; Poetics, Poetry, Tragedy, etc.;
English Literature, Arabic Literature, and other literatures; and
a few authors (Boccaccio, Faulkner, Goethe).

11/86 Religion Index Two: Multi-Author Works. 1978--.
Covers 1976--. Annual. Indexes by author and subject essays in selected
    books.

11/87 Adams, Charles J., ed. A Reader's Guide to the Great Religions.
    N. Y.: The Free Press/London: Collier-Macmillan, 1977. 521 pp.
2nd ed. 1st ed. 1965. Thirteen bibl. essays on religions or regions
    (China, Japan, the native religions of the Americas).
EcumR 30 (1978):78-80--"the most helpful single guide"; RelSt 15 (1979):
    562-64

11/88 Griffin, Ernest G. Bibliography of Literature and Religion. Ed-
    monton: Dept. of English, U. of Alberta, 1969. 40 lv.
Not seen.

11/89 "Bibliography." In Christianity and Literature.
In each issue (4/yr.) 31:1 (Fall, 1981):79-102, entries 6640-6778, by
    period. Books and arts. in English chiefly, on writers in English
    chiefly. Abstracts of 1-4 sentences. To 22:2 (Winter, 1973)
    called Conference on Christianity and Literature Newsletter.

• HANDBOOKS •

11/90 Brandon, Samuel George Frederick, gen. ed. A Dictionary of Com-
    parative Religion. London: Weidenfeld and Nicolson, 1970. 704 pp.
Short entries, signed, with bibls., mostly of books, but incl. refs. to
    the standard specialist encyclopedias. Art, Sacred: 1 col. text,
    with many cross-refs., 1/2 col. bibl.; Earth-mother: 1/2 col.
    Butterfly: 1/4 col. Synoptic Index, listing arts. under names of
    16 religions. General index of names and terms.

JAAR 40 (1972):390-92--noting lack of comparative approach within arts.;
   HistRel 12 (1972/73):288-90; JSSR 11 (1971):305-06

11/91 Encyclopaedia of Religion and Ethics. Edinburgh: Clark/N. Y.:
       Scribner's, 1908-26.
James Hastings, ed. 13 vols. Long arts. on religions and on religious
   and social practices, past and present. Melancholy: 7 3/4 cols.;
   Revenge: 4 1/4 cols., incl. a brief bibl. citing Plato, Seneca,
   Aquinas, Butler and several early 20th c. philosophers; Mountains
   and Mountain Gods: 9 cols.; Birth: 53 cols., in 13 separately
   signed sections on regions or religions.

11/92 Die Religion in Geschichte und Gegenwart: Handwörterbuch für
       Theologie und Religionswissenschaft. Tübingen: Mohr, 1957-65.
3rd ed. 7 vols. Signed arts. on people, movements, gods, practices,
   ideas. Index of names and topics in vol. 7. K. Galling, ed.

11/93 The Oxford Dictionary of the Christian Church. London: Oxford U.
       Pr., 1974. 1518 pp.
2nd ed. 1st ed. 1957. Frank L. Cross and E. A. Livingstone, eds. Brief
   arts., most 1 col. or less, few more than 2 cols. Biographies
   and other topics. Augustine: 3 cols., plus 1/2 col. bibl.
JBiblLit 93 (1974):481-82

11/94 Reallexikon für Antike und Christentum: Sachwörterbuch zur Ausein-
       andersetzung des Christentums mit der Antiken Welt. Stuttgart:
       Hiersemann, 1950--. Theodor Klauser, ed.
11 vols. to date, through Gottesnamen. Arts. on people, gods, symbols,
   objects and practices in Greek, Roman, Jewish and Christian reli-
   gions. Abraham: 9 cols. in 8 sections, on Jewish, pagan and
   Christian aspects, plus 1/3 col. bibl.; section 8: Abraham in
   Christian art: 1 1/2 col. Apollon: nearly 5 cols. Gold: 35 cols.
   Altar: nearly 44 cols., with illus. and bibls. Gladiator: 22 cols.
JTS ns 31 (1980):615-20

11/95 Hastings, James, ed. <u>Dictionary</u> <u>of</u> <u>the</u> <u>Bible</u>. N. Y.: Scribner's,
       1963. 1059 pp.
Rev ed., by Frederick C. Grant and H. H. Rowley. 1st ed. 1909. Brief
       arts. on names, places and other topics. Hastings also edited a
       <u>Dictionary</u> <u>of</u> <u>the</u> <u>Bible</u> in 4 vols. and suppl. (N. Y.: Scribner's,
       1898-1904), a <u>Dictionary</u> <u>of</u> <u>Christ</u> <u>and</u> <u>the</u> <u>Gospels</u> in 2 vols
       (N. Y.: Scribner's/Edinburgh: Clark, 1924) and a <u>Dictionary</u> <u>of</u> <u>the</u>
       <u>Apostolic</u> <u>Church</u> in 2 vols. (N. Y.: Scribner's, 1922).

11/96 <u>The</u> <u>Interpreter's</u> <u>Dictionary</u> <u>of</u> <u>the</u> <u>Bible</u>: <u>An</u> <u>Illustrated</u> <u>Ency-</u>
       <u>clopedia</u> <u>Identifying</u> <u>and</u> <u>Explaining</u> <u>All</u> <u>Proper</u> <u>Names</u> <u>and</u> <u>Signifi-</u>
       <u>cant</u> <u>Terms</u> <u>and</u> <u>Subjects</u> <u>in</u> <u>the</u> <u>Holy</u> <u>Scriptures</u>, <u>Including</u> <u>the</u>
       <u>Apocrypha</u>, <u>with</u> <u>Attention</u> <u>to</u> <u>Archaeological</u> <u>Discoveries</u> <u>and</u> <u>Re-</u>
       <u>searches</u> <u>into</u> <u>the</u> <u>Life</u> <u>and</u> <u>Faith</u> <u>of</u> <u>Ancient</u> <u>Times</u>. N. Y.: Abing-
       don, 1962-76.
4 vols. and suppl. vol.

● ● SOCIAL SCIENCES ● ●

● BIBLIOGRAPHIES ●

11/97 White, Carl M., et al. <u>Sources</u> <u>of</u> <u>Information</u> <u>in</u> <u>the</u> <u>Social</u> <u>Sci-</u>
       <u>ences</u>: <u>A</u> <u>Guide</u> <u>to</u> <u>the</u> <u>Literature</u>. Chicago: ALA, 1973. 702 pp.
2nd ed. 1st ed. 1964. Essays with bibls. on 9 areas, and an essay on
       the social sciences in general. History: pp. 83-137, citing more
       than 500 books and journals. Anthropology: pp. 307-74, appr. 550
       entries (bibls., dictionaries, encyclopedias, histories and book-
       length studies of major topics and regions). Other sections cover
       geography, sociology, psychology, political science, economics and
       business administration, and education. Index of authors, titles
       and subjects.

11/98 <u>Literature</u> <u>and</u> <u>Society</u>, <u>1950</u>-<u>1955</u>: <u>A</u> <u>Selective</u> <u>Bibliography</u>.
       Coral Gables, Fla.: U. of Miami Pr., 1956. 57 pp.

Thomas F. Marshall, ed. 284 entries.

11/99 Literature and Society: A Selective Bibliography. N. p.: n. p..
       1962. 71 pp.
Thomas F. Marshall and George K. Smart, eds.

11/100 Literature and Society, 1961-1965: A Selective Bibliography.
        Coral Gables, Fla.: U. of Miami Pr., 1967. 160 pp.
Paul J. Carter and George K. Smart, eds. 691 entries, by scholar, list-
     ing arts., chiefly in English. Brief annotations. Index of names,
     titles and other subjects. This and the preceeding 2 entries were
     sponsored by the Modern Lang. Assn. of America, General Topics 6
     group.

11/101 Social Sciences Index. 1974/75--.
4/yr. and annual cumulation. Companion to Humanities Index (1/12).

11/102 Social Sciences Citation Index. 1973--.
3/yr. and annual cumulation. Companion to Arts and Humanities Citation
     Index (1/13).

● HANDBOOK ●

11/103 International Encyclopedia of the Social Sciences. N. p.: Mac-
        millan & The Free Press, 1968.
16 vols. and index vol. David L. Sills, ed. Often lengthy arts. on
     theories and theorists in all the social sciences. Biographical
     suppl. (vol. 18), 1979, on modern theorists. Orig. ed.: Encyclo-
     paedia of the Social Sciences, N. Y.: Macmillan, 1930-33, 15 vols.

● ANTHROPOLOGY ●

11/104 International Bibliography of Social and Cultural Anthropology.
        1958--.

Annual. Covers from 1955. Classified arrangement. Section G: folk-
     culture, incl. art, performance and literature.

● POLITICAL SCIENCE ●

11/105 International Bibliography of Political Science. 1953--.
Annual. Covers from 1952. Classified arrangement. Some coverage of
     the history of political theory.

● SOCIOLOGY ●

11/106 International Bibliography of Sociology. 1952--.
Annual. Covers from 1951. Little direct attention to literature. Sec-
     tion 13100 covers culture and related matters. Subsection 13820
     covers literature.

11/107 Sociological Abstracts. 1952--.
12/yr., with annual index. Section 1300: Sociology of the arts; subsec-
     tion 1300/30: sociology of language and literature.

● PSYCHOLOGY ●

11/108 "Bibliography." In Literature and Psychology: A Quarterly Jour-
     nal of Literary Criticism as Informed by Depth Psychology. 1
     (1951)-23 (1973)
The last installments appeared in issue no. 4, were arranged by journal,
     and offered abstracts.

11/109 Kiell, Norman. Psychoanalysis, Psychology and Literature: A
     Bibliography. Metuchen & London: Scarecrow, 1982.
2 vols. 1269 pp. Vol. 1: 965 pp., 19,674 entries, listing books and
     arts. in English and other langs., by topic, incl. the genres
     (sections 3-10). Vol. 2: indexes, incl. Authors (literary authors
     studied and authors of the studies), and other subjects.

Montaigne: 21 refs., under 14 subheads. Mirrors: 8 refs. Death:
2 1/4 cols. of refs., all specifically qualified. See also Kiell's
Psychiatry and Psychology in the Visual Arts and Aesthetics: A
Bibliography, Madison: U. of Wisconsin Pr., 1965, 250 pp.
JAAC 24 (1964/65):325--ref. to Visual Arts.

11/110 Rothenberg, Albert and Bette Greenberg. The Index of Scientific
    Writings on Creativity: Creative Men and Women. Hamden, Conn.:
    Archon, 1974. 117 pp.
3145 entries, listing books and arts. as found in Psychological Ab-
    stracts (11/111), Grinstein's Index to Psychoanalytic Writings,
    Index Medicus (11/114) and other bibls., through 1973. Covers
    writers, musicians, artists, etc. Rimbaud: 18 entries, incl. sev-
    eral European diss. Ibsen: 39 entries, incl. a number on specific
    plays. See also their Index to Scientific Writings on Creativity:
    General, 1566-1974, Hamden, Conn.: Archon, 1976, 274 pp.
MusicR 38 (1977):228; N&Q ns 23 (1976):480

11/111 Psychological Abstracts. 1927--.
Monthly, with semi-annual cumulated index of subjects and authors.
    Cumulated indexes covering periods of 3 years or longer, through
    1977. Current subject headings incl. Literature, Autobiography,
    Biography, Poetry, Prose, Drama, Myths. July-Dec., 1981: Drama: 2
    entries, Peer Gynt and Endgame; Literature: 25 entries, incl. 2 on
    D. H. Lawrence and one on W. Irving and on David Copperfield.
    This index can be searched through a computer service.

11/112 Bleich, David, et al. "The Psychological Study of Language and
    Literature: A Selected and Annotated Bibliography." In Style 12
    (1978):113-210.
Pt. 2: "Subjectivity, Language and Epistemology in Literature and Criti-
    cism," by Bleich, pp. 164-203, entries 426-819.

● MEDICINE ●

11/113 Trautmann, Joanne and Carol Pollard. Literature and Medicine:
    Topics, Titles and Notes. Hershey, Pa: Dept. of Humanities, Her-
    shey Medical Center, Penn. St. U., 1975. 209 pp.
Pp. 1-151: a list of novels, stories, poems, plays, etc., incl. essays
    and autobiographies, most by English or American writers, but incl.
    some transls. In 6 chronological periods, Classical to 20th c.
    Gives plot summaries. Medieval: 5 pp., 56 works, Beowulf to
    Chaucer, incl. 6 tales from the Decameron. 20th c.: 49 pp.
    "Topic List," pp. 152-209, listing the works under 39 broad head-
    ings. Four of Petrarch's Canzoniere would be found variously under
    The Body, Sexuality, Grief and Suffering.

11/114 Index Medicus. 1960--.
Monthly, with annual cumulation. Subject headings incl. Literature;
    Biography; Literature, Medieval; Medicine in Literature; Mythology;
    Creativeness. Medicine in Literature, 1980: 28 refs., incl. Chau-
    cer, Kafka, Boethius, Joyce, Andrić and Parzival. Continues sev-
    eral earlier indexes which index medical research from 1879. This
    index can be searched through a computer service.

● ● GENERAL SOURCES ● ●

11/115 Sheehy, Eugene P., comp. Guide to Reference Books. Chicago:
    ALA, 1976. 1015 pp.
9th ed. 1st ed. 1902. Suppl., Chicago: ALA, 1980, 305 pp. Classified
    arrangement. Annotated. Index of scholars, titles and subjects.
    This guide, and the ones by Walford, Malclès and Totok (below),
    list and describe national bibliographies, general collections of
    biographies, dictionaries of English and foreign languages, and
    many other basic and important general sources of information not
    listed here. Lengthy sections on all major disciplines, incl. the
    arts, humanities, social sciences and sciences. Lengthy section

on literature, emphasizing English and American literature, incl.
some titles not listed here (especially quotation books,
anthologies, lists of novels, plays, etc., but also incl. some
handbooks, histories and bibls. of research which may be of use).

11/116 Walford, A. J. Guide to Reference Material. London: Library
    Assn., 1973-77.
3rd ed. 1st ed 1959. 3 vols. I. Science and Technology. 4th ed.
    1980. 697 pp. II: Social and Historical Sciences; Philosophy and
    Religion. 1975. 647 pp. III: Generalities, Languages, the Arts
    and Literature. 1977. 710 pp. Probably more concerned with
    scholarly research than Sheehy (11/115), which divides its atten-
    tion between academic and public libraries. The classification
    system is based on a variation of the Dewey Decimal System, with
    sometimes odd results--directories of publishing houses are to be
    found in Vol. 1, in the Technology section. Each vol. has an
    index of names, titles and subject categories, with a cumulated
    index of subject categories in vol. 3.

11/117 Malclès, Louise-Noëlle. Les Sources du travail bibliographique.
    Genève: Droz/Lille: Giard, 1950-58.
3 vol.

11/118 Malclès, Louise-Noëlle. Manuel de Bibliographie. Paris: PUF,
    1975. 398 pp.
3rd ed., rev. by Andrée Lhéritier. 1st ed. 1963.

11/119 Totok, Wilhelm, Karl-Heinz Weimann and Rolf Weitzel. Handbuch
    der bibliographischen Nachschlagewerke. Frankfurt am Main:
    Klostermann, 1972. 367 pp.
4th ed. 1st ed. 1954.

INDEXES

• INDEX of NAMES •

of bibliographers, editors, compilers, etc.

Diacritical marks are ignored in alphabetizing.

• SELECTIVE INDEX of TITLES and INSTITUTIONS •

D

E

J

K

L

M

• INDEX of SUBJECTS •

Please note: (1) This index lists the sections and subsections of this book which are associated with a subject. There are headings for chronologies, fiction, the Romantic Period, 164 authors, and so forth, but not for bibliographies, handbooks or other forms of reference sources. (2) It notes individual books and other works, when their subject is more precise or otherwise different from that of the section in which they are placed. (3) It does not duplicate the information contained in the outlines which precede each section. (4) Although it sometimes includes references to special features or parts in books, it does not include any of the many articles, bibliographies or reviews of research which are mentioned in the annotations merely as illustrative of the sort of information to be found in a work. (5) The references under the headings for periods and centuries lead to the sections or specific works which deal precisely with that period; omitted are those sections or works which combine that period with the period preceding or following.

A

B